ASPECTS OF BARNSLEY 5

Aspects of BARNSLEY

5

Discovering Local History

Edited by
Brian Elliott

Series Editor
Brian Elliott

Wharncliffe Publishing

First Published in 1998 by
Wharncliffe Publishing
an imprint of
Pen and Sword Books Limited,
47 Church Street, Barnsley,
South Yorkshire. S70 2AS

Copyright © Wharncliffe Publishing 1998

*For up-to-date information on other titles produced under the
Wharncliffe imprint, please telephone or write to:*

>   Wharncliffe Publishing
>   FREEPOST
>   47 Church Street
>   Barnsley
>   South Yorkshire S70 2BR
>   Telephone (24 hours): 01226 - 734555

ISBN: 1-871647-45-2

A CIP catalogue record of this book is available from the
British Library

Cover illustration: Royston Parish Church, from an anon oil painting c. 1840

Printed in Great Britain by
St. Edmundsbury Press, Bury St. Edmunds, Suffolk.

CONTENTS

INTRODUCTION

by Brian Elliott

Wharncliffe Publishing has, over the last decade or so, established a well-earned reputation as a publisher of high quality local books. The widely acclaimed *Aspects Series* continues to be at the forefront of their expanding catalogue of new titles. The publication of the fifth volume of *Aspects of Barnsley* is a remarkable achievement for a town and district that is occasionally but erroneously perceived as having 'little history'. Since its inception in 1993 the *Aspects of Barnsley* series has attracted some 77 articles by 41 contributors. The very eclectic range of subjects, presented in a popular but authoritative style, enhanced with excellent graphics and illustrations, has been so well received by both the public and a variety of institutions that the *Aspects* formula has been successfully established or launched in Rotherham, Doncaster, Sheffield and Leeds; with new volumes planned for Wakefield, Huddersfield, Bradford, East Yorkshire and Lancashire.

Previous Barnsley volumes have always included contributions of an autobiographical nature and have recognised the importance of well-researched oral history. This volume extends this process and will hopefully result in other local life stories and accounts of culture and tradition coming forward. Athron 'Dick' Bedford's willingness to talk to myself about his early life also encouraged him to write down some of his most vivid memories. The result is a fascinating insight into an almost forgotten era. Eileen Umpleby's recollections of her work at the Town Hall is the kind of cameo account that provides us with what would otherwise be an underestimated not to say ignored aspect of wartime Barnsley. Many local people born during, just after and certainly before 1945 will have fond memories of some the characters and personalities associated with Barnsley's Theatre Royal. Pamela Watson, has skilfully collected some these recollection together in her contribution which contains photographs of some of the 'star' as well as 'up and coming' acts. Trevor Polding's short history of Barnsley's trams is bound to promote some memories as well as providing the kind of technical information of interest to any one interested in this revived form of transport. Oral history has been successfully combined with literary research in Rose Johnston's perceptive study of George Orwell's visit to Barnsley in the 1930s. Pigeon keeping and racing has long been associated with mining communities and Jack Wilde's crusade to place on record the old traditions of an almost vanished specialist aspect of the sport has already stimulated interest from other parts of the country.

Locally, many of our recent cultural traditions have understandable roots in mining along with associated industries and communications. John Goodchild's account of the astonishing spread of collieries 'Up Wakefield Road' during the nineteenth and early twentieth centuries serves as an indispensable guide for anyone wishing to understand the industry even though so much of its visual remains have gone. There are few better places for us to appreciate the communal impact of industry and associated aristocratic influence than at Elsecar, the subject of Ian Medlicott's detailed and well-researched article; whilst Melvyn Jones makes excellent use of the 1851 census in his study of a 'sponsored migration' into Elsecar and Hoyland township. Roger Glister in partnership with the Barnsley Canal Group again provides us with an interesting and superbly illustrated description of our local waterway.

Penistone Market and Cloth Hall is the subject of David Hey's contribution which adds to several other excellent *Aspects* articles about this moorland town and district whilst, returning to Barnsley, Alan Whitworth investigates the influence and assesses the importance of local architect John Whitworth.

Many people will remember Barnsley footballer Gordon Pallister's 'Temperance Bar' situated in Back Regent Street, perhaps a last reminder of a movement that in the last quarter of the nineteenth century included Cocoa and Coffee Taverns, the subject of Kate Taylor's original study. Finally, Brian Elliott, using ecclesiastical records, examines aspects of the work of the church courts with reference to the ancient parish of Royston.

Once again the book would not be possible without the help, support and skills of all members of the Wharncliffe team at the Drill Hall. Thanks in particular are due to Charles Hewitt for his continued support and also to Barbara Bramall, Mike Parsons, Roni and Paul Wilkinson and Paula Brennon. As usual the Archives and Local Studies department at Barnsley Library have provided an excellent service to *Aspects* researchers; as has John Goodchild's Local History Study Centre.

1. WAR TIME AT THE TOWN HALL: A PERSONAL MEMORY

by Eileen Umpleby

I BELONGED TO A GROUP of young people who were very politically minded. We were appalled by the events of the Spanish Civil War and the subsequent appeasement of Hitler and Mussolini by the British Government. There was palpable unease about the situation and it was becoming clear that Britain would have to go to war to resolve it. In fact, there was a sense of relief from the tension of uncertainty, though tremendous apprehension, when war was declared.

I got my first job in July 1939 when I was appointed as a clerk in the Education Department at the Town Hall, Barnsley (Figure 1). It seemed apposite that I should be taking the place of a young man who had been conscripted into the Armed Forces under the Military Training Act of May 1939. This required young men of 20 and 21 years to undertake military training for six months. The six months was, of course, over-ruled by events and they did not return to civilian life for several years. The Education Offices occupied a prestigious position on the ground floor of the Town Hall, to the left of the main doorway. Later, when I was secretary to the Director, I had my own office. It is interesting to note that there were only nine members of

Figure 1. Bransley's new Town Hall in the the late 1930s   *Brian Elliott Collection*

staff in those days, including the Director. The Director, then Mr H S Magnay, wore many 'hats'. Some of them were: Head of the Juvenile Employment Bureau, Secretary to the Governors of the Girls' High School, Examinations Secretary and Chairman of the National Savings Committee to name but a few. Later he was Chief Air Raid Warden.

I had only worked there for two months when war against Germany was declared on 3 September 1939. Like most office workers then, staff worked on Saturday mornings, the afternoons being precious time off. In the middle of Saturday morning on 2 September a letter arrived from the Board of Education, stating what was to happen about schools in the event of war. All members of staff were asked to stay on and the Director and Chairman of the Education Committee met to decide how to inform the Head Teachers of the Borough schools. By the middle of the afternoon, the staff were taking out letters which had to be given into the hands of the Head Teacher concerned. It was quite difficult to contact some of them as schools were officially on holiday. At 6.30 pm although the job was unfinished, the Director dismissed everyone and asked us to return on Sunday morning. I was glad to get away, for I had a date to see the film *Pygmalion* with Leslie Howard and Wendy Hillier - good escapism. Coming into the streets after the film was quite a shock. Street lighting was officially switched off on Saturday 2 September, so this was the first experience of the lack of lighting. Transport too, had to have headlights partially blacked out. In addition to walking home in complete darkness, there was a tremendous electric storm and it seemed as if Armageddon was nigh.

Sunday morning, by contrast, was a beautiful autumn day. The office staff returned to the Town Hall and continued to try to reach the Head Teachers not yet contacted. I was at the outskirts of the Borough, when Mr Chamberlain's announcement of the declaration of war on Germany was made. His grave voice could be heard from radio sets through open doors and windows as I sped along the streets. The directive from the Board of Education was that schools must remained closed until arrangements could be made for the accommodation of the school children in a safe place during an air raid. There was such a problem in finding the space for this, that some schools had to resort to part-time education for a long time. The building of public air raid shelters was going ahead. The government had allocated 85 per cent of the cost of these in February 1939.

One of the first things which had to happen at the Town Hall was the black-out of all the windows during the hours of darkness. This

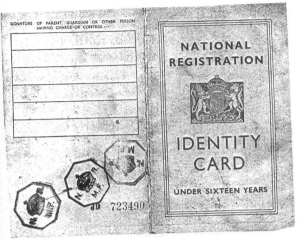

Figure 2. Identity Card

was a mammoth task, but one which had to be tackled quickly as autumn was already upon us and the Town Hall had to be a good example to other premises. Prominent buildings and air raid warden's posts had to be surrounded by sandbags. In addition to the blacking out of windows, householders were advised to put sticky tape on windows to minimise the effect of bomb damage. A National Register had been compiled and Identity Cards were issued on this basis in September to be carried at all times (Figure 2).

With the out-break of war, people were anxious to do their bit to help the war effort. This was in their spare time and on a voluntary basis. The Civil Defence Service included Air Raid Wardens (Figure 3), telephonists, Special Police and Auxiliary firemen attached to the regular fire service (Figure 4). Men too old for conscription in to the

Figure 3. Civil Defence Workers reviewed by Lord Harlech, Town Hall steps.

Figure 4. Members of the Auxiliary Fire Service with Mayor Walton.
Barnsley Chronicle

armed forces, and often soldiers in the last war, joined the Home Guard (Figure 5). Boys joined organisations like the ATC, Sea Scouts or Boys' Brigade (Figure 6). All the Town Hall staff were gathered into air raid preparations. The female staff were to man the telephones in the Civil Defence Control room and the men took part in other services. However, there would soon be few men left at home available for Civil Defence as more were conscripted. The National Service (Armed Forces) Act was passed on the first day of the war making men between 18 and 41 years liable to 'call-up'. In December 1941, unmarried women of 20 to 30 years (19 years the following year) were given the choice between the Auxiliary Services (WRENs, WAAFs or ATS), the Land Army or jobs in Industry. Certain jobs were reserved

Figure 5. Home Guard led by Captain Wilson. Somme Sunday, 19 June 1941 *Barnsley Chronicle*

as were those in the Education Service. By 1942, most of one's circle of friends, male and female were away from home.

The ARP Control Room was in the cellars of the Town Hall, which had been reinforced to withstand bomb blast and this is where we had to be on telephone duty. We often wondered how we would get out of

there if the Town Hall was bombed as it seemed a very prominent target. One of the stories circulating was that German 'planes used the building as a landmark to find their way on bombing raids to Sheffield, Manchester and Liverpool. The pale Portland stone must have shone very brightly under a 'bomber's moon'.

The Control Room was rectangular in shape, a large-scale map of the Borough occupying one long wall, covered by curtains when not in use (Figure 7). On the opposite wall was a row of telephone booths where we sat during a raid, awaiting calls. When messages about bombing incidents were sent in by Air Raid Wardens etc the appropriate service had to be alerted to send help and the incident was plotted on the map. The warnings of approaching enemy air-craft were coded as yellow, purple or red, in that sequence of danger. The sirens were sounded for the whole town to take shelter on a red alert. Barnsley people were used to sirens (buzzers) sounding at such places as the Ceag and the Star Paper Mill to announce the starting and finishing times of work. These now had to stop and the Paper Mill was chosen to sound the siren for an air raid. This was very different – a stomach churning, swooping wail. The siren sounded on one note for the 'All-clear'.

At first we left our offices during the day to man the Control Room on a 'purple' alert, but this became so disruptive to the work on hand, that the

Figure 7. Me in the Control Room, in front of the curtains covering the map of Barnsley, 1943.

Figure 6. The Air Training Corps on parade, Town Hall steps, 16 July 1941.

order was changed to going on duty on a 'red' alert. The times of duty were managed on a rota system – 6.am to 9 am, 5.30 pm to 6.am. However, this became such a burden on top of a hectic working day that staff were going down like nine-pins. It was decided to appoint a full-time staff to cover the night shift, 9.pm to 9.a.m. The Town Hall staff, plus the female staff of the Borough schools then worked rotas to cover evenings, Saturdays and Sundays. This was much easier: I was usually on duty one evening per week and sometimes a Saturday or Sunday. There were long periods when nothing happened. There must have been miles of knitting done during slack periods – comforts for the troops, sweaters for ourselves. These were a useful addition to the wardrobe in the time of stringent clothes rationing. There was a great deal of 'Make do and mend'. Jumpers were unravelled and knitted into other things; damaged parachute silk could be bought in Barnsley Market and made into pretty underwear. Of course, in addition, there was endless letter writing.

There were many training sessions during this time – on how to take messages and dispatch the correct service to the incident, fire-fighting practice and not least, lectures on gas attacks and recognising the different types, mustard and phosgene. There was a real fear that the Germans would use gas on the civilian population. Gas was used by the Italians in Abyssinia in 1936. Gas masks had already been issued to the whole population and it was advised that they should be carried at all times (Figure 8). The small square cardboard container was part of everone's dress. I always found the regulation gas mask suffocating and was quite relieved when the Control staff were issued with larger Civil Defence masks.

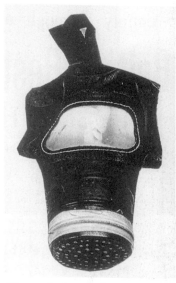

Figure 8. Gas Masks had to be carried at all times.

I was not on duty during the devastating raids on Sheffield in December 1940, but staff who were had a very lively time, sending the appropriate help. Walking home from evening classes, the sky was criss-crossed with the beams of search lights as they tried to pin-point enemy air-craft as a target for the anti-aircraft guns. Flack from the guns rained down on Barnsley streets.

When I first went to the Education Office there were no coffee or tea breaks. Older members of staff used to send out for a tray of coffee from Goodworths at the top of Market Hill. This seemed the height of sophistication and I wondered when I would be able to afford to do the same. However, there were now so many people in the Town Hall at all times of day that a Canteen was opened on the top floor to cater for coffee breaks and to serve High Tea to those staying on ARP duty after office hours. Ration Books had been printed before the war and rationing became necessary from January, 1940 (Figure 9). The German 'U' boats were wreaking havoc, sinking our merchant ships bringing supplies from the Empire. The rationing

Figure 8. Gas Masks had to be carried at all times.   **Figure 9.** Ration Book and Clothing Coupons.

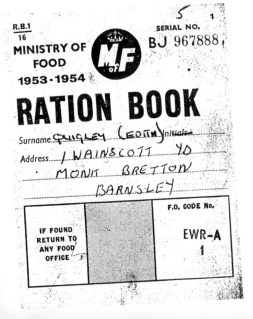

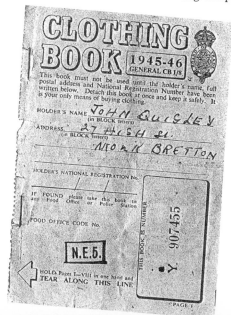

County Borough of Barnsley

British Restaurant

PUBLIC HALL

BARNSLEY'S FIRST BRITISH RESTAURANT, in the Public Hall, under the auspices of the War Emergency Committee, will be OFFICIALLY OPENED on WEDNESDAY NEXT, the 12th November, 1941, at 11.45 a.m.

The Opening Ceremony will be performed by the Chairman of the Social Welfare Committee (Mr. Councillor Mason, J.P.).

Immediately after the opening ceremony meals will be available for the public on the premises at the following prices, approved by the Ministry of Food, viz.:—

Meat & Vegetables - 6d.

Meat & Vegetables (for children)   - 4d.

Soup   -   -   - 1d.

Sweet   -   -   - 2d.

Cup of Tea   -   - 1d.

Bread   -   -   - Free

Town Hall,
BARNSLEY.
6th November, 1941.

A. E. GILFILLAN,
Town Clerk.

3184

Figure 10. Price List, British Restaurant (Public Hall, Eldon Street).

of bacon, butter and sugar were the first items to be restricted, followed by meat and tea in March and July. Restaurants and Works' canteens were allowed their own supplies of food, so this was a useful addition to the food rations for those who could afford it. A real innovation was the British Restaurant. Local Authorities were urged to promote these to provide cheap, nutritious food on a non-profit making basis. A Barnsley British Restaurant was opened in the Public Hall on Eldon Street (Figure 10). It took a while for Barnsley folk not used to eating out, to take advantage of this.

I did not stay in the General Office long, before I took the place of one of the men who had been conscripted, working out the wages of manual workers and other financial dealings. One of my duties was to go to the Barnsley Girls' High School to collect tuition fees which many pupils paid for their education. I then walked back to the Town Hall with a bag full of money. What a contrast with today when there would have to be a security van.

The Education staff took on many extraneous duties apart from ARP. One job which occurred very early in the war was to take a party of young evacuees who had arrived from the Channel Islands, unaccountably without footwear, to the Co-operative Society Shoe Department to get them fitted out.

Barnsley was regarded as a 'neutral' area, rather than 'safe', so we did not get other evacuees, except by private arrangement, until the Germans started to launch flying bombs. These were coming over from French sites from June 1944. They mainly affected the south of England, but occasionally a stray one came our way. These V.1's were quite terrifying. As soon as the noise of the propulsion stopped, the bomb descended. It was the random nature of these which was scary. We soon got news that evacuees were to be sent to Barnsley. Members of the Education staff over twenty-one years of age were hastily appointed as Billeting Officers and asked to attend a Reception Centre. It was a Sunday morning and a group of mothers and babies were expected to arrive from a maternity hospital in the London area which had been badly damaged by a V.1 (nick-named 'buzz bombs or doodle-bugs). We waited a long time before the sorry party arrived. These mothers were looking very frail and exhausted, having given birth to their babies one or two days before and then experienced the trauma of being bombed; some also had toddlers with them. I think our hearts went out to all of them. The Billeting Officers were given the addresses of houses which had been registered as having spare rooms. It was compulsory to accept the evacuees allocated. Most of the houses concerned were in the north of the town. The householders had only been given a short warning of what to expect. I escorted the first of my mothers and babies by taxi to the address given to me and could not help noticing the look of dismay on the face of the house-holder and the apprehension of the mother concerned. I did follow up the progress of these evacuees and some returned to the south of England quite quickly. Others gravitated to the other end of town where they felt more comfortable, if more crowded.

There were more pleasurable escort duties. London shows now came to perform regularly in Leeds and Manchester and my colleagues and I were able to see good plays and ballet. The 'B' companies of the Royal Shakespeare and Sadlers Wells Ballet sometimes came to the Barnsley Girls' High School to perform for schools. On these occasions, we had to meet the actors and dancers at the railway station and escort them to their hotels or digs. This was a glimpse into a completely different world. Another time, I had to meet Dr Edith Summerskill, a member of the Government, and take her to the Girls' High School Speech Day.

There were on-going fund raising efforts for the Red Cross and other charities and the departments of the Town Hall were quite competitive about this. We mainly organised Whist Drives and tried to provide refreshments, which was difficult from our own rations. However strange, people would always eat everything provided. One of the Education Department's more enterprising efforts was a Brain's Trust. The BBC *Brain's Trust* was a very popular programme on the radio Home Service, a bit like *Any Questions* today. In those days the personalities were Professor Joad, Dr Julian Huxley, Commander Campbell to name but a few. We contacted as many 'big' names as we could and were pleased when Professor Joad agreed to take part. He was quite a personality by this time. Local dignitaries formed the rest of the team.

Most young people of my generation were keen on ballroom dancing. Apart from the cinema, it was the most popular entertainment. I was taught to dance by my mother in the Tower Ballroom, Blackpool, to the strains of Reginald Dixon on the organ. In our teens, the best and cheapest dances were held at the Technical College. They were on Saturday nights and organised by the different departments. However, as the war wore on, most of the males of our age had been called up for war service. It was about this time that the female staff of the Town Hall were invited to dances at the military camp at Cawthorne Park. The camp was first taken over by the Canadian Army. Apparently, the Commanding Officer thought that the Town Hall employees would be 'nice types' to invite. Transport would be sent to the Town Hall to take us to Cawthorne and bring us back at a reasonable time. I think we went out of curiosity and were surprised how well things were organised. There was a good dance band and, of course, plenty of partners. There was a very strict protocol about not leaving the dance hall – some girls did with disastrous consequences. The biggest surprise of the evening was the buffet supper. There was a great variety of food and of quality which had not been seen since before the war; most of it had come from Canada. After that the

Figure 11. Visit of King George VI and Queen Elizabeth on the Town Hall steps.

Figure 12. 'Eyes Left': A contingent of ATS march pass the Town Hall, Mayor Walton inspects, 4 July 1941.

suppers became an incentive to attend.

After the dark days of the previous years, things seemed more promising for 1944. The Town Hall was spruced up for the visit of King George VI and Queen Elizabeth in that year – always a morale booster (Figure 11). The Town Hall always made a splendid background as a saluting base for a march-past. (Figures 12-13).

It was also clear by 1944, that the 'second front' was imminent and there was talk of 'D' Day landings in Europe. For a long time, none of us had known where our relatives and boyfriends were, because there was a complete black-out of news. We heard later that the whole of southern England was a vast military camp. It seemed very momentous when it was announced on the BBC News that landings had started in France on 6 June. So we watched cinema newsreels for information about it and were astounded at the heroism of those taking part.

It was a sign of optimism generated by the better war news, when there was important planning by the government for post war. The planning affecting the Education Department was the Butler Education Act of May 1944. It was to be the most impressive shake-up in the education world since 1902. The President of the Board of Education was to become the Minister of Education, giving him more importance. Basically, the Act said that LEA's were to provide three stages of education: Elementary, Secondary and Further. The school leaving age was to be raised to fifteen years and later to sixteen years. School fees were to be abolished in LEA Grammar Schools, school

Figure 13. The Army displaying their tanks in front of the Town Hall.
A J Roberts

dinners were to be provided for those who required them and there was to be free milk for all. Plans for implementing the Act were to be sent to the Ministry as soon as possible. To this end, I spent long hours taking shorthand dictation from the Director of Education, Mr H V Lightfoot, about his ideas for the reorganisation. Education was only one area of planning for post-war Britain.

I do not remember finishing work at the statuary 5.30 pm except during August when the schools were on holiday. However, it was never boring working in the Education Office because of the variety of the work. Of course, all the staff went through some very anxious times. Most males between the ages of eighteen and forty-one were fighting in one war zone or another. There were frequently times when letters were long delayed and we at home had no news of what was happening. There were many casualties and not many families escaped having at least one member killed, or taken prisoner of war. In the early days of the war, all the women in my family (the men being in the forces or on war work), foregathered with my Grandfather on

Sunday evenings. This was particularly to listen to the now famous speeches of Winston Churchill on the radio at 9 pm. Also known for its calm commonsense was the *Postscript* after the 9 pm news, often delivered by J B Priestley, in his bluff Yorkshire voice. His *Postscript after Dunkirk* was memorable. Life did become easier as the tide of the war turned in our favour. From September 1944, Civil Defence was virtually disbanded, though it was not formally discontinued until May 1945.

We were given a day's holiday for V E Day on 8 May 1945, and there were street parties and dancing in the streets, and general rejoicing that the War in Europe was over. But it did not seem the same as it would have done if all our friends had been there and not abroad or away on war work. Even after V J Day in August, it was almost unbelievable that this long war was over at last. The cessation of war was an anti-climax in many ways because things continued in the same way for a long time. It took several years before all the different categories of the armed forces were demobbed. Rationing, in fact, became very much worse and went on until the 1950s.

At the beginning of 1946 my husband returned from abroad, having been demobbed early under Class 'B' release, and I left the Education Office to take up the next part of my life. We went to live in London and were faced everywhere by extensive areas of bombed-out buildings, with the ubiquitous Rose Bay Willow Herb growing through the rubble. I then realised that we had been lucky in Barnsley to have had no more than a stray bomb.

Acknowledgements

My thanks to Barnsley Archives and Local Studies Department and Sheffield Reference Library. Also to Kath Parkin of the *Barnsley Chronicle* for publishing an appeal for memorabilia about the Second World War – and to Mr J Walton for his response.

2. THE INVASION SCARE OF AUGUST 1805

by Harold Taylor

THURSDAY AUGUST 15, 1805: the whole of Barnsley had been astir from an early hour, and for very good reason. In the small hours men had been urgently moving through the town and surrounding villages – beating drums – calling out the members of the Staincross Volunteer Infantry. The French had invaded at last! 'Boney' was coming! The Beacon on Woolley Edge (Figures 1-2) had shone out its

Figure 1. Woolley Edge, looking northwards over rising ground towards Beacon Hill. H Taylor (1960)

Figure 2. Woolley Edge and the location of Beacon Hill; the Ordnance Survey Sheet of 1851 - Six inches to One Mile. Note the height of 575 feet in the Beacon field compared with heights below 400 to the north and east.

warning some hours before in response to a blaze at Pontefract, the next beacon in a chain which stretched across the county.

Colonel Spencer-Stanhope, Commander of the local Regiment of Volunteers, had set the call-out in motion from his base at Cannon Hall, the messengers moving in great haste, some of them having long journeys to make, for the catchment area of the Regiment extended over the thirty-eight townships of the Staincross wapentake, from Thurlstone, out in the west, to Hemsworth in the east (Figure 3). Despite these long distances the response had been quick and efficient:

> To the immortal honour of the Volunteers, every man flew immediately to arms who was not prevented by sickness or absence from home, reported the Sheffield Iris newspaper.

By the end of that Thursday morning all were present on Market Hill, in uniform and armed with musket and bayonet. Old John Gill, a weaver, had been moving among the men, tears in his eyes, begging as many as he could reach to hasten to his cottage and drink the ale his wife had just brewed 'so that the French should not have the pleasure of drinking it.'

Soon the Volunteers would begin their march to Pontefract to join other Companies, and all the military training carried out in recent years and months would be put to the test.

Figure 3. The Staincross Wapentake and its Townships.

Fellow Citizens,

B ONAPARTE threatens to invade us : He promises to enrich his soldiers with our property : To glut their lust with our Wives and Daughters : To incite his Hell-hounds to execute his vengeance he has *sworn* to permit every thing. Shall we merit, by our cowardice, the titles of sordid Shopkeepers, Cowardly Scum, and Dastardly Wretches, which in every proclamation he gives us : No ; we will loudly give him *the lie* : let us make ourselves ready to shut our Shops and march to give him the reception his malicious calumnies deserve : Let every brave young fellow instantly join the Army or Navy ; and those among us, who, from being married, or so occupied in business, cannot, let us join some Volunteer Corps, where we may learn the use of arms and yet attend our business ; let us encourage recruiting in our neighbourhood, and loudly silence the tongues of those whom Ignorance or Defection (if any such there be) lead them to doubt of the attempt to invade, or inveigh against the measures taken to resist it. — By doing this, and feeling confidence in ourselves, we shall probably prevent the attempt, or, if favoured by a dark night, the enemy should reach our shores, — our Unanimity and Strength will paralize his efforts and render him an easy prey to our brave Army. Let *us*, in our families and neighbourhood, thus contribute to so desirable an event, and the *blood-stained banners of the vaunted Conquerors of Europe will soon be hung up in our Churches, the honourable Trophies of our brave Army:* — an Army ever Victorious when not doubled in numbers; and the only Army who can stand the charge of Bayonets. — What *Army* ever stood THEIRS!!! — *Let the welfare of our Country animate all — and " come the World in Arms against us, and we'll shock 'em !"*

A SHOPKEEPER.

Thee, Haughty Tyrants ne'er shall tame,
All their Attempts to pull thee down
Shall but arouse thy gen'rous flame
To work their woe and thy renown. ---

RULE BRITTANIA.

PRINTED FOR J. GINGER, 169, PICCADILLY,
Price SIXPENCE per Dozen, for Distribution, or one PENNY each.

Figure 4. Leaflet to promote recruitment of Volunteers. *Sheffield Archives*

After a brief peace, war with France had been resumed in the spring of 1803. Napoleon had now turned his attention to England and was threatening invasion. How would he cross the Channel? Imaginative forecasts had been put about suggesting that the invaders would use fleets of balloons as well as an armada of boats and that they might even construct a tunnel.

Government leaflets (Figure 4) and posters, aimed at encouraging men to volunteer for the defence forces, painted lurid word-pictures

AT a Meeting of the principal Inhabitants of this Town, aſſembled to conſider of the Meaſures neceſſary to give effect to the Defence Act.

Joſeph Beckett Eſq. in the Chair.

Reſolved that a Troop of Forty Cavalry excluſive of Officers ſhould be raiſed in this, and the adjoining Townſhips, for the internal defence, and ſupport of the civil Power within the Wapentake of Staincroſs and within twelve miles of the Town of Barnſley.

That the ſaid Troop ſhould conſiſt of none but ſubſtantial Houſeholders, willing to clothe, accoutre, train and diſcipline themſelves; and their Horſes. (Government finding Arms and Ammunition.)

Reſolved that an aſſociated Body of two hundred Infantry ſhould be raiſed within this, and the adjoining townſhips, for the purpoſe aforeſaid; and to be called out and embodied, if his Majeſty ſhould think proper, in caſe of actual invaſion to act in any part of the County of York: but not elſewhere.

That the ſaid Corps of Infantry, ſhould attend once a Week or oftener, if thought neceſſary, to learn the Uſe of Arms (Government providing Arms and Ammunition.)

That the neceſſary Officers ſhould be choſen by the ſaid Corps; and recommended to the Lord Lieutenant of this Riding for his Majeſty's Approbation.

That the ſaid Corps ſhould be independent of any other Corps, to be raiſed within the Riding.

That, as the ſaid Corps will not be able to organize itſelf without Aſſiſtance, and it appearing from Mr. Secretary Dundas's Letter to the Lord Lieutenant to be conſiſtent with the views of Government to grant allowances for clothing the Men and paying them on the Days of Exerciſe. That ſuch Allowances ſhould be applied for.

That Application ſhould alſo be made to Government, for an Adjutant and a proper number of non-commiſſioned Officers, for the purpoſe of training and excerciſing the Men in the ſaid Corps.

That if the reſpective Townſhips in the Wapentake, as well as the adjoining Townſhips, chuſe to join this Aſſociation and to extend the Aſſociation, thro' the Wapentake, ſuch extenſion would have the beſt effect.

That the Chairman do write to the principal Inhabitants of the reſpective Townſhips, requeſting that they will attend an adjourned Meeting for the purpoſe of conſidering whether they are willing to join or not.

That this Meeting be adjourned to Wedneſday next the ninth inſtant.

Figure 5. Meeting resolved to raise Volunteer Cavalry and Infantry, 1798.
Sheffield Archives

of the likely fate of the population, should Bonaparte's men prevail. His soldiers would be 'enriched with everyones' property' and worse – 'they would glut their lust with our women and daughters.'

Earlier in this August of 1805 the Government had received news of large bodies of troops embarking on the coast of Holland and of increased preparations at Boulogne. The threat was clear. The invasion was on !

The need for a 'Supplementary Militia' in the Barnsley area, a Volunteer Infantry to reinforce the regular Regiments of the Army, had been realised seven years before, and action taken at a meeting of 'the principal inhabitants of the town', chaired by Joseph Beckett (Figure 5). With the country on a war footing again in 1803, renewed efforts were now made to recruit volunteers. Lists of 'eligible' men were now available too, after a Defence Act of that year had required all parish constables to record the names and occupations of all able-bodied men aged eighteen to sixty who were not already engaged in a military capacity. Subsequently the upper age limit had been reduced to forty-five.

There were two meetings at Barnsley in August 1803 to organise the recruitment and support for a 'volunteer corps' in the wapentake. In mid-August a 'numerous and respectable meeting of the inhabitants of Staincross wapentake' resolved that a Corps should be raised and that subscriptions be invited to defray the expenses. Small and large sums would be equally welcome since 'High and Low, Rich and Poor, had everything that was dear to them at stake.' By the end of the month a further meeting, chaired by Godfrey Wentworth of Woolley Hall, was able to work out details. This high-powered gathering included Walter Spencer-Stanhope, James Stuart-Wortley, Francis Edmunds of Worsbrough Hall, Sir Francis Wood of Hemsworth, Joseph Beckett and William Elmhirst. There were to be ten infantry companies, of sixty to seventy men, each with a proportionate number of officers, and the meeting could immediately name sixteen gentlemen who would expect to serve in that capacity, among them Francis Wood, Spencer-Stanhope, already an experienced Captain of a troop of the West Riding Gentlemen Yeomanry Cavalry, Joseph Shaw of Staincross Hall and James Cockshutt of Wortley.

It is of great interest, in view of Barnsley's 'radical' politics and stormy labour relationships, especially in connection with its large population of handloom weavers, that the Volunteer Corps – like the Yeomanry Cavalry – would not only be required to serve in defence of the Realm but to help 'suppress any Rebellion or Insurrection in this country'. Men with property were casting anxious glances

Wapentake of Staincrofs.

AUGUST 17, 1803.

*S*UBSCRIPTIONS *entered into in aid of Government-Allowance, at a Meeting held this day at Barnsley, for promoting a Volunteer Corps of Infantry, under the General Defence Acts, for the said Wapentake.—To be returned in case the Corps is not formed.*

	£.	s.		£.	s.
G. W. Wentworth	500	0	Day & Acomb	1	1
W. Spencer Stanhope	300	0	Iohn Ward	1	1
Francis Wood, part of 200£.	125	0	Iohn Leadman	5	5
Francis Edmunds	100	0	Iohn Kay	1	1
I. Beckett	50	0	Thos. Atkinson	1	1
W. Elmhirst	50	0	Joseph Todd	5	5
Charles Bowns	25	0	John Dixon	3	3
Jeremiah Dixon	21	0	Thomas Marriot	5	5
Henry Clarke	21	0	Geo. Clarke	35	0
Iohn Moore	25	0	Mrs. Cawood	5	0
Wm. Jackson, (Bankend)	10	10	Miss Alderson	5	0
Iohn Pinder	10	10	Ino. Clarke, Jun. volunteer in Yeomanry Cavalry.	5	0
Cha. Stringer	21	0			
Charles Marshall	21	0	Richard Raywood	5	5
Iohn Pickering, Junior.	21	0	Richard Dunn	5	5
Iohn Fletcher	10	10	Ino. Cordeux	2	2
Richard Gill	25	0	Joseph Hall	5	5
Richard Crookes	10	10	Mrs. & Miss Clarke	5	5
Mrs. Cotton, (by I. Baron)	50	0	Job Townsend	5	5
John Micklethwaite	30	0	Thomas Cockshaw	2	2
Samuel Thorp	25	0	Jonas Clarke	21	0
William Parker	21	0	Thomas Hardy	2	2
James Carr	10	10	Richard Senior	2	2
George Guest	1	1	Iohn Addy	1	1
Joseph Bewer	10	10	Iohn Haxworth & Co.	5	5
David Wood	5	5	Geo. Alletson	3	3
William Railton	21	0	James Lister	1	1
Joseph Shaw, Staincross.	25	0	Thomas Bellamy	1	1

Figure 6. Part of the Subscription List issued in Barnsley, August 1803.
Sheffield Archives

towards France, and indeed, some years earlier, in December 1792, a meeting at the Moot Hall, chaired by Spencer-Stanhope, had condemned the 'excesses of the French Revolutionaries and the outrageous opinions prevalent among the revolutionaries of France.'

The response to the call for subscriptions was indeed encouraging, a list of one hundred names being drawn up at one of the August meetings (Figure 6). The large sum of £500 pledged by Godfrey Wentworth, heading the list, is a measure of the perceived threat. Among the more modest subscriptions were those from a number of the town's linen manufacturers – Edward Taylor, Jonathan Haxworth, Richard Raywood and Jonathan Cordeux.

Matters developed quickly. By the latter end of September a 'Return of the Staincross Volunteer Infantry' planned for two Barnsley Companies and one each associated with the townships of Cawthorne, Darton, Denby, Felkirk, Hemsworth, Royston, Thurlstone and Wortley. The principal officers of the Barnsley Companies were Lieutenant Colonel Walter Spencer-Stanhope, Commandant, Lieutenant Colonel Sir Francis Lindley Wood and Major John Hammond Lees. Charles Yates would serve as Surgeon and John Goodair as Chaplain. Each Company would have two Drummers.

Despite the initial fervour, however, there appears to have been some difficulty in the collection of subscriptions in subsequent months (Figure 7). By the spring of 1804 reminders were being issued

Figure 7. Request for payment of Subscriptions to support the Yeoman Cavalry - July 1803. *Sheffield Archives*

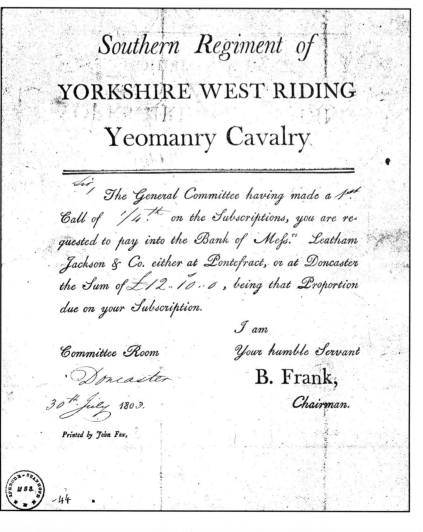

Militia List for the Township of Carlton —
First Class
Men Under Thirty Having no Children

No of men	persons Names in Alphabetical Order	Rank Title or Occupation	Age	Exempt or not Exempt from militia	Grounds of Exemption	Effective volunteer &c or Yeoman	Licensed Teacher &c none
1	Allon John	Servant	25				
2	Barber Ric.d	Servant	20	—			
3	Batey Tho.s	Husbandman	28				
4	Brooke Jon.n	Servant	18	Preempt		volunteer	
5	Cash Jon.n	Servant	20				
6	Crosland Joseph	Husbandman	20				
7	Chalenger Tho.t	Servant	24	Exempt		volunteer	
8	Clark John	Farmer	25	Preempt		by substitute	
9	Cutt John	Servant	24	Preempt		volunteer	
10	Fyre Jon.n	Servant	18				
11	Fox Joshua	Carpinter	23	—			
12	Fox Sam.l	weaver	20				
13	Hawksworth Wm	Farmer	22	Preempt		yeoman	
14	Hatham Joseph	Husbandman	20				
15	Hargreaves John	Canponeman	20	Exempt		Apprentice	
16	Holland Wm	Servant	20	Preempt		apprentice	
17	Hinge James	Servant	29				
18	Senior John	Carpinter	20	Exempt		Apprentice	
19	Senior Beny.n	Servant	21	Exempt		volunteer	
20	Slack John	Husbandman	24				
21	... John	Sergeant	28				
22	wandright Jos.h	Farmer	26				
23	wainwright Isaac	weaver	23	Exempt		by substitute	
24	Walker Jonas	mason	23				

Second Class
Men above Thirty Having no Children

25	Eastwood John	Farmer	35				
26	Eastwood Ric.d	Inmate	31	Exempt	—	Informs	

Figure 8. Part of the Militia List of 1806 for the Township of Carlton. Anyone claiming exemption from the Militia was instructed to appear at the *White Bear Inn* in Barnsley on September 17th at 'ten in the forenoon', bringing a Surgeon's Certificate of their Inability. *John Goodchild Collection*

to defaulters requiring them to pay at the bank of Messers Beckett & Clark at Barnsley before the twentieth of April.

Recruitment for the Volunteer Infantry too was very uneven. Allowing for the very considerable differences in population totals, the initial response in 1803 varied greatly from township to township. The list gathered from the parish constables in August showed that only 40 out of the possible 787 men in Barnsley had offered their services. In Wortley, however, 103 out of 133 had come forward and 43 out of

91 in Kexborough, but only 15 out of 212 in Cawthorne.

For whatever reasons totals changed remarkably, however, in the next few years, the numbers being revealed in detail in the Militia Lists of 1806, which fortunately have survived. By this time the contingents from both Barnsley and Cawthorne had more than doubled and Kexborough's fallen to less than half its previous number. There had been a more uniform response from most of the townships around Barnsley of 20% or more of those eligible, but volunteers were very thin on the ground in Barugh, Cudworth, Carlton and Silkstone.

It is not surprising that in almost all the townships the great majority of the volunteers were younger men, under the age of thirty and without children (Figure 8). These appear in the Militia Lists as Class One men. Nevertheless in Barnsley about a third of the Volunteers belonged to Class Four – men aged over thirty with at least one child under the age of fourteen. In Hemsworth there were almost equal numbers from Classes One and Four – men aged over thirty with at least one child under the age of fourteen. In Hemsworth there were almost equal numbers from Classes One and Four, among the latter John Levit, a labourer with three children, one of nine men listed as 'Poor'. Such a man would have been exempt from compulsory 'call-up' into a Militia Regiment on grounds of poverty alone. In Barugh too the Volunteers included John Pickering, 'Linen man' aged thirty-nine and father of four children.

Evidently patriotism was not the only motivation. With such wide-spread poverty – in Darton township, for example, 78 of the 98 men in Class Four are described as 'Poor' – the chance to earn extra pay must have been hard to resist. Privates in the Volunteer Infantry would receive one shilling a day when on duty or in training carried out in their own district, and double that amount if called outside it. In 1803 a man would serve at least twenty-four days in the year unless excused by the Medical Practitioner to the Corps, and there were other opportunities to earn further pay. The Lord Lieutenant of the County might call for an extra ten days training, and an annual inspection could involve six days with the Volunteers. Such additional days, moreover, were to be chosen so as to cause least interference with the 'general occupations' of the men – their basic sources of livelihood.

There was another important consideration. Men who joined the Volunteer Infantry were no longer liable to conscription into a Militia Regiment but would be required only for the limited number of occasions in their local area unless, of course, they were called to meet an invasion emergency. They would be able to follow their usual occupation and continue to live at home with their families. A man who had not joined the Volunteer Infantry was – unless infirm or serving an apprenticeship – liable to be conscripted into the Militia if his name was drawn by a system of balloting, though he could escape service by paying a fee for a substitute to take his place. a man might well feel attracted to such a role since the family of a 'Substitute' would be supported in his absence through the local rates. The Quarter Sessions records for 1805 and 1806 include court orders for the family of the Barnsley 'Substitute', Abraham Orme, to receive sums of £14.18s.6d. and, on two occasions, £3.18s.0d. Nevertheless, any Militia man could be away from home for long periods and involved in all the mortal dangers and privations of campaigns against the French.

No doubt some young men would be prompted to join the Volunteer Infantry by the expectation that their uniform would impress the young ladies.

In Darton township, which included Mapplewell and Staincross, notable centres of the hand-made nail industry, the Volunteers included no fewer than nineteen nailmakers. They would certainly have been keen to earn extra money through their military service. It was hard work even to make a poor living. Though supposedly paid by the thousand nails, the nailmaster's 'thousand' amounted to twelve hundred, and some paid their workers in 'tokens' rather than in cash, coins redeemable only at the master's own shop, where enhanced prices might well have been charged.

Short spells of duty with the Volunteers would have fitted in partic-ularly well with the nailmakers' habits. Being on piecework, it had been traditional for them to leave the nailshop to earn extra money when opportunities arose, such as at haytime and harvest time on local farms, or to take time off to work their own vegetable gardens. There may have been a problem for some of them, however. Drill sessions were sometimes arranged for Sundays. Men with 'religious scruples' could transfer the session to a weekday but without pay, since Sunday was not regarded as a 'day of work'. There were two Methodist chapels in Mapplewell/Staincross by 1805 and some very ardent chapel-goers among the nailmakers !

Barnsley linen weavers too were on piecework and perhaps more than willing to escape now and then from their damp and and dismal cellar-loomshops and be paid for it. Certainly weavers were numerous among the Barnsley Companies of the Volunteer Infantry.

Away to the west of the wapentake, handloom woollen weavers from the cottages of Denby and Thurlstone townships were prominent among the local Volunteers, perhaps for the same reasons.

Whatever the motivation, the Volunteers had embarked on a serious

Figure 9. 'Supplementary Cavalry and Infantry; the New Levies of 1796.' (Cartoon in the British Museum) A less than respectful contemporary view!

business. A man who refused to turn out could, like men in the regular army, be punished as a deserter. 'Improper conduct' on duty or failure to obey orders earned a substantial fine of five shillings for each offence or a week's imprisonment. Selling, pawning, losing or damaging clothes or equipment could lead to a forty shilling fine, or hard labour in prison for failure to pay. Refusal to pay could also result in a magistrate's order to seize the defaulter's goods and chattels.

As the threat of invasion appeared to grow, training of the Volunteer Infantry went on apace (Figure 9). In October 1804, a time chosen so as not to interfere with the harvest, and 'likely to be a dry spell', the volunteers were called for training to Wath Wood. This was considered to be 'ground not bad for the purpose and as central as can be picked upon'. On the recommendation of Wentworth-Fitzwilliam 'men were to go through some evolutions', and there was to be a 'day of inspection'. Evidently it was to be a long day, for the phase of the moon – in

Figure 10. Walter Spencer Stanhope as a young man. *(by kind permission of Simon Fraser)*

its second quarter – was cited as another favourable circumstance. Importantly, the use of horse-drawn transport was to be tried out. Corps 'coming from a distance' were to ' muster their wagons'.

Among some of the Volunteer Companies the need for drill and the practice of battle formations – advancing and retreating in line, firing, and rear-guard actions – was evidently pressing by the spring of 1805. Francis Lees at Gunthwaite had reported to Spencer-Stanhope in April that the Cawthorne Company was

falling off with regard to attendance at Drill, leaving much to fear unless Mr. Stanhope could come and animate them.

Walter Spencer-Stanhope (Figure 10) was in fact noted for his inspirational powers! On the occasion of presentation of new colours to the Staincross Volunteer Infantry Regiment in 1805 he had made a 'soul-stirring' speech to his men, which not only 'thrilled his hearers' but 'evoked an almost unparalleled outburst of applause throughout England' when reported. One sentence from this was 'long quoted':

The Chief Consul of France calls us a nation of shopkeepers. Let us, as shopkeepers, then melt our weights and scales and return him the compliment in bullets.

There had been other grumbles at Cawthorne too. Evidently the proposal to enlarge the Drum and Fife band with 'three brass drums, a long drum and four-octave flutes' had not met with universal approval.

As for the readiness of the wagon transport, those earmarked in the Staincross wapentake for military duty had not yet been fitted out with cross-seats, as recommended. Francis Wood, writing to Colonel Stanhope after the alarm of August 1805, had stressed the urgency of this work as the best means of delivering the men to the rendezvous. Travel by this means, moreover, rather than long marches would, he urged, 'diminish the incentive of the thirst' and so prevent drunkenness on the way. He feared that the officers could expect a 'rap on the knuckles' for this neglect.

In February 1805 James Cockshutt had expressed other worries. He had been to watch the Leeds Volunteers on a 'Field Day' and had gone home afterwards with

very unpleasant ideas of our great inferiority compared with the steadiness in manoeuvring and firing of these men. Indeed, he could not guess when the Staincross Volunteers might be properly qualified to act with these men.

Hopefully some, at least, of these deficiencies had been put right by the late April of 1805, when the Staincross Regiment assembled at Doncaster for a period of exercises. They were unlucky with the weather, however, the drill on the sixth day, Monday, being carried out after a heavy fall of snow which had left a covering six inches deep.

The raising of the infantry regiments had formed only part of the preparations for defence of the kingdom. In 1794 Thomas Richard Beaumont of Bretton Hall had provided the main initiative in the formation of a regiment of Light Horse – four troops of sixty men – and Walter Spencer-Stanhope had been chosen as Captain of the Barnsley Troop. Four years later renewed efforts were made to recruit for a

Troop of Forty Cavalry exclusive of officers...for the internal defence and support of the civil Power within the Wapentake of Staincross and within twelve miles of the town of Barnsley.

The troop was to consist of none but 'substantial householders', willing to clothe, accoutre, train and discipline themselves, and to provide their own horses, the Government to find arms and ammunition.

The local gentry were well represented among the Yeomanry Cavalry but there were substantial local farmers and professional men among there numbers also. In Worsbrough township Francis Edmunds headed the list, supported by six yeoman farmers and two others – George Tattersall and Joseph Tweedale – as well as an articled clerk, William Allen. Two Kexborough farmers, Francis Swift and Francis Scholefield, had joined, and the Barnsley Yeoman included the surgeon, Richard Rock. In full uniform they must have presented an impressive sight, in their scarlet jackets faced with green, their buff vests and breeches, their boots and spurs, green capes and cloaks of blue, and hat adorned with a feather. An impressive effect on the pocket too, for contemporary accounts record alarm at the rising cost of this uniform!

Careful preparations of other kinds had been made also to prepare the district for the eventuality of an invasion. Owners and masters of boats and barges were to make their vessels available for the transport of troops and stores. To this end forms had been returned detailing their likely locations, their tonnage and whether decked or not. All this information was very relevant for canals had recently been constructed in the Barnsley area. By 1805 the Barnsley Canal had been extended to the Barnby Basin and the Dearne and Dove to basins at Elsecar and Worsbrough.

Lists had been compiled too of available wagons and carts in each township detailing whether drawn by two, three or more horses. It was strongly recommended that spade, pick or billhook be attached to the vehicles so that Pioneers would be able to clear obstacles, enabling them to achieve the expected distance of twenty-five to thirty miles a day. The returns, dispatched to Godfrey Wentworth in January 1805, listed for Barnsley no fewer than19 wagons, 89 carts and 223 horses, whilst Darton could provide from totals of six wagons, 39 carts and 92 horses, surely a superabundance of transport resources! In fact each Company would have one wagon on the march and local magistrates were expected to order vehicles along the route so that each would not need to be taken not more than one day's journey from the owner's base – a laborious procedure!

Food supplies would have to be maintained throughout an emergency. To this end lists had been drawn up of bakers in the county who had:

> *faithfully promised to bake and deliver in case of invasion such quantities of good, wholesome and well-baked fresh bread in loaves of three and four and a half pounds as stocksof flour allowed.......over and above the Ordinary Consumption of our Customers.*

Details were added of the amount of fuel required required to keep each oven constantly in use, and millers had been told how much flour would be expected to supply.

If the defence forces were to be overwhelmed, what amounted to a scorched earth policy had been proposed in 1796 and again in 1801. All means of subsistence in parts of the country in imminent danger of falling to the enemy were to be consumed or destroyed, compensation to be paid to the owners in happier times. However, the enormity of the task of putting this into practice had been realised by November 1803 and the plan abandoned. Nevertheless old John Gill had entered into the spirit of this policy on that August morning in 1805, and on his own initiative!

By the summer of 1805 the threat of invasion seemed very real. Rumours from Holland and France indicated that French generals had been ordered to report on the Channel coast. Napoleon himself was believed to be on his way to Boulogne.

On the fateful day of the Alarm the very first man to report on Market Hill, ready in uniform, was George Uttley, a stonemason. The various Companies gradually assembled and by nine o'clock on that morning they were ready to march off down Old Mill Lane on their way to Pontefract. 'All the town' had turned out to see them, the keener ones - especially the wives and sweethearts – walking as far as Burton Bank before sadly turning back.

The Quartermaster had ridden ahead, reaching Pontefract by eleven, to demand billets for 700 volunteers. An hour later the Barnsley Troop of Cavalry arrived in the town.

Other Companies were on the move also. By six in the morning the Sheffield, Rotherham, Ecclesfield and Wath Wood Infantry, along with three troops of Yeoman Cavalry had all been mustering. The Sheffield Iris was able to report later that

> *in an instant, and without the delay of a single moment, the whole of the Volunteer Force, Cavalry and Infantry, ...was put in motion, and prepared with an astonishing alacrity and spirit, to go out to meet and repel their audacious and insulting foes who, they understood, had either landed or were on the point of polluting the shores of Albion by a mad attempt to land.*

A meeting of the 'principal inhabitants of the town' in Barnsley later in the month would likewise congratulate the Volunteers on their display of loyalty and on their heroism and zeal.

The arrival of forces from Barnsley prompted the Pontefract authorities to bring out their own drummers to call out the local Volunteers (Figure 11). Meanwhile, however, some of the Barnsley Cavalry had been talking to the keeper of the Pontefract Beacon and surprised by his replies. He had seen the Woolley Beacon from his post the evening before, but as his orders were to fire only on 'appearances eastward and not westward', he had not fired his own. The truth dawned upon them. It had been a false alarm!

There had been uncertainty about the firing of the Woolley Edge Beacon long before this, however. Parson Dixon of Woolley, who was a magistrate and responsible for the Woolley Beacon, had sent a messenger to Cannon Hall on the Wednesday evening at nine o'clock:

> *The Beacon at Pontefract is lighted but not that at Bilham, from whence Woolley Beacon is to take alarm. Probably by the time the servant with this letter reaches you our Beacon will be lighted. Mr.*

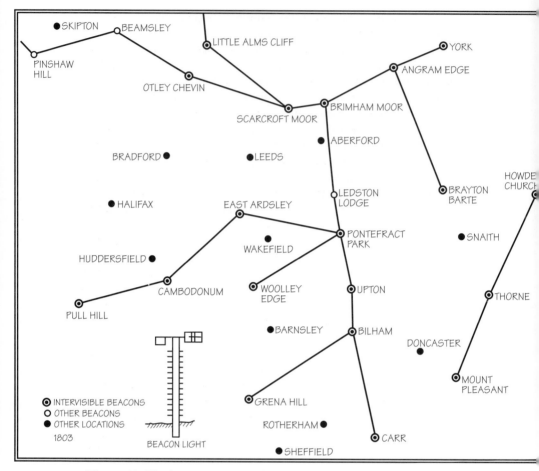

Figure 11. The beacon network of 1803. *West Yorkshire Archives*

> *Wentworth is away at Farnley. Any assistance I can render you as Inspector of Division in the absence of the Lieutenant of the Division I shall be happy to give.*

Now very concerned, Dixon dispatched another message at five a.m. and yet another an hour later:

> *I have ordered the Woolley Volunteers to wait upon you in Barnsley. I have no further intelligence than the Beacon of last night. I shall wait at home for information.*

Reports differ about the cause of the blaze which had been seen from Woolley Edge. Perhaps it had been the firing of a brick kiln, it was suggested, but most likely it had been the burning of rape straw after the crop had been harvested.

In Pontefract no time was now lost. The chief constables were dispatched with counter orders, an urgent task, since around 3,500 men and 100 wagons were thought to be on their way. Meanwhile the marchers from Barnsley had reached Hemsworth. It was a very hot day and 'the gallant troops had been offered hospitality at taverns on the way'. It was at Hemsworth that the news of the false alarm reached them and where – no doubt amidst feelings of relief and anticlimax – they were treated to a meal of cold beef, bread and ale through the generosity of Sir Francis Wood, officer in charge of the Hemsworth Company of the Volunteers. On their way back they were 'feted by farmers and offered the loan of wagons' and 'all the way home the countryside turned out to present them with refreshments.'

The men from Sheffield were less fortunate. Although they had been cheered by the local inhabitants on the way out, they were mocked on the way back and 'subjected to ribald banter for years afterwards.'

Those returning to Barnsley were met at Old Mill Lane by wives and others, who enquired anxiously how the battle had gone and whether anyone had been killed or wounded.

Despite all the fears and worries about preparedness during the preceding months, the Volunteer Infantry had done well. Only 9 out of about 560 men had been missing from the ranks, and these were accounted for by either illness or absence from home.

Moreover the men were proud of their achievement and of their

leaders, marking the event with a presentation of a silver cup, appropriately inscribed to Colonel Spencer-Stanhope to 'testify to their regard and attachment to their Commander' (Figure 12). As a further bonus for the occasion each man received the Government bounty of two guineas, as was due and, should he have had access to one of the Sheffield or Leeds newspapers of the day he could bask in the glory of his accomplishment: 'It is impossible to do

Figure 12. The Volunteers' Vase or urn presented to Walter Spencer Stanhope in 1805. *(by kind permission of Simon Fraser)*

justice', commented the *Leeds Intelligencer,*

> *to the prompt spirit and alacrity of our brave countrymen, who have thus mustered on the first moment of alarm, and evinced a display of loyalty and patriotism worthy of British Volunteers and British soldiers, a spirit not to be subdued by the most powerful efforts of our daring foes.*

By the end of August Napoleon had abandoned his idea of invading England – for the time being at least – had turned his back on the Channel and marched his armies eastwards to fight the Austrians and to achieve his great victory at Austerlitz, rather as many years later in the 1940s, another would-be invader had second thoughts and turned his eyes eastwards. On both occasions the local Volunteers remained watchful and ready.

Sources

Contemporary documents and printed material, the latter as either Government or Barnsley publications (i) in the Brotherton Library, University of Leeds (MSS & Special Collections Section): Woolley Hall Papers 60: letter Lord Mulgrave to Earl Fitzwilliam 8/1803; Authorizing Act of Parliament 8/03; Return of Wagons and Carts 3/04 and 1/05; subscription list 8/03 and 12/04; Return of Wagons and Carts 3/04 and 1/05; rendezvous for the Township Companies; Return of Numbers of Volunteers in Staincross Wapentake 8/03; Resolution made at Barnsley meeting 8/03;Plan for rendering the Body of the People instrumental to the general Defence in Case of Invasion. (ii) in Sheffield Archives: Spencer-Stanhope Papers 60565/6:recruiting poster; inspection at Barnsley 1803; call for Yeoman Cavalry to pay arrears of subscriptions 7/03; letters Cockshutt to Spencer-Stanhope 2/04, 5/04, 12/04, 6/05; Cavalry equipment 4/04; letters Francis Wood to Spencer-Stanhope 1/05, 4/05, 8/05; letter Lees to Spencer-Stanhope 4/05; minutes of meeting at Barnsley 8/05; drummers' allegiance document. (iii) in the John Goodchild Archive at Wakefield: Militia Returns for Staincross Wapentake 1806; subscription lists Staincross Wapentake; list of Staincross Volunteers accepted 8/03; arrears of subscriptions 4/04; Extract from General Defence Act so far as relates to Volunteers (service requirements and punishments); requisition forms issued to bakers, barge owners and owners of carts and wagons; typescript copy 'Volunteers of the West Riding of Yorkshire' detailing the August alarm of 1805. Quarter Session Records are in the West Yorkshire Archives at Wakefield, also the map of Beacons of 1803. Microfilm of *Leeds Intelligencer* at Leeds Central Library and of *Sheffield Iris* at Sheffield Central Library. Eli Hoyle's *History of Barnsley* and Burland's *Annals of Barnsley* in the Local Studies section at Barnsley Central Library. Reference was also made to R P Berry's *History of the Volunteer Infantry;* J R Western's *The English Militia in the Eighteenth Century,* I F W Beckett's *The Amateur Military Tradition 1558-1945* and Barry Jackson's *Cawthorne 1790-1990.*

Acknowledgements

I thank the staff at Sheffield Archives for permission to reproduce items from the Spencer Stanhope Papers and for their help in locating material. I am grateful to John Goodchild for making available his private archive and for permission to reproduce the Militia List for Carlton township. I thank Maurice Hepworth of Barnsley Local Studies Library, the staff at the Brotherton Library Special Collections section and also Barry Jackson for their help in locating sources. I thank the staff at the Local History Libraries in Leeds and in Sheffield for their help and I am grateful to the staff of the West Yorkshire Archive Service for permission to copy the Beacon Map of 1803 (Wakefield Reference P3/13). I am grateful to the Trustees of the British Museum and to Routledge Ltd for permission to reproduce the illustrations for the 'New Levies of 1796'. Finally I thank Professor David Hey for kindly reading and commenting on the typescript.

3. DEVELOPMENT AND DECLINE OF THE BARNSLEY CANAL

by Roger Glister

THE OPENING OF THE BARNSLEY CANAL from the river Calder to the basin at Old Mill was heralded with much jollity as reported in the *Doncaster Gazette* on the 14 June 1799,

> *On which occasion the Proprietors of the Aire and Calder Navigation, ordered two of their sloops completely rigged, and furnished with men, guns &c to attend. These sloops left the river Calder about nine o'clock in the morning with cargoes of yarn and other merchandise, and proceeded to Barnsley, amidst a vast concourse of spectators, miners, & manufacturers, who expressed the most lively joy'*

The remainder of the line to Barnby Basin did not open to traffic until the beginning of 1802 when the pumping engine, installed by the Low Moor Company to pump water back up the five locks at Barugh, was commissioned. The coalfield at Barnby Furnace, operated by the Low Moor Company, was now able to develop and its product made up fifty percent of the coal carried down the waterway to the Calder. Manufactured goods were also carried away from Barnsley while a good return trade was soon established transporting building materials, agricultural produce and limestone. The latter was brought up the canal from Brotherton and Knottingley in large quantities to be burnt in kilns built at Barnby Basin and Barugh.

Despite the authority to build the essential tramroads from the Silkstone collieries being included in the Act of Parliament granted to construct the canal, only the Low Moor Company had so far taken advantage of the clause with a half-mile long tramway from the colliery at Barnby Furnace to the canal head. By 1804 its output had reached 10,000 tons but due to geological faults the mine was closed by the end of 1806. At the time only one other colliery was producing coal in any quantity. This was the Silkstone Colliery operated by Samuel Thorp of Banks Hall which had very precarious transport links with the canal along a roadway that was impassable in wet weather. During 1807 it was quite usual to find between five and ten boats waiting in Barnby Basin for loads and be idle for anything up to a week at a time.

This sorry state of affairs soon began to tell on the Canal Company's finances and the situation deteriorated to the point where the treasurer reported debts amounting to some £44,000 with less than £10 in hand with which to discharge them. The Company felt it necessary to issue a statement to the shareholders which read,

> It therefore becomes a Duty incumbent on the Committee to declare to the Proprietors that the Company's Affairs are at present exceedingly embarrassed and that their Difficulties are increasing.

These 'Difficulties' were also felt further down the ladder when the annual pay of Mr Benjamin Shillito, a lock keeper, was cut from £54.60p to £36.40p. Desperate measures were urgently required, and thus at a special meeting of the shareholders in October 1807 the Company sought approval to raise the £43,000 extra capital needed to satisfy the main creditors and build the tramways to serve the working collieries in the Silkstone coalfield.

During 1808 the lines were surveyed, land was purchased and construction put in hand. Some of the land belonged to Walter Spencer-Stanhope, the principal shareholder and chairman of the Barrnsley Canal Company and who, despite the Company's difficult situation, had no qualms about charging £100 an acre for it. The resultant tramway was built to a gauge of four foot two inch using cast iron double flanged rails spiked to stone sleeper blocks laid diagonally to the line. It ran for two miles from Barnby Basin to Silkstone Bridge and was fully operational by mid 1810. The three foot long rail sections came mainly from the Low Moor Company's foundry but some were obtained at the Wakefield foundry of Isaac Aydon. The cost of the railway was about £4,500 made up of materials at £2,193, labour £1,294 and the remainder being the land cost. At the time of opening two concerns were using the new railway, Samuel Thorp and Jonas Clarke. The former had made preparations for the arrival of the railway by the construction of a short branch line to his already operational pits at Banks Hall. Jonas Clarke, however, had awaited the coming of the railway before developing his colliery at the south end of the village of Silkstone.

Their monopoly was short lived due to the arrival of Thomas and Daniel Wilson who re-opened the colliery at Barnby Furnace and developed pits to the east of the line. Another short branch to Norcroft Bridge was constructed by Richard Stringer and Joseph Popplewell, with rails provided by John Darwin & Co. at Elsecar Ironworks, to serve another new colliery. These four coal companies provided the bulk of the trade for the Barnsley Canal for the next ten years. Nearly half of the product from the Silkstone coalfield only used the Barnsley Canal as far as the junction with the Dearne and Dove where it proceeded to the Dun Navigation at Swinton and thence to Lincolnshire. The rest travelled the full length of the Barnsley Canal and made its way to the Ouse via the Aire and Calder Navigation. A not inconsiderable tonnage of coal from the collieries around Worsbrough was also using the Barnsley Canal to reach the markets of the Vale of York and an unusual sight on the upper reaches of the Dearne and Dove Canal would have been laden coal barges passing in both directions.

The development of the Silkstone Railway was the saving of the Barnsley Canal in its early years. From an annual tonnage of coal in 1808 of 34,673 it rose without fail each year to 85,355 in 1813, and with some slight faltering to 114,353 in 1820. This was some consolation for the long suffering shareholders who enjoyed a steadily rising dividend, in 1820 the Company paid a princely seven-and-a-half percent.

Throughout the early years both the Barnsley and the Dearne and Dove canals had been plagued by a shortage of water and the first of several steps to alleviate the problem was taken in 1807 when the reservoir at Cold Hiendley was enlarged. In 1854 a second reservoir, Wintersett, was built adjacent to the original and this in turn was increased in size by 55 acres in 1874. At this time a pumping engine was installed at Cold Hiendley to raise excess water from this lower reservoir into the larger Wintersett reservoir. This beam engine made by Harvey's of Hale was still working shortly after the Second World War. Coal for the steam plant was delivered to the site by narrow boats that navigated the feeder that ran from the canal near Haw Park Mine Bridge and was one of only a few roles played by such craft on this broad canal.

In 1828 the Aire and Calder proposed to rebuild the line of the Calder to enable the passage of larger vessels from the Humber to Wakefield and beyond. The Barnsley Canal Company supported this scheme and to this end Joseph Atkinson, the resident engineer appointed in 1823, made an announcement that he would be raising and re-aligning most of the bridges on the canal, 'to enable that Description of Sea-going Vessels called Billy-boys to navigate up the Line'. He was of the opinion that these craft would be capable and willing to transport Silkstone coal direct from the West Riding of Yorkshire to coastal ports without trans-shipment. Unfortunately, Mr Atkinson died before his plan was fully implemented and it was his successor, Mr W T Hall, who made the declaration in January 1830 that all the necessary alterations having been made to the bridges, 'all BILLY BOYS, COASTING and other VESSELS of not more than 14 Feet 10 Inches Beam, may now pass along the whole of the Canal for Silkstone Coal, Merchandise, &c'. So reported the *Doncaster Gazette* on 8 January, 1830.

Billy Boys were basically sea going vessels carrying 80 to 100 tons and built along the same lines as the better known keels. Being of clinker construction with very bluff bows and more pronounced shear they were about 63 feet long with a beam of some 18 feet and, like the keels, carried leeboards. They were twin masted with a bowsprit and carried sloop style rigging which was not the most convenient of sailing rigs to dismantle and stow on deck whilst the craft navigated a low bridge on a canal. As the Billy Boys drew considerably more water than a keel and were more than four feet wider it would be reasonable to assume that none took advantage of Mr Hall's extensive alterations to the infrastructure of the Barnsley Canal. They did, however, make occasional visits to Leeds and Wakefield using the up-graded Aire and Calder Navigation.

The first signs of the storm clouds gathering on the horizon came with the proposed North Midland Railway line from Derby to Leeds and the Barnsley Canal Company found itself objecting to the Bill in order to ensure that any bridges over the canal were built to the same dimensions as those on the Goole Canal should they wish at a later date to increase its capacity. This they did in September 1836 by deepening the canal to seven feet by raising the banks and lock walls. The reservoir at Cold Hiendley also had its capacity increased by heightening the embankment. The North Midland opened in 1840 and was quickly followed in 1841 by the Great North of England Railway that ran from Darlington to York and it was this concern that heralded the decline of the Barnsley Canal.

An entry in the Proprietors' Minute Book on 6th July 1842 illustrates the early inroads made by the new railways into the canal trade. It was recorded that this line from Darlington was carrying

> *a considerable quantity of Coal into the neighbourhood of Ripon, Boro'bridge, York etc. which was formerly supplied by Mr. Clarke's Silkstone Coal to the extent of about Fifty thousand Tons per Annum.*

Coal tonnage on the canal continued to fall as more and more cheaper coal from outlying coal fields arrived by rail to satisfy the needs of the Barnsley's former customers. By 1844, the Great North of England Railway had cut its rates to 1/4d per mile with which neither the Barnsley Canal nor the Aire and Calder Navigation could compete.

After several acrimonious meetings with both the Aire and Calder and the Don Navigation the Barnsley Canal remained independent in a chaotic, cut-throat world of railway expansion where both the old and the new transport systems were fighting for survival. When the Don Navigation took over the Dearne and Dove Canal in January 1846 after long negotiations they cut their tolls by more than fifty percent damaging the Barnsley even further and this proved to be the final straw; they began looking for a buyer. A period of horse-trading then commenced between the Manchester and Leeds Railway, the Manchester, Sheffield and Lincolnshire Railway and the Aire and Calder Navigation. The Barnsley Company flirted with each of the bidders in turn but failed to reach an agreement during which time the Company's position was steadily weakening. The tonnage of coal carried by the canal had dropped from 204,000 tons in 1844 to 84,000 in 1853 owing to the amount of trade taking advantage of the cheaper tolls on the Dearne and Dove. As the Barnsley Canal was a source of trade for the Aire and Calder and, like the Don Navigation, it wanted to protect the Silkstone coalfield from total exploitation by the railways a strong representation was made to the Company which, at last recognising the futility of independence, capitulated. A Bill authorising the transfer was introduced in 1856 but the Barnsley Company remained in existence to carry on some of the formal business.

The trade to York was still diminishing in an alarming fashion; from 19,840 tons in 1851 to 958 tons in 1870. To balance this the tonnage to Hull and the coastal trade had dramatically increased from 579 in 1851 to 46,424 in 1870 whilst that to Goole had grown slightly and stood at 24,950 tons in 1870. During this period of its life the Barnsley Canal was in need of constant and costly maintenance due to the silting up of the channel and the large accumulation of weed in some lengths of the cut. The Barugh locks were in a very bad state of repair despite £7,000 being spent on improvements and on 6 August 1861 the scourge of the Barnsley Canal gave notice of its future intentions.

On this fateful day the canal bank burst at Royston due to subsidence and deposited a loaded sloop, complete with her crew, in a field some 400 yards away. During the three weeks it took to reopen the canal over one hundred boats were queueing up to continue their journeys. The sinking of the land due to coal extraction from beneath the canal was eventually to lead to its downfall; banks had to be continually strengthened and the channel dredged to overcome the changing contours of the canal bed. In 1866, according to an entry in the Barnsley Canal Minute Book of 4 July, the committee went to

Figures 1-2. Two picture postcards showing the 'bursting of the Barnsley Aqueduct' capture the drama of the occasion. 20 November 1911. *Courtesy of Barnsley Canal Group and the Author*

inspect the aqueduct and reported

> *considerable damage caused by the sinking of the land. Great caution will be required in preventing both the fissures in the rock and the cracks in the arches of the aqueduct becoming larger.*

However, the Aire and Calder still had faith in the Barnsley when between 1879 and 1881 they lengthened all the locks up to Barugh from the original 66 feet to 84 feet but leaving the width at 15 feet in an attempt to accommodate the newer 79 feet long barges of iron construction that were now taking the place of the wooden built keels, though some boat builders remained faithful to wood for many years to come.

By 1893 the five locks and the canal above Barugh wharf had been abandoned when maintenance costs far out-weighed the tolls received from the scant trade on this section of the canal due to the monopoly of the railway serving the Silkstone coal field.

The second major breach occurred on 20 November 1911 when the embankment adjacent to the aqueduct failed due to the ever present subsidence and caused the closure of the canal until 10 July 1912. The following graphic account appeared in the *Barnsley Chronicle* of Saturday 25 November 1911:

> *A miner named Oscar Cooper, of Harborough Hills, was on the spot when the water began to break through. He was taking a short cut, about 5.30 in the morning, to get to his work at the Barnsley Main Colliery, when he noticed water working itself through the banks. He crept back and warned other colliers who were following. They considered it dangerous to attempt to cross* [the aqueduct] *and Cooper went to call the canal bank man. The water rapidly increased in volume, and at ten minutes to six the men saw the bank collapse. Cooper says, 'There was a rumble like thunder, and then the bank all came down'. A man named Sykes, who lives at the lock house close at hand, says that between five and six he was awakened by a rumbling noise, and went out to see what was a matter. On getting out on the bank he heard a sharp crack. He saw that the bank had given away, but at the time according to his estimate, the breach was not more than five feet wide. The water, however, was making short work of the soft earth; soon the clay puddling in the bed of the canal gave way and before long the gap had extended fifty yards. A long stretch of the canal, estimated at about twelve miles, was draining away through the gap with terrible force.*

Again, in September 1922 the canal was closed for four months

Figure 3. This fine view looking towards the aqueduct and the distant town of Barnsley was taken by Norman Marshall, from a train crossing the railway viaduct at Hoyle Mill, 23 February 1954.

during a servere drought. Despite the trials and tribulations the canal trade held up reasonably well with the total tonnage peaking in 1895/99 at 257,798 and in the four years leading to the outbreak of war had fallen to 192,406 tons. Between the wars traffic steadily declined mainly due to the collieries along the line being worked out.

A breach close to the aqueduct on 13 June 1945 caused the flooding of Mottram Wood Colliery and the resultant compensation cost the Company £2,375; a sum it could ill-afford. This leak was repaired but by November the general manager was warning of further trouble in the area of the aqueduct where the subsiding ground was forcing the banks to be built ever higher to maintain the navigable depth. Exactly

a year later, on 22 November 1946, the canal burst at Littleworth which caused 53 million gallons of water to flood the fields and a nearby housing estate. This time compensation was set at £3,500 and made the Aire and Calder consider the viability of the Barnsley Canal.

In January 1947 a Bill was put before Parliament applying for the nationalisation of the Aire and Calder and this opportunity was taken by the board of directors to recommend the abandonment of the waterway. The Ministry consented and abandonment was applied for under the *Railway & Canal Traffic Act of 1888*. The last boat passed through Royston on 7 December 1950 and 10 June 1952 saw the last one to use Heath Lock with the warrant granted in 1953.

The canal quickly deteriorated with the aqueduct being demolished as being 'unsafe' very shortly after closure and the earth's surface compensating for the havoc wreaked far below. The demand for the

commodity that had built the Barnsley Canal had finally destroyed it.

The waterway languished in a very sorry state for many years until in 1984 the Barnsley Canal Group was formed with the intention of highlighting the plight of this piece of our heritage and campaigning for its restoration and return to navigable status. A full report on the state of the canal and a presentation of the case for restoration was published by the Group later in the year. Since then their tireless efforts have at last started to bear fruit and both the Barnsley Canal and the Dearne and Dove Canal are no longer being viewed as linear rubbish tips but as potential water-based amenities giving pleasure and employment to many along the waterway corridor.

The illustrations (Figures 1-10) that follow are from the extensive archive of the Barnsley Canal Group and private collections as acknowledged in the captions.

Figure 4. Demolition in progress at the Barnsley Aqueduct, Spring 1954. This excellent photograph by Norman Marshall helps us to appreciate both the scale of the original engineering achievement and the great loss to the local landscape. Monk Bretton 'castle' can be seen on Burton Bank in the distance.

Further reading.

Copies of *The Barnsley Canal - a forgotten waterway?* at £2.50p (including postage) can be had from Roger Glister, 2 Moorside Court, Cowpasture Road, Ilkley, LS29 8UF.

Hadfield C, *The Canals of Yorkshire and North East England,* 1973.
Baxter B, Stone Blocks and Iron Rails, 1966.
Slatcher W N, The Barnsley Canal and its First Twenty Years, *Transport History,* 1968.
Smith P L, *Canal Craft,* 1979.

Figures 5-7. This excellent and fortuitous set of photographs by Norman Marshall record the demolition of the Barnsley Aqueduct in the Spring of 1954. The weight of the crane and the condition of the masonry suggests that the structure was in fact far from unstable. Survival would have ensured that the aqueduct remained as a most important example of canal industrial archaeology; and a spectacular centre-piece of the restoration and development of the canal.

Figure 8. The canal basin at Old Mill. *Barnsley Canal Group*

Figure 9. A 'pleasure barge' at Harborough Hill bridge, Old Mill (bound for Cold Hiendley?) probably an outing from a local church or chapel, c1940. *Barnsley Canal Group.*

Figure 10. Barges on the canal at Redferns Glassworks, Old Mill, c. 1950. *Barnsley Canal Group.*

Figure 1. Extract from the six-inch to one mile Ordnance Survey map of 1890. In the short distance from Smithies to New Lodge several collieries are clearly marked: East Gawber Hall, Primrose Main, Wharncliffe Carlton and Wallsend, along with sites of 'Old Shafts'.

4. UP WAKEFIELD ROAD: COLLIERY DEVELOPMENTS

by John Goodchild M Univ

A TRAVELLER BETWEEN BARNSLEY and Wakefield in the last decades of the nineteenth century would have been visually and aurally impressed or even horrified, if not a local – by the number of independent collieries which he passed between Old Mill and New Lodge (Figure 1). In few other areas locally was there such a concentration of working pits, and the noise as well as the visual impact was considerable. All were relatively newly opened, but they differed in the seams which they worked and in their size (and hence outputs and employment figures), while some were shaft pits and others drifts. This essay attempts briefly to explain why, how and by whom this complex of local collieries developed; the study is entirely based on manuscript material in the John Goodchild Local History Study Centre at Wakefield.

Geological, economic and transport factors governed the development of coal mining in this area as in others, and a particular combination of these resulted in this instance in a short-term but concentrated working of the coal within a quite limited area. The Barnsley seam of coal was that worked by the largest of these concerns, although others worked the thinner seems too; the Barnsley Bed hereabouts provided some seven feet of workable coal of the best quality, but the seam dipped away from its outcrop on the further side of the Dearne valley, so that it was left for large-scale exploitation until after the more accessible and shallower (and hence more readily and cheaply got) Barnsley Bed coal there was within foreseeable exhaustion.

The new markets for coal which were opened up by the new steam railways – within Yorkshire, in England and abroad – were available to Barnsley coal from the opening of the first local line in January 1850, but access to the new railway and older canal (opened in c 1800 here), both of which also lay on the opposite side of the valley of the Dearne, was somewhat physically difficult. There is no evidence of even modest coal workings alongside the main road from Barnsley towards Wakefield, until the 1850s: distance from a means of transport other than the road and the depth of the Barnsley seem, combined to retard working in this area, although a little further along the same Dearne

valley side, coal was being worked in the Darton area long before the
new railway-borne era which opened in 1850.

It was in January 1854 that Robert Craik & Co began sinking their
colliery which was then apparently known as **New Lodge Colliery,**
but was soon to be known by its coal-market-orientated name of **East
Gawber Hall Colliery**. A lease of some 208 acres of Barnsley Bed
coal had been obtained, and sinking was undertaken by Messrs Jagger
– one of the usual itinerant firms of pit sinkers - on the New Lodge
estate. Coal carriage by road to the nearest railway station was costly,
and negotiations were opened with the new lessees of the Barnsley
Canal for the use of their waterway, guaranteeing a minimum of
25,000 tons a year; the canal would provide the necessary connecting
facilities. Discussions involving the point of meeting with the canal
were followed by a proposal by the canal to promote a railway which
would have connected up all the collieries from Woolley to a basin at
the north end of the canal aqueduct near Barnsley, but that proposal
was unsuccessful, and early in 1858 Craiks agreed to a line laid out by
the canal's engineer, following the shortest possible route to the canal.

The Barnsley Bed was won at East Gawber in February 1856,
although the upper seams were already being worked – the Woodmoor
and the Mapplewell. Coal was advertised at six shillings at the pit, and
7s 8d delivered in Barnsley; and negotiations over a railway having as
yet proved unproductive, the firm advertised the letting for three
months of the carting of 100 tons daily to the canal at Old Mill Wharf,
and of 50 tons daily to the Barnsley railway station.

By the end of 1858, Craiks had sent some 7,000 tons of coal down
the canal, much of which had come to Leeds, and increasing areas of
coal were being worked and the associated royalty payments made.
When an attempt was made to increase the ratability of the new
colliery from £152 to £1,125 in 1860, sales were some 1,200 to 1,300
tons per week by canal and only 10 to 15 tons by land. Railway access
was now wanted, and in 1863 agreement was reached to cross the
canal (by increasing the minimum canal tonnage) and build on
upwards to the Lancashire & Yorkshire's branch. Pit head selling prices
in this period were:

best hards	22 cwt to the ton	7s
softs	24	6
clay seam	24	4
screened slack	30	2
smudge	30	1s

In 1864 the firm had 260 employees, which was to rise to some 800 before the 1883 explosion and then drop to about 450 in the later 1880s. A plan of the Carlton Coalfield, adjoining upon that in lease to Craiks, made by Henry Holt of Wakefield and dated August 1856, shows 'Engine Pit New Lodge Colliery' in the land of J F Carr esq and south of New Laithes; Lord Wharncliffe was having his own Carlton township coalfield tested by borings for coals, and in due course a lease of a major part – the upper or western part of the coal-field – was granted to Craiks, while from March 1857 some 86.5 acres of the Barnsley Bed were also leased from the Earl of Shrewsbury's Hospital Trustees, lying in Monk Bretton township and at £570 a year for the first seven years, £760 for the second seven and £1140 for the last seven, as minimum coal rents, plus an extra acreage rent of £300 per year.

Craiks were always financial penny-pinchers, and Charles Morton, the Government Inspector of Mines, had a sad tale to tell in relation to the partners in 1861:

Explosion of fire-damp at Craik and Co's East Gawber Colliery

Soon after the horrible catastrophe at Lundhill in 1857, I persuaded the owners of East Gawber Colliery, which was but modestly ventilated, to prohibit naked lights and indiscriminate blasting of coal in their pits;and they continued for a while to follow this wholesome advice.

Unfortunately, however, the same mistaken prejudice and short-sighted economy which had rejected safety lamps at Lundhill, and thereby produced such awful calamities at that colliery, again became paramount at East Gawber, and wrought very mischievous consequences for Messrs Craik and Co. and their servants, in 1861.

By degrees, and for the sake of cheapness, the use of safety lamps was unwisely abandoned; candles were generally re-introduced; and gunpowder was employed as freely and imprudently as ever.

The natural result was, that apparently unimportant flashes and faint explosions of inflammable gas gradually became more frequent and less thought of.

On different days during the last week of July 1861, two such ignitions of fire-damp were produced in a 'heading', by blasting the coal; – the first did no damage, but the second set fire to the Barnsley Thick Bed; and two valuable lives were sacrificed and others jeopardized in the abortive attempt to arrest the flames. With a view to check the spread of the fire to adjoining parts of the mine, the underground-viewer (Mark Ward) *and his deputy* (John Warhurst) *commenced building a couple of stoppings, to exclude air from the burning mass; and whilst thus engaged, another explosion occurred which burnt them so severely as to cause their death.*

The injured persons and the horses were then speedily brought to the surface; the mine was abandoned; and the mouths of the two shafts were covered as tightly as possible; leaving open the top of the upcast or furnace shaft, situated about 340 yards to the rise of the other two pits.

Explosive shocks were felt above ground twelve hours afterwards, but they were not strong enough to remove the shaft coverings.

Subsequently, apart from the explosion of 1883 (Figure 2) which killed 22, the colliery's fatal accident record was, by local standards, a not altogether black one.

From its earliest days, as we shall see, East Gawber Hall had had to contend with the output of other new and large collieries which were developed in the Barnsley area at exactly its own period of opening.

Papers of the middle of 1865 refer to a proposed lease allowing of the building of cottages: a number of three-roomed, single storey cottages with very long chimneys at Hill Top, near the site of the East Gawber Hall Colliery, remained by the side of the Wakefield Road until after the end of the 1939-45 War and were some of the few in the West Riding, other than those at Pilley of the Wharncliffe Silkstone Company, of the single storey type. In 1865-66 it was proposed to extend the Lord Wharncliffe lease to sixty years 'to justify erection of Iron Works by Craik & Co.' and a site had been chosen for this major new development. Nothing came of it, but the lease area was extended into the Carlton coalfield, Lord Wharncliffe agreeing to join the partners in proving the coal, and in 1867 references occur to the sinking of a new engine pit. The lease was in fact extended in November 1867 for a further term of forty-two years from July 1865.

Figure 2. Engraving of the scene at the disaster at Wharncliffe Carlton Colliery, October 1883.

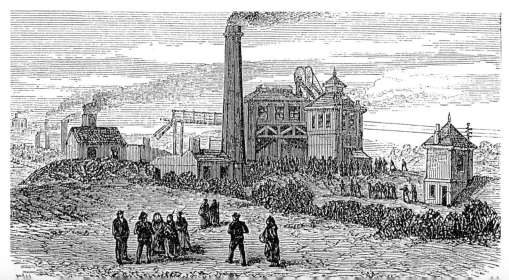

The colliery's prospects were vastly improved by the opening of the Barnsley Coal Railway, delayed though that development was to prove. The necessary Act was obtained in July 1861, but it was not until January 1870 that the line was opened through to Applehaigh from Stairfoot, and further connections at each end were made subsequently. The new lease had presumably allowed of an increased output, and it was now possible to abandon the awkward tramway which connected with the canal and with the railway beyond it. At East Gawber Hall the shaft was 155 yards to the Barnsley Bed, which itself divided

softs	3'6"
dirt and coal	1'2"
hard coal	3'6"
soft coal	1'1"

A new shaft was sunk adjoining the mainline railway, with the title Wharncliffe Carlton, about 1872. A full report of a visit made to the new pit in 1874 was published in one of the Barnsley newspapers, and gives details.

East Gawber Hall was one of a number of Barnsley area collieries begun by successful Barnsley linen manufacturers. Robert Craik, the founder of the business, was an interesting fellow: 'a self-made man: the sole architect of his own fortune', as he was described by the *Barnsley Chronicle* at his death. He was a Scot from Kirkcudbrightshire; he was apprenticed to a draper in Dumfries and at 20 he came as an assistant to a Barnsley draper on Market Hill. He was said to have been

a young man of remarkably frank and engaging manner, and one who at once secured the confidence and commanded the respect of those with whom he came into contact occupying a much higher social position,

and about 1828 he became an employee of the large linen manufacturing firm of Jackson & Hodgetts. In 1832 he both married and set up in business as a linen manufacturer with the title of Craik & Wood, the firm opening an account with the Wakefield Banking Co, but Wood leaving the partnership about 1834. In 1840 Craik took the tenancy of the Old Mill bleach works, and carried on bleaching along with linen cloth manufacturing, and in about 1854, as we have seen, took a lease of the New Lodge estate coal, about 208 acres of the Barnsley seam. Subsequently, with partners, he took extensive areas of coal from Lord Wharncliffe and others, all carried on 'with remarkable success'.

Robert Craik was a Barnsley Police Commissioner and at the first election of a Local Board for Barnsley, in 1853, he was elected a member, although he retired after three years and later took little active part in public affairs. He served as churchwarden, as an overseer of the poor, and he was active in philanthropic concerns. He died at Buxton in 1868 and was buried in Barnsley Cemetery. His home was in Church Street, although he had lived at Fairfield House until 1859.

Craik's elder and, it is said, more domineering son, William, subsequently headed the firm. Of his life little is known except that he became a town councillor in 1871 and remained such until his death in 1885, although it was then said that ill health had latterly prevented him from attending the meetings of the Corporation very regularly. He died at only fifty, and apparently unmarried, of dropsy, which had first shown itself in October 1884 and since the appearance of which he had been confined to the house. His brother Thomas survived him.

George Sidebottom had 'had entire control' of the working colliery, as neither Mr George nor Mr Tom (Craik) had any knowledge of technical matters. Tom Craik had apparently taken over nominally on Sidebottom's leaving, but the view of J H Wood the mining engineer, who measured the East Gawber Hall Wharncliffe Estate coal for both lessor and lessee, was that Mr Tom 'more than once evinced to me' his ignorance 'when looking over the plans with him'. The colliery was being worked by the early 1880s in a 'very unworkmanlife manner'. The pillars left to support the underground workings were being partly worked through and reduced in strength, the lessor's surveyors not being informed, and hence that coal not paid for; Craiks alleged that the pillars were crushed and hidden by a years-old creep to which the workings were in part subject, thus hiding the area from which the coal had been irregularly got. Craiks also used the excuse of the 1883 explosion to keep secret any knowledge of the south side workings of the Main Gawber Plane. The main level needed thirty foot posts on each side and the lease provided for a main level and three permanent bord gates: their permancy ceased as they were allowed to become impassable. Coal had been improperly shaved in thick layers from posts, and when a decision to work back was implemented, it was found that the coal was crushed and worthless. When Craiks negotiated for **Bromley Colliery** (near Wortley), their East Gawber Hall Colliery rent for pillars was reduced from £275 to £225 per acre, but returned to the high figure when Bromley was given up.

Craiks had been initial members of the South Yorkshire Coalmasters' Association from 1861, but their workmen seemed to have been reluctant members of the miners' unions until the 1880s, when the following were the Craik men's figures:

	Contributions £			Entrance Fees £		
1885	34	0	0	14	12	6d
1886	39	4	0	2	12	6
1887	35	15	3		5	0
1888	48	12	8	0	0	0
1889	149	4	11	0	0	0
1890	343	12	9	3	6	6

The mineral records of the Earl of Wharncliffe's estate indicate the amount of coal got in each year from and including 1874:

	at East Gawber Hall			at Wharncliffe Carlton			rental payments		
	a.	r.	p.	a.	r.	p.	£.	s.	d.
1874	6	2	33	4	2	36		5893	11	9
1875	13	2	12	5	0	9		5123	11	10
1876	8	2	25	4	2	21		3671	4	11
1877	5	2	17	1	2	1		1955	9	9
1878	4	3	14	4	2	25		2611	3	6
1879	4	2	0	2	0	8		2215	9	4
1880	9	3	14	1	2	23 & posts 3.3.19	3465		
1881	8	2	39	5	1	19	2.2.0	4577	14	1
1882	15	1	20	6	3	11		5731	8	9
1883	10	3	29	6	0	27		3529	6	11
1884	16	0	5	1	1	16		2823	12	2
1885	17	0	7	0	3	16		3271	18	0
1886	20	2	20	0	2	9		3460	1	3
1887	21	3	22	0	3	5		3516	7	8
1888	21	1	24	1	1	32		3410	14	6
1889	18	2	31					2595	19	11
1890	13	1	19					2510	17	4
1891	16	0	20					2318	11	10
1892	13	0	2					2401	8	9
1893	no rents charged								
1894	7	2	4					1160	7	6
1895	6	3	16					1589	16	0
1896	6	0	26					1092		
1897	6	1	4					1103	1	2
1898	2	3	9					416	5	0
1899	1	1	0					188		

Beyond this date the estate mineral rent book is indecipherable, owing to decay through damp. A few figures which give gettings in the various owners' estates which were worked from East Gawber and Wharncliffe Carlton and passed as subject to wayleave rents to Wharncliffe are interesting as being the only means of judging both overall output and any relationship between coal outputs from Wharncliffe's and others' coal worked:

1879	Wharncliffe estate	6a	2	8p
	Mrs Carr's	5	1	34
	Mrs Daly's	1	3	35
	Shrewsbury Hospital estate	0	0	12
1881	Wharncliffe Estate	18	3	16
	Mrs Carr's "	4	1	30
	Shrewsbury Hospital estate	4	3	38

In 1892 wayleave was charged on 6a 0 33p of Mrs Daly's coal passing through the Wharncliffe estate. Allowances were made in 1882 for 'Slips in Coal' and for 'Bad Tops', but coal left to support roadways underground was charged to the tenant. The seam was an average seven feet in thickness, and produced an average of 9,000 tons an acre.

Craiks were for some years also manufacturers of railway wagons. This business was begun in 1863 and was turned into a limited liability concern only in 1876, when G W and T Craik retained a large part of the capital of £10,000. The concern paid ten per cent in December 1876 and another five per cent in September 1877, but nothing there-after and soon went into liquidation. The linen manufactory was given up by Craiks, according to trade directories, between 1857 and 1861, but bleaching continued, latterly at the Greenfoot Bleachworks: Craiks are mentioned as bleachers in the 1897 directory, but not in that of 1904.

The Craiks worked a colliery other than East Gawber Hall, that at Bromley in the township of Wortley, to the south of Barnsley. The colliery was owned by Lord Wharncliffe, who sent from it coal to London via the GNR in increasing tonnages in 1869 to 1871, rising to 38,674 tons. In 1874, on the crest of the coalmining boom, agree-ment was reached to let the colliery to G W and T Craik; Lord Wharncliffe had some 90 men and boys working at the time.

Craiks ceased working the mine in 1879-80, but a new agreement was reached in May 1881 and the colliery was subsequently worked, although only until later in that year, as The Bromley Silkstone Co. In the following year, Craiks owed the Barnsley Banking Company a large but unstated sum: judgement was obtained by the Bank against

Craiks and Lord Wharncliffe, although the Bank's directors refused 'to crush Craik':

The Bank has allowed this man [Craik] *to trade on Lord Wharncliffe's credit, entirely without his Lordship's knowledge or authority, & now they require him to pay the amount due to the Bank.*

It is not entirely clear as to whether this related to East Gawber Hall or to Bromley, although probably the latter. In July 1882 Lord Wharncliffe had paid the Bank £1500 on account of the colliery's debt to it; there was at the time a larger arrear of coal rent due to Wharncliffe for East Gawber from the Craik brothers.

At East Gawber, a new colliery was opened by the same partners in c1873, in the coal boom and close to the new railway, with the title Wharncliffe Carlton: the success of the colliery was said in 1874 to be owing to 'the persevering industry of Mr Thomas Craik (the junior brother)'. But in 1883 there occurred at **Wharncliffe Carlton** a great explosion, by which 22 were killed and 800 men and boys were – as the underground workings were connected up with those of East Gawber Hall – thrown out of work. An engraving shows the colliery at this time: it was described as having been sunk for some ten years, having two winding engines by Messers Coupe, engine builders of Wigan, each of 65 hp. The shaft was 130 yards and there was a cubical engine house; the shaft was 13 ft in diameter, bricked from the surface to about 35 yards and then tubbed or bricked. A six-inch diameter pipe took steam to an engine plane, and below there were two engines (again by Coupe), each of 40 hp. The colliery was worked 'longwall', and Stephenson lamps had always been used. Interestingly, a representative of Pope & Pearson, of West Riding Colliery at Altofts, had visited the colliery after the explosion with a view to getting employees for his own firm.

As has been seen, the fatal accidents record of Craiks was not a bad one: in the years 1868 to 1888 inclusive, apart from the 22 killed in the disaster of 1883, only 19 died, the largest number being six in one year. However, the concern had to struggle, and not only with the financial and markedly deteriorated physical conditions which were results of the explosions and which may have closed Wharncliffe Carlton for coal getting in 1889, but also with the long-continued depression of the 1870s and 80s.

In 1884 the Wharncliffe mineral agent wrote that

the Lessees had been struggling with great difficulties, but...those

> *difficulties are consequent upon their own mismanagement, and the want of proper mining skill and judgement in the working of the Colliery, and the conduct of the business.*

There were said to have been at least seven managers since the colliery was opened and there was in 1883 not one under-manager or deputy who had been there three years earlier – and none were recollected to have left to better themselves! The manager, Sidebottom, who had been there ten or twelve years, had claimed that his wages were in arrear, and that the general complaint was that G W Craik,

> *who had no practical knowledge, browbeats them in reference to the work, or the wages. Mr Tom Craik has very little practical knowledge and he is entirely subordinate in his opinions & acts, to Mr G W Craik.*

As to getting of the coal, it was said by the agent that Craiks worked 'the best first'.

However, despite these difficulties the colliery continued, and in 1890 a new Shrewsbury Hospital lease was taken by Tom Craik alone. A major lawsuit in the 1880s with Wharncliffe resulted in the preservation of a whole series of plans of the workings at East Gawber Hall and Wharncliffe Carlton. By 1893, however, the money owed to the Wakefield & Barnsley Union Bank was causing the Bank some concern and matters were brought to a head when, under the terms of a distraint for rent, the colliery was advertised for sale by Lancaster & Sons, the Barnsley auctioneers. At this time S H Headley was manager and Bury & Walker were solicitors for Craik. The projected 1893 sale was prevented by the colliers arming themselves with pick shafts and chasing the bailiffs away. However, a new tenant was found in the person of John Edey, who paid a still-substantial Barnsley Bed

Figure 3. Heading from a Memorandum – dated August 17 1898 – of the Wharncliffe and East Gawber Colliery Company made shortly after John Edey had taken over from 'R.Craik & Co'.

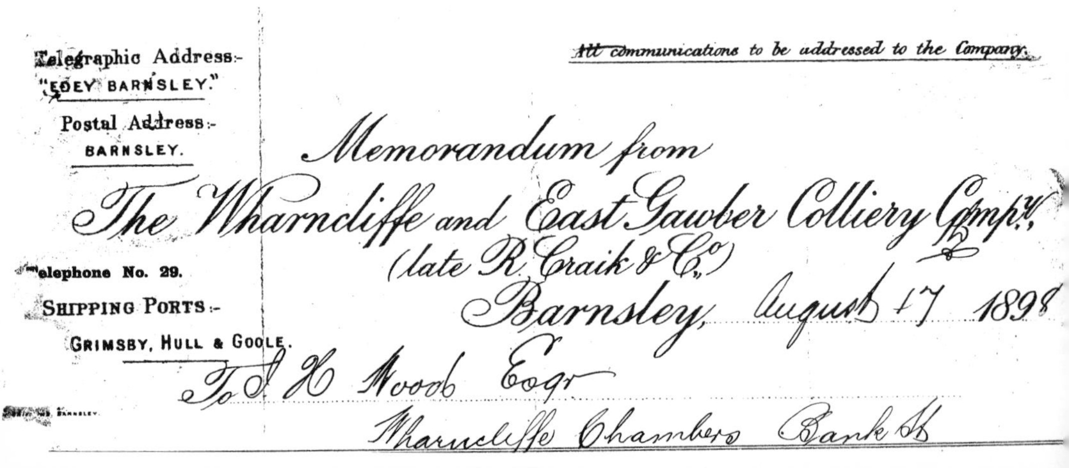

Telegraphic Address:-
"EDEY BARNSLEY."
Postal Address:-
BARNSLEY.

All communications to be addressed to the Company.

Memorandum from
The Wharncliffe and East Gawber Colliery Compy
(late R. Craik & Co)

Telephone No. 29.
Shipping Ports:-
Grimsby, Hull & Goole.

Barnsley, August 17 1898

To J H Wood Esqr
Wharncliffe Chambers Bank St

coal rent to the Wharncliffe estate in 1894, even though his rent was now but £150 an acre as against the £275 which had been charged upon Craiks in the 1880s (Figure 3). John Edey was a chartered accountant from Sheffield, who took over the running, probably as liquidator, of the extensive but unsuccessful Silkstone & Haigh Moor Collieries at Allerton Bywater, near Castleford, which under him increased their employees from 400 or 500 to nearly 2,000, and the output was increased to nearly 500,000 tons a year, with heavy shipments from Hull and Goole; the collieries were lit throughout by electric light in 1892. An account of Edey published in that year and accompanied by a photograph of him suggests

> *strikes and disputes...[are] practically unknown...A more just, fair-minded or considerate master than Mr John Edey it would be extremely difficult to find... Mr. Edey is also proprietor of the Seaborne Coal Company, is largely interested in the coal trade of London and the Continent, and is a shipowner. He is, moreover, the principal proprietor of Walker & Co., Limited, Wakefield [brewers], and is a member of the London Chamber of Commerce...he is possessed of a most courteous and considerate manner.*

and he was a Tory and churchman. This account of John Edey differs however from the recollections of him of P C Greaves, who comments that Edey as liquidator

> *ran the pit for some years, as chief liquidator...The litigation took place and, after nineteen days hearing, it was proved that Mr Edey has done something which did not conform to the Bankruptcy laws. It was very involved and he came in for a good deal of condemnation from the judge. He had to leave, and a new company was formed.*

Edey was unable to make his new concern at East Gawber a success either, and the coal rentals book shows a decline in the coal worked during the 1890s; only one and a quarter acres of Barnsley coal was worked in the year 1899 and coal ceased to be worked there in January 1901, the Barnsley Bed workings being formally abandoned in the following months, as exhausted. Edey however retained the lease; although he did not work the mine (according to the 1901 and 1903 lists of mines at work), he was charged the minimum rent of £150 a year up to January 1908.

During 1893, negotiations resulted in Edey, who lived now in Barnsley, agreeing to take the lower seams, but he seems not to have worked them. In 1907 Lord Wharncliffe's mineral agents wrote to Edey in London, hoping to be able to help him to find another coal-

RULES

OF THE

Primrose Main Colliery

WORKMEN'S

SICK & ACCIDENT

SOCIETY.

Barnsley:

R. E. GRIFFITHS, PRINTER AND LITHOGRAPHER, CHURCH STREET,

1905.

Figure 4. Title-page from Rules of the Primrose Main Colliery Wormen's Sick and Accident Society, printed and published in Barnsley, 1905.

field, and in May 1908 it was believed that a purchaser could be found for the colliery plant. A couple of months later, T W Ward's offer for the plan was turned down, as it was thought by the Earl's agents that they had found a tenant to take the collieries, while in the same month negotiations were in hand as to the taking of Wharncliffe Carlton by the nearby **Central Silkstone Colliery**. Workings in the Winter seam of coal at East Gawber Hall Colliery were officially abandoned in 1916 and 1921.

Not far from East Gawber Hall Colliery, but in St Helen's Lane, was the small **St Helen's Colliery**, 72 yards deep to the Woodmoor seam. This is not listed in 1853, but it is shown on a plan of 1858; it was short-lived and in not either the directory of 1861 nor the list of collieries of 1864. In a similar situation, W C Daglish worked the **Melton Silkstone Colliery** in 1929-30.

On the hillside above the road and railway, and close to the lane leading to Burton Bank Quarry, a shaft is shown on the Ordnance and Geological maps, 35 yards deep to the Winter seam; on the later OS maps levels are shown in the nearby field, opposite to Primrose Main Colliery. Nothing of the history of these levels seems to be recorded, although it is always possible that some memory of their working has been passed down orally. **Primrose Main Colliery** (Figure 4) was a drift mine, and one which had a chequered history in the less than fifty years of its existence. It was opened by James Linsley & Son and its first sod was cut by the chairman of the Monk Bretton Local Board early in 1885. Some 100 acres of coal had been leased from the Earl of Wharncliffe, and the colliery worked the thin seams – the Winter (or Four Foot) and Summer (or Two Foot). The owning partnership became Linsley & Bastow, and from 1891 J Sugden. It then probably closed for a short time, and was re-opened in 1892 by Percival Muschamp & Co's Primrose Main Colliery Company Limited: Muschamp was a Barnsley mining engineer. A coalyard was opened at Wakefield, to which place coal could be taken direct by rail from 1884, and a much larger area (661 acres) of coal was leased from Lord Wharncliffe in 1898. But the colliery was short of capital in Muschamp's hands, and the lease was transferred to the Barnsley Coal & Bye Products Company Limited, of which Muschamp was managing director, a method of enlarging the colliery which proved successful, as by 1903 there were 114 underground workers and, in 1911, 300. But continuing financial success proved elusive; in 1913 the manager wrote that the firm had

> *consistently sustained heavy losses, so much so that they have under consideration the question of stopping altogether,*

which did indeed happen, a receiver for the debenture holders taking charge at the end of that year, and by the end of 1914 the colliery's plant, rails, sleepers, wagons etc had been cleared away, and nothing remained but two empty brick engine houses, the chimney, offices, lamp cabin and two further small brick buildings. The pit – a day hole leading to an underground incline – had collapsed about fifteen yards from the entrance. But in 1913 and under W Laycock & Company, the colliery re-opened, working the Summer Bed, and in 1919 they sold out to Messers Vickerman of Bradford – presumably the yarn agents and merchants of that name – who worked both seams. All is said to have been closed down and sold off about 1930, although the colliery is not listed in the Colliery Year Books of 1923 and 1926, not are any abandonments of workings at Primrose Main listed up to and including 1932.

Thomas Marsden's paper works, Smithies Valley Paper Mills, stood close to where Smithies Lane crosses the Dearne; there is no reference in 1872 to the business also owning a colliery, but in 1874 a drift mine worked by Marsden had ninety employees. A first fatal accident occurred at **Smithies Colliery** in 1878, and others followed in 1883 and 1888. The colliery adjoined the Barnsley Coal Railway and worked the thinner seams – the Winter, Summer and Top Beamshaw – and it may have been shut down by Marsdens in 1897, when the men were on strike and the pit was certainly closed. The pit had been variously known as **Smithies Main, Marsden Main** or (popularly) the **Sludge,** and it soon became also known as **Wallsend Main**, utilising the name of Tyneside coals well-respected in the market. In 1901 the new Wallsend Main Colliery Company employed nineteen underground workers in the Winter seam and worked alum shales (which were also worked at Primrose Main). By 1903 there were fifty men and boys working below ground and producing about 26,000 tons a year. It was now proposed that this become a much larger colliery, increasing output to over 200,000 tons and taking up a large coal lease area; under the new title, the **Central Silkstone Collieries Limited** (again making use of a well-known coal's name);it installed electricity by 1906, put in sidings to the adjacent railway, had fifty ten-ton capacity railway wagons in 1903, and by 1911 had 252 underground workers. But in 1913 a receiver for the debenture holders was appointed, and the end was in sight. Anderson & Son Ltd, who owned Central Silkstone, were members of Sir Joseph Hewitt's Barnsley & District Colliery Owners' Association, which brought together many of the thin-seam pit owners. But the colliery revived as the **Silkstone Colliery Co.Ltd**, whose chairman was Sir William Bulmer of The Grange at Cullingworth. By 1923 there were some 300 underground workers and its printed price lists for underground work go up to 1925; but the colliery closed thereafter, and its workings were officially abandoned in the Spring of 1927.

The **Rosa Colliery**, although not sunk until about 1869, was part of an older colliery undertaking which was expanding its working area as demand increased and older areas were exhausted. Sinkings had been begun at Mount Osborne alongside the Pontefract road in 1837, by Richard Day, a Monk Bretton bleacher and John Twibell, under the supervision of Charles Hawcroft: during 1838 Day & Twibell opened Mount Osborne and **Old Mill** Collieries, both working the Barnsley seam and both feeding coal to the canals. Day was succeeded at his death in 1844 by his nephew William Day, trained as a mining engineer, while John Twibell took a very active part in the affairs of the Yorkshire Coal Masters' Association in the late 1840s and 50s, dying in 1867 at 71, after some years of retirement. William Day sank both **Agnes** and Rosa collieries after Twibell's retirement – the former in 1861-62 and the latter in about 1869. Rosa was to be a large pit, and in 1874 there were some 200 men and boys in its Barnsley Bed workings at 115 yards, while Mount Osborne, Old Mill and Agnes had been connected underground in 1868. In 1871 the colliery sold coal at five shillings a ton. All the pits of this firm were poorly situated for railway transport until the opening of the Barnsley Coal Railway, but the quantities sent by the Barnsley Canal increased from 20,000 tons (in 1861) to 62,000 (1870). In 1870 some two-thirds of the firm's coal was going to Hull, as good Barnsley Bed coal for foreign trade.

Meanwhile, William Day with partners was developing an entirely new area of Barnsley Bed coal at **Monk Bretton**, where the first sod was cut in the middle of 1867 and the Barnsley Bed reached in mid 1870 at some 300 yards. The older pits near Barnsley were worked out by the mid-1880s and the colliery stopped in January 1884, the workings being officially abandoned that same year.

Mottram Wood Colliery worked the thin coal seams – successively the Winter, the Summer and the Melton Field. Production probably began in 1905, the date of its Special Rules, and it was worked initially by the Mottram Wood Colliery Company Limited. Numbers of underground workers were quite small – 68 in 1911, 30 in 1918, 46 in 1923 – and in 1923 the annual output was said to be 5,000 to 10,000 tons a year. The present writer has the colliery's printed Price List of 1924. The colliery is said to have been sold in 1930 to W C Daglish, and after some two years to the Barnsley Syndicate Ltd, a Sheffield concern with various members of the Boot family prominent in it. Four drifts were worked altogether. In 1939 there were some 100 underground employees and the colliery was electrified, working only the winter seam. But in the Spring of 1939 the bank of the nearby Barnsley Canal collapsed and the colliery was inundated; the 1940 List of Mines gives seventeen underground workers, but the inundation caused the colliery to be discontinued and eventually closed.

Thus ended less than a century's working of the collieries 'up Wakefield Road'. As always round Barnsley – and of course elsewhere too – the best quality coal had been worked first, and the nature of the industry had resulted in piecemeal working, leaving some areas unworkable on account of the adjacent worked areas being filled with water when their working ceased. Now little remains to see on the ground, but a walk along the route of the Barnsley Coal Railway, especially when armed with an older edition of the Ordnance Survey, reveals much of interest. Indeed, here as elsewhere in the Barnsley area documents, maps, illustrations and personal recollections survive in some quantity alongside remains on the ground, awaiting the attention of historians of this once great and significant industry.

Author's Note

The source material made use of in this essay are wholely in John Goodchild's Local History Study Centre at Wakefield.

5. A History of Barnsley Trams

by Trevor Polding

IN 1896, ON 26 OCTOBER, the British Electric Traction Company was registered as a Limited Liability Company for the chief purpose of carrying passengers, goods and the generation and distribution of electric power. Authority was subsequently obtained to construct and operate tramways in various parts of the country. In Barnsley, tramways were constructed through two regulations: the Barnsley and District Light Railway Order of 1900 and the Barnsley and District Extension Order of 1902. These powers were transferred to a new company, The Barnsley and District Electric Traction Co which held its first board meeting on 12 March 1902, appointing Sir Thomas Pilkington, Mr E Garke, Mr W I Greer and Mr A E Paris as directors.

Even before the formation of the company, councils had been making decisions about the tramway. In January 1902 Barnsley Town Council approved the design of the span pole and feeder pillars while Monk Bretton RDC decided in favour of a narrow gauge. In February the Streets, Buildings and Improvements Committee made the following decisions:

1. The line should be laid down in the centre of Sheffield Road.
2. The position of the two passing places be altered.
3. The road level under the railway bridges in Eldon Street and Eldon Street North be lowered.
4. The position of the poles be arranged between the company, the Borough Engineer and the Borough Surveyor.

In June the Borough Engineer informed the committee it would cost £250 to have wood blocks between the tracks and it was decided that no further action would be taken. There followed a number of irate letters in the *Barnsley Independent,* complaining about the Traction Company laying rough stone instead of wooden setts in Sheffield Road but eventually, on 11 June, wood setts were reinstated.

In July 1902 a notice appeared in the *Barnsley Chronicle* to the effect that the Barnsley Traction Company would prolong the time limit for completion of the work to 11 November 1902. At this time the Board of Trade confirmed the Barnsley and District Light Railway Order, allowing the construction of light railways in the Urban Districts of Worsbrough, Hoyland Nether, the parish of Tankersley and the Rural District of Wortley.

The original scheme was for a tramway along Eldon Street, up Regent Street and along Huddersfield Road, to the limit of the residential area. The possibility of a bridge over the Great Central Railway at Worsbrough to enable a service to be run to Hoyland and Tankersley was explored but dropped in 1904. Services to Stairfoot and to Kingston via Racecommon Road were considered but not pursued.

In August 1902 Barnsley Town Council were complaining about the length of the time the road had been up at the corner of Pontefract Road and it was announced that the machines installed at the Electricity Works were ready for supplying power. On 11 October the *Barnsley Independent* was able to announce that the works were virtually complete.

The great day arrived at last and on Sunday, 12 October 1902 trial trips were made in the Worsbrough direction to test the brakes of Car Number 1. The next day this was repeated and three more trams ran over the line to join Nos 1 & 2 in the Upper Sheffield Road depot. In the afternoon of the 14 October a trip to test the car and overhead was taken, the VIP party including Mr G W Robinson of the Tramway Company, Mr P W Thompson, Resident Permanent Way Engineer, Mr S Bastow (Borough Engineer) and Mrs Bastow; and Mr and Mrs Pearson. The historic run was through Worsbrough Cutting to Worsbrough Dale, through New England and then to the *Melbourne Hotel*. Photographs were taken at Cutting End and New England.

On 1 November 1902 the Board of Trade carried out its inspection. Colonel von Donop and Mr A P Trotter made the inspection, running two cars, the first carrying the inspectors, the second carrying representatives of the Local Authorities and the tramway company. They proceeded first to Worsbrough Dale and New England, and then to Old Mill. The journey took two hours, the inspectors having plans of the system with them, were able to make a careful survey of track and overhead, alighting from time to time for a closer look. Apparently satisfied, they approved details for the service to commence on 7 November.

Ten cars would be in service. There would be a ten-minute service from May Day Green to Cutting End with alternate cars to Worsbrough Dale and New England; and a twenty minute service to Old Mill. The one penny fare stages were:

Old Mill to May Day Green Queens Hotel (Eldon Street) *to Fountain* (Sheffield Road). *Fountain to Worsbrough Dale or New England*

Early cars were run for the workmen at Barrow Colliery between 5 am and 6 am with extra cars back in the afternoon at a fare of one penny from May Day Green to Worsbrough Dale or New England. The through fare from Barnsley to these destinations was two pence and although the fare was varied greatly to try and increase revenue it reverted back to two pence just prior to the Great War and the same fare still applied on Yorkshire Traction buses in 1952! By way of further comparison, before the tramways started a horse-drawn wagonette plied between the Ebenezer Church in Sheffield Road and Cutting End. The fare was three pence if the weather was fine but doubled to six pence if it was bad !

On 7 November 1902 the first car ran in normal service. It left Eldon Street in the direction of Worsbrough at 3 pm. The driver was Mr Jesse James Hammond and the conductor Mr Sam Jones. Mr Rigby, a local chemist, purchased the first ticket for the sum of five shillings, a considerable sum in those days. He was determined to be the first man over the track after the official opening so he took a seat at the front of the car and leaned over the top deck so that he was ahead of the driver. He can be seen at the front of the car in Figure 2, taken

Figure 1. Jesse Hammond, driver of Barnsley's first tram, in his B & DET uniform. *Courtesy of Hammond Family*

outside the *Wellington Hotel*. In this photograph it can be seen that Mr Hammond, the driver, is wearing his own clothes since the uniforms had not yet arrived.

The following day, 8 November 1902, the tramway had a rather spectacular mishap when shortly after 8 pm Car No 5, on an outward journey to Worsbrough Bridge and very heavily laden reached Cutting End but proceeded no further since the driver had found that the brakes were not working properly. The passengers were ordered off the car where they joined an already large crowd hoping to return to Barnsley. As the conductor was reversing the trolley pole the crowd made a concerted rush to board the car, knocking the driver from the platform in the process. The car began to run away down the slope with the driver in hot pursuit. He had just managed to board and was

Figure 2. The first service tram outside the Wellington Hotel. James Hammond, the driver, is wearing civilian clothes as the uniforms had not arrived in time for the start of the service. Mr Rigby, the chemist, is sat at the front of the top deck. *Courtesy of Hammond Family*

trying to bring it under control when he was again flung to the ground by the rush of panic-striken passengers leaving the car, some even leaping from the top deck. Lightened by the sudden departure of the passengers, the came came to stop of its own accord. The result of all this was a bent trolley pole and two severely shaken passengers (presumably top deck leapers), minor consequences in the circumstances.

By 15 November it was noted that only four cars were running on the Worsbrough section and two on the Old Mill route. A demi-car was purchased for use on this section (Figure 3).

In March 1908 Barnsley Council approached the Tramway Company with a view to extending the system to Monk Bretton. The Tramway Company also had similar requests from the citizens of

Cudworth, Shafton, Brierley and Grimethorpe who argued that the extension would serve an increasing population of 6-7,000. A deputation was appointed to argue the case. The Council complained in April that the promises to extend services from Old Mill to the *Sportsman Inn* (Wakefield Road) had not been kept. They also noted that opposition to the tramway had started in the form of a motor bus service to Hoyland Common.

At the seventh AGM of the Barnsley Electric Traction Company, on 2 May 1908, it was revealed that a profit of £1609 had been made the previous year but on 16 May of the same year the secretary of the company announced that no further extensions to the system were possible. The company had obviously decided on a change of direction, buying its first motor bus in 1913 and ultimately becoming the Yorkshire Traction Omnibus Company. Whilst the route mileage remained static, the tramways were not neglected. Two new cars of a more modern design were bought after the Great War and the older cars rebuilt in a variety of ways.

Between 1913 and closure in 1930, with one exception, nothing happened to the tramway that the local newspapers regarded as worth reporting. However, there was one notable exception. In early December 1914 a double deck tram on the Old Mill service was stood at the Eldon Street terminus when some mischievous paper boys rang the bell and the conductor - thinking it was the driver's signal – pulled out the shoe brake (a type of scotch), causing the tram to begin

Figure 3. The demi-car in service on the Yorkshire Woollen District as their No 59, before being sold to the Barnsley and District. *Roy Brook*

moving down the slight slope. As the conductor collected the fares inside he thought the speed of the tram was rather high, finding to his horror that there was no driver! Seeing how close they were to the curve fro Eldon Street into Old Mill Lane, he went into a blind panic and pulled the trolley from the wire, plunging the car into darkness. The car left the rails at the Prince of Wales, ran across the road and plunged into the front of a grocer's shop. There were five fatalities and a number of injured, some of whom had jumped from the doomed tram. Both the driver and the conductor were dismissed.

On 31 August 1930 Barnsley said farewell to its trams. The last tram from Smithies was to have been driven back up the hill by Charlie Thomas but as Jesse James Hammond was on board Charlie felt that

Figure 4. Car No 1 on last day with the last type of top cover rebuild with five windows upstairs but looking rather more integral with the rest of the body than the earlier types. The crowd is of course the 'top brass' vying to drive the last tram. *Roy Brook*

it was only right that Jesse, driver of the first tram, should have the honour. Jesse drove up the hill to Eldon Street where the 'top brass' were assembled to have the privilege of driving the last tram into the depot. Mr Jesse Hammond, son of Jesse James Hammond, related to me that Mr G W Robinson, the General Manager, drove the last tram up Sheffield Road and was to have driven the last tram into the depot. However, Inspector Wood, driving the preceding tram, dropped his passengers at the depot and drove, out of sight, round the bend towards Worsbrough. After Mr Robinson had put his tram away Inspector Wood drove his 'last tram' triumphantly into the depot. I have since learnt from Inspector Wood that his triumph was short lived as Mr Robinson promptly took his tram out again and once more drove 'the last tram' into the depot and immediately had the traction current turned off. Thus ended the trams of the Barnsley and District Electric Traction Company (Figure 4).

Appendix I

Early Personnel

1902: the first Traffic Superintendent was Mr C D Pearson. The first Electrical Engineer was Mr S E Barstow who was also Borough Electrical Engineer.

In February 1903 Mr A E Paris became the Managing Director. He was also the MD of Yorkshire Woollen District Tramways which lead to close cooperation between the two companies. In 1904 Mr Paris resigned from the B & DT and Mr W H Moorhouse became manager until 1907. In October of the same year Mr P H Marco took over and continued until he left to join the forces in October 1914. It wasn't until March 1915 that Mr W E Nicoll took the post that he kept until August 1919. The final General Manager was Mr G W Robinson, appointed 1928. The last Traffic Superintendent was Mr A Wood who continued to serve the company for many years. He joined the company in March 1903 as a driver, becoming an Inspector in 1908, Chief Inspector in 1912 and serving as Traffic Superintendent from 1919-1945.

Appendix II

Routes

The Worsbrough route ran from Eldon Street via Kendray Street and May Day Green to Sheffield Road, as far as Cutting End where it divided, one line proceeding to Worsbrough Dale, the other to New England. In the Smithies direction the line ran down Eldon Street North into Old Mill Lane, terminating just short of the railway bridge over the Barnsley Coal Railway at the bottom of Old Mill Lane. The track was of standard gauge and was double between Eldon Street and the bottom of New Street, the rest being single with passing loops. The overhead had two trolley wires throughout to avoid the need for points in the wiring.

Appendix III

Tramcars – Double deck Cars, 1-10: technical description.
Double-deck open top cars with three window saloons built 1902-3 by Brush Electrical Engineering Co of Loughborough. Length 27' 5", width 6' 6", fitted with 90 degree reversed stairs. Seating for 22 passengers inside and 26 outside, later increased to 34 outside by fitting double instead of single seats. They were fitted with two 32 Hp Brush motors and controllers.

Trucks: Brush Type A of six foot wheelbase. Brakes: Hand wheel brake and rheostatic brake. Later fitted with mechanical track brake. These cars were of the standard Brush/BET type supplied to other BET tramways such as Yorkshire Woollen District & Peterborough. Three of the Woollen District cars ran in Barnsley on hire during 1904 and there is a story that the two may have remained, being renumbered in to the Barnsley fleet, although no documentation has come to light to support this. The cars were originally, fitted with to covers from 1904 onwards. These were of three types – three side windows; six side windows and two end windows with narrow planks; and six side windows and three end windows with broad planks. Some of the six side window type were fitted with semi-circular ends to cover the balconies by 1914. The open-top type trolley standard was retained and projected through a hole in the roof.

The two post-war cars were of top covered type with open balconies fitted with Bill trucks. At the beginning of the 1920s the earlier cars were rebuilt into a similar form with a rather more integral looking top deck, but can be distinguished by the fact that they retained their reversed stairs and three-window lower saloon. These top covers were built by Charles Smith of Barnsley who built similar ones for the Woollen District cars.

Single deck demi-car No 13, technical description: single deck vestibuled four-wheeled one-man demi-car, built in 1904, probably by the British Electric Car Co for Brush Engineering & Raworths Traction Patents Ltd. Length, 20' 6", width 6' 6". Seating for 20 passengers, 14 inside and 6 on platforms. Electrical equipment by Raworth Traction Patents Ltd. Two 17 Hp Brush motors and Raworth

Figure 5. A group photograph at the Tram Depot, Upper Sheffield Road. The gentleman in the bowler hat is believed to be Mr Moorhouse. *Courtesy of Hammond Family*

controllers. Truck: rigid frame suspension 6ft wheelbase. Brakes : hand wheel brake, mechanical track brake, regenerative brake. This car has an interesting history. The Yorkshire Woollen District Tramways (who operated in Dewsbury and surrounding area) faced with what they considered to be excessive charges for the electricity they bought from Heckmondike Council's Electricity Works, decided to take steps to minimise power consumption on the section concerned. They bought one Raworth regenerative demi-car, to be their No.59. Among its features was a lifting bar across the passenger doorway that when lifted to allow passengers to exit or enter cut off power and applied the brake. It ran in service on the Heckmondike-Hightown route and proved so satisfactory that the YWD bought eight more sets of Raworth equipment for use in larger cars. The demi-car having served its purpose was no longer required by YWD and was lent to the Barnsley and District in September 1905 (Mr E A Paris having close connections with both companies and two months later was sold to the Barnsley and District for £500. It was used on the Eldon Street-Smithies route as a one man car. The special control was of the regenerative type that fed power back into the overhead when running downhill and was controlled by one lever. The car was very under-powered and Mr Wood told me that, as a driver, his main problem was keeping children from running after the car and riding on the fender as it struggled at walking pace up the steeper reaches of Old Mill Lane and Eldon Street North. By the time he had stopped the car and applied the hand brake the children were long gone. In Barnsley the car was known as 'Little Willie'.

Appendix IV

Passengers Carried, 1902–1930

Year	Miles Run	Passengers
1902*	No record	No record
1903	198,100	2,444,292
1904	204,982	2,096,123
1905	203,765	1,715,762
1906	201,544	1,720,411
1907	206,884	1,800,308
1908	196,314	1,820,245
1909	196,473	1,716,373
1910	196,042	1,762,252
1911	219,146	1,910,955
1912	211,500	1,860,156
1913	247,207	2,147,091
1914	238,623	2,050,107
1915	210,894	2,074,125
1916	210,344	2,289,799
1917	213,230	2,632,083
1918	213,155	2,897,556
1919	208,377	2,896,488
1920	218,651	3,016,126
1921	208,834	2,751,591
1922	220,360	2,696,896
1923	221,283	2,677,848
1924	231,276	2,792,311
1925	235,513	2,615,333
1926	162,571	1,765,768
1927	197,870	1,982,507
1928	199,335	1,877,469
1929	199,315	1,915,530
1930*	133,629	1,241,253

Figure 6. An early photograph of an open-top tram at May Day Green.
Courtesy of Hammond Family

Acknowledgements

My thanks to Rex Medley of the Yorkshire Traction Company, without whose help and interest the project would not have progressed. The fact that he was the same Rex Medley who was a classmate at Wilthorpe Council School was a decided bonus. Thanks also to Jesse Hammond and family for their hospitality, personal recollections and the loan of family photographs;and to former Chief Inspector A Wood who, at the age of eighty, remembered vividly the early days of the tramway. To Roy Brook of Huddersfield, thanks for the benefit of his extensive tramway knowledge, particularly of the links with Yorkshire Woollen, and access to his photographic collection, which has been invaluable. A final thank you to my late father, Alf Polding of Gawber, who, on my behalf, spent many hours in Barnsley Reference Library poring over old newspapers, seeking any mention of tramways.

Figure 7. Car No 2, bound for Worsbrough, passing Cheapside.
Courtesy Roy Brook

Figure 8. Staff at depot, c.1908. Mr Marco is the man in the light suit with Chief Inspector Wood seated next to him. Jesse James Hammond is the driver second from the right on the back row. Above him on the top deck of the 'Smithies' tram is Jesse Hammond, his son, who was to drive buses for the Yorkshire Traction Company. *Courtesy of Hammond Family*

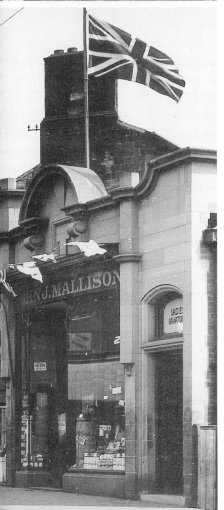

Figure 9. Commercial postcard showing Eldon Street and Public Hall looking towards the Eldon Street terminus, a scene still recognisable today.

Figure 10. Bottom end of Sheffield Road, showing double track merging into single track. *Roy Brook*

Figure 11. Commercial postcard showing Sheffield Road. The style of poles and the use of two trolley wires over the single track can be clearly seen. The poles were used for lighting purposes long after the trams had gone.

Figure 12. Barnsley bound car passing Fountain in Upper Sheffield Road. *Roy Brook*

Figure 13. Car No 6 at Worsbrough Bridge terminus showing passing loop. *Roy Brook*

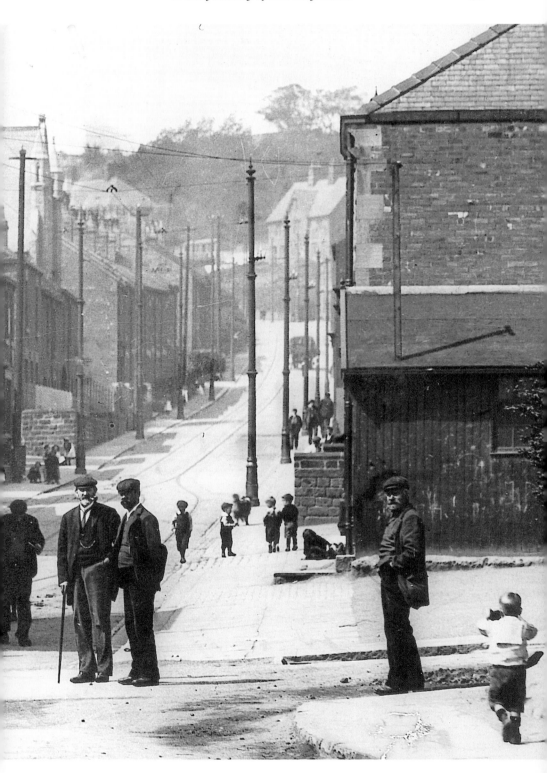

Figure 14. Mr P H Marco and Chief Inspector Wood with some of their crews at the Eldon Street terminus. The car is fitted with a top cover inside the original handrails. *Courtesy Hammond Family*

Figure 15. Another May Day Green scene, a location that was popular with local photographers. *Roy Brook*

6. PLOUGH BOY TO CHEESE FACTOR: SOME MEMORIES OF MY EARLY LIFE

By Athron 'Dick' Bedford

Introduction by Brian Elliott

Autobiographies of ordinary people - even within the confines of an edited extract such as the example that follows - can provide us with a most interesting inside view of working life. This is certainly true with regard to the recollections of Athron or 'Dick' Bedford (Figure 1) whose memory extends back to before the outbreak of the Great War. Dick was first introduced to me about three years ago as 'a most interesting Barnsley character' who bought and sold cheese. This extract is based upon the resultant taped interview and a subsequent written 'auto-biography'. Dick's paternal forebears came from a farming background but were also involved with other local activities : his grandfather, George Smith Bedford, in partnership with Messers Bonson and Drake, produced grindstones from the Oaks Quarry at Pinder Oaks, near Stairfoot (Figure 2) whilst his father was involved in the building of properties on Bismark Street and Bedford Street area of town. Dick recalls with great

Figure 1. Athron 'Dick' Bedford, photographed at Pule Hill Hall Farm, Thurgoland, in April 1995. *Brian Elliott*

Figure 2. Trade card advertising 'The Original Oaks Quarry, near Barnsley'.

THE ORIGINAL
OAKS QUARRY.
NEAR BARNSLEY,
(LATE HAYWOOD'S.)

THE PUBLIC are respectfully informed, that they may be supplied with GRIND-STONES of *first-rate Quality*, and of *any Size*, from the above Quarry, at PRICES stated on the other side of this Card.

The celebrity of the OAKS QUARRY STONE for GRINDSTONES, &c. has been so long known, and is so fully and so justly established, as to render comment altogether unnecessary.

☞ **Apply to Messrs. Bedford, Bonson, Drake, & Co.,**
OAKS QUARRY, BARNSLEY.

affection his own memories of farm work more than eighty years ago, followed by a somewhat surprising 'late' education at a well-known Wakefield school. An interesting account of his early business life follows, developing and expanding into unexpected quarters though not far removed from a farming context. Dick's reminiscences end here in the 1930s but suffice to say the cheese business survived the Second World War, post-war rationing and in fact Dick diversified into the selling of milking machines, and eventually moved premises from Britannia Street to Doncaster Road subsequent to retirement in the early 1970s; a later life that could be regarded as 'another story'. I would like to thank Joan and Ronnie Warttig of Pule Hill Hall Farm, Thurgoland for introducing me to 'Uncle Dick' and of course to Dick himself for being so willing to share his memories.

Rockley Abbey Farm

THE FIRST TIME THAT I SAW DAYLIGHT was on 26 March 1907 at Rockley Abbey Farm, Worsbrough. At the time Captain Bruce Wentworth of Stainborough [Wentworth Castle] owned the land and reared thousands of pheasants for shooting parties. The birds used to play havoc with the crops. I can just remember my father throwing something to frighten them away, although I heard my mother say we were well paid for the damage that they caused. I also recall milk being delivered daily from the farm to the town workhouse at Pogmoor.

White Cross and Swaithe Hall Farms

I was two years old when we left Rockley to take up farming at White Cross and Swaithe Hall farms (Figures 3-5) which my family farmed until 1920 when my father - at the age of 60 - decided to retire. Sadly,

Figure 3. Old Swaithe Hall Farm. *Brian Elliott, 1974*

Figure 4. The young Dick Bedford, gun in hand, in the grounds of Swaithe Hall. Some of our family and father's nurses looking on.

he died three months later. At the age of five or six [1911/12] I began to notice matters relating to the working of the farms.

Farming was a lovely life, although there was no ending to the work when livestock were kept. The job entailed milking thirty to forty cows night and morning and then the milk had to be delivered to the Kendray Hospital, father being paid one shilling [5p] a gallon. It was a long job, taking nearly two hours. At seven years old I could help but rather slowly. When the War [1914] broke out most of the milkers had to be sold since nearly all pasture land had to be ploughed up for growing crops.

At the age of eight I tried my hand at ploughing. Arthur Jackson, one of the men that lived-in, gave me a few lessons how to handle two horses with one line tied to the 'bit' on the horse on the right. Arthur used to fix the rigging and plough one furrow for me. My first attempt went well until I got to the end of the furrow but I eventually got the knack of turning at the next furrow. After such good tuition everything went well and I had two very good horses that were used to the task.

After my Father heard about my ploughing he was rather uneasy since I was only small and if the plough blades came into contact with

Figure 5. Family group and nurses at the doorway of Swaithe Hall, 1920. Left to Right (standing): Professor George Bedford, Elizabeth Varah Bedford (mother), Nurse for father (who had just died), Bruce Bedford (brother), Nurse, Agnes Jane or 'Topsy'(sister), Betty May Elizabeth (sister), Louise (sister), Percy Bedford (brother); left to right (front): Arthron 'Dick' Bedford, William Bedford (Percy's son) and 'Shep' (dog).

some rock my ribs could be damaged. However, it was a field of sixteen acres, taking two of us with a single furrow plough three weeks to complete. The field that I did not want to plough was the one adjoining the Wombwell Road, near the Brickworks. Here, the soil was light in texture, consisting mostly of ashes. It was used for the dumping of midden ash and night-soil. Most houses had privies which were emptied at the dead of night when not in use. Some had two seats, one large and one small, a few even had three - large, medium and small. The contents were spread on the land by some arrangement. However, the light soil made it easy to drill and was sowed with savoy cabbage seed. We always had good crops, the land being perfect for the growing of root vegetables. The savoys grew to a tremendous size, some as large as set-pots. Mother wouldn't have any in the house, knowing where they had been grown!

When the savoys were ready they were cut and loaded on a four-wheeled waggon which had large side boards, the load being about one and a half tons. Not wanting low wholesale prices for them, a door-to-door method of disposal was decided. My brother, two workmen and myself called at rows of houses through Wombwell as far as the 'Concrete' houses that have since been demolished. I just hated all the affair, every winter Saturday having a large savoy in each hand, calling at houses and asking if they required a cabbage. I used to be cold handling them since some were even covered with ice. They were sold for two [old] pence each. At 'dinner' time we had two old pennyworth of chips wrapped in newspaper but never saw the likes of fish.

After all the savoys were sold the field was left vacant so the night-soil men could resume spreading the midden ashes and privy contents. It must have been an awful job. Luckily we lived in the Hall where there was a water toilet.

Two of the farmhands joined the army which left us with only a couple of men living-in. They had the warmest room in the house as it was above the kitchen where the cooking range was located. One of them stayed with us for seven years.

We got rather short of labour so employed two land girls for the light work. Father also applied to the War Ministry for some extra help. Two men were sent in army uniform, but knew little about farming , unable to plough and handle horses, so were employed muck spreading. and other casual work.

Sunday was usually a quiet day when the animals were fed. Mother, my sister and I used to attend St Thomas's Church at Worsbrough Dale each Sunday morning and evening. Father stayed at home smoking his pipe and making use of the ale in the cellar. On one occasion when we came home from church there was a fire at the rear of the house. Father had collected all the cushions, a chair, even some sheets from the beds in the room above the kitchen where Arthur and Willie slept, including the two soldiers that had been sent to help us out. Father had felt rather itchy. After careful examination of the cushions he found lice, clusters of them creeping about, so in haste fired anything that was loose in the kitchen. The lice had been brought by the soldiers who had been in the trenches. Even the locals told us that they had seen the soldiers in the fields with their shirts off, burning the seams of their clothes with matches, trying to rid themselves of the infestation.

There was always plenty of work to do, especially at harvest time. We employed Irish labourers to help out. Two of them, John and and

Patrick, arrived each year at harvest time and lived in the Saddle House, a one-up-and-one-down at the end of the stables adjoining the Carriage House and had been originally built to accommodate the groom of the Hall. John probably lived in a crofter's cottage in Ireland where conditions were very bad. He was a kindly man of about 50 years old. John and Patrick amused me in the early days. They never bothered using a table cloth but made do with a sheet of newspaper, placing another sheet on top after each meal, so that by harvest time was over there was a huge pile of papers many inches high. Their temporary home was never cleaned but they didn't seem to mind. On Saturday nights they shopped for beef, bread and vegetables, much of it free but their main diet was potatoes which they boiled unpeeled in a large iron pan. Often not bothering with plates, they would simply dig-in with a fork. A kind of mixed soup or grill was also consumed with a spoon direct from the pan. At times I could see them eating from the same plate. Drink was taken in pint mugs which were never washed. After a meal they would sit in a relaxed position, legs crossed, smoking stubby clay pipes in a lordly fashion causing the place to smell of stale tobacco. Harvest finished, John could be seen packing a tin travelling chest, though what he packed heaven knows since the only clothes I saw were working clothes, the same he wore when he arrived. John would say to father 'We are now ready, boss to return to Ireland' and father would pay what was due and off they would go, with the words ' all being well boss, we'll see you next harvest'. To me they were unusual characters, neither of them liked spending money, but saved as much as they could to take back to Ireland. They were good workers with a jolly disposition with not a care in the world. After John and Patrick left their place was thoroughly washed with carbolic soap and used for storage until the next harvest.

At various times a dray load of spent grain was collected from Clarkson's Brewery, along with six half-barrels of ale. Ephram had told the Irishmen he would bring them a pint or two. However, Ephram took a milk can with him to hold the ale, but couldn't resist and drank it himself on the way home.

Back to School

My eldest brother, George, was rather concerned about my having lost the education owing to working on the farm and decided that I ought to have lessons somewhere. I was twelve-and-a half in 1920, so too old to return to Council School; but George managed to get me a place at Queen Elizabeth Grammar School at Wakefield (Figure 6).

School seemed rather strange to me, after working on the land so it

Figure 6. 'Wakefield Grammar School' class of 1921. Dick Bedford can be seen, standing, on extreme right of third row from the back (no other figure behind him).

took a few weeks to settle in. We had breakfast and lunch with the headmaster, Mr Spilsbury, and their two daughters. I was made most welcome and everybody appeared very respectful. The first few weeks were a problem as I had been placed in the senior part of the school owing to my age but found it tough going as some of the subjects were too complicated for me to understand because of my years of missed schooling. However, with help, I began to make headway, though my first term's report was very poor. Two-and-a-half years later my report included a comment that my 'reading was good' and 'much progress' had been made. By then I was growing tired of all the routine, the lessons such as Algebra and Languages were getting even harder and with the hour 'Prep' each evening I was beginning to get sickened of the whole affair.

As a boarder it was usually the custom to join the Army Cadet Corp, wearing the proper Khaki uniform, including putees, hat, haversack and rifle. Three evenings used to be 'square bashing'. This I didn't mind as it avoided having to do the usual hour of Prep' which I hated. We used to have many route marches, some five to ten miles long. I think we were all rather proud when marching through Wakefield. People used to stop and stare as we must have looked smart, all in step, with the officer walking in front in officer's uniform. He was one of the masters who had served in the war.

Sport days were Tuesday and Thursday afternoons but not being an enthusiast, I avoided rugby and, if possible, would sneak off to the swimming baths. I couldn't see much fun in being kicked about. Often three or four of us would get up at about 5.30 a.m., run all the way down Northgate to have a swim before breakfast. I didn't go to learn as I already knew how to swim, having learned in the canal that ran through our land at Swaithe.

After considering matters carefully I decided to give my notice in as I had tired of all the routine. Having finished with the Khaki uniform which was rather an expensive outfit, I sold it for a nominal sum to a new boarder.

End of farming and memories of 'Tommy Wallocks'.

After the sale of 8 March 1920 everywhere was so quiet and forlorn, all the stock and implements having gone. We had grown very fond of some of the animals and felt sad to loose them. A few weeks afterwards Father wasn't feeling well but kept soldiering on. Suddenly he became very ill and was taken to his bed. After day and night nursing he passed away. My eldest brother George, from Reading, came over. It was a very sad time for us all, especially since he was looking forwards to his retirement. My brother, George, took responsibility for winding up the estate. He came across a building society book where two shillings a week had been paid in for me, for work I had done on the farm.

Mother was very disappointed at my leaving such a good school. The school fees were expensive and the cost of my board had had to be paid. I realised that I had lost a chance in a lifetime and felt sorry that so much had been spent on my education.

I never recall my Father giving me any money. I had over 50 bantams scratching about the farm, so I got some money from the sale of eggs. At times the bantams would go missing, to return weeks later with a brood of chicks. Food was cheap but people had little money to spend. After harvest was over Father would allow the people living in the village to glean for any heads of wheat that had fallen on the ground from the binder, which they used to feed a few fowls that they kept.

During the school month holiday three of the boys from the village came asking me if my Father would give them a job. Father came out and to his surprise asked their age which was seven years. He most have felt sorry for them since he gave them a job of weeding between the rows of potatoes at a shilling a day. They were good little workers, managing to clear the field of weeds before going back to school. I noticed that all they had for dinner was a slice of bread and dripping. When Mother found out she sent them meat sandwiches and jugs of tea.

Our produce was sold at very low prices: cwt of turnips would be 2s 6d, cwt of potatoes 2s and wheat about 3s. After ploughing up land for the war effort we were left with a large amount of straw, too ample for our needs and this was sold for a very low price.

A jolly chap called Smith came for a load of oat straw with a pony and flat dray. On one occasion, on reaching the Bull Bridge cross roads, Mr Smith was confronted by the policeman on duty, mentioning that the load of straw was too heavy for such a small pony. After some arguing Smith simply released the pony from the dray, pulling the load himself up Bull Hill to show that it was not too heavy for the pony. The buyer of straw was also known as 'Tommy Wallocks'. It was said that Tommy, a strong chap, once wheeled a piano on a hand cart all the way to Huddersfield but the story is far from being true. At one time, when he hadn't a pony he did wheel a piano to Dodworth but when he got there and mentioned the charge the owner refused to pay him, so he had to wheel it back.

Returning to the 1920 sale, we had a black horse called Fanny, 15.3 hands tall and very fast. She belonged to my brother, Percy, but owing to not reaching the reserved sale figure, was withdrawn. Fanny had been in the army for a year or two when my brother purchased her. I used to ride her around the fields. Having given up farming Fanny was kept in the garden where there was ample grass in an area of more than an acre. At times I would take her for a few trots to give her some exercise but rode bare-backed as the saddles had been sold in the sale. Occasionally I made her gallop for a short distance. One day I took a friend with me, so Fanny had double the weight to carry. On reaching the railway bridge at White Cross I decided to give her a gallop over the bridge. My sister Annis happened to be going to see my Mother walking along the bridge, she stared at us, shouting 'You silly fools !' Some days later there was a knock at the door and to our surprise it was Mr Smith ('Tommy Wallocks') who had not come for straw this time but to buy Fanny. My brother must have put her up for sale. Percy wanted £15 for the pony but Mr Smith only offered £11. They were arguing for some considerable time but about an hour later I saw Smith leading Fanny away which saddened me as she had given me so many happy hours.

Mr Smith was a likable sort of person, very respectful and well known around Barnsley with his horse and flat dray, doing handy jobs that came his way. No doubt also by selling the oat straw that he bought from us for a pound or two. How he came to be called 'Wallocks' we never knew but he became one of Barnsley's characters. The last time that I saw him was in 1932 or 1933. He was well-dressed, walking along Doncaster Road, pushing someone in an invalid chair.

Butcher's boy

After leaving the grammar school much of my time was spent going for long walks with a girlfriend that I met when having dancing lessons. She became my dancing partner for a few years. On Saturdays we often went to the gym in Dodworth Road to learn any new dances. Mr Howard [later of Rose Cottage siege fame] and his daughter gave us lessons.

I was still at a loose end, wondering what the future might hold for me but was given the chance to help my sister Annis at their butcher's shop in Sheffield Road. I did not like being a butcher, my wage being ten shillings a week, less than I got as spending money when I was at grammar school. I liked animals but did not like seeing them killed, so decided to leave.

In business! my tobacconist shop by the Corn Exchange

I passed my time walking and having a dance or two at the gym. One day, strolling down the street, I happened to notice a little shabby shop

Figure 7. The Corn Exchange can be seen at the top (left) side of the market place, at the junction with Shambles Street in this delightfully informal picture postcard, the image dating from about 1900. *Brian Elliott Collection*

adjoining the Corn Exchange on Market Hill in Barnsley (Figure 7). I looked through the window and noticed that there was a counter and fittings and it appeared to be just one room, unoccupied for some time, in a shocking state. I had the idea that it could be renovated and made respectable, so inquired at a Barnsley Corporation office and was told that the rent was eight shillings [40p] a week which I accepted. I engaged a decorator to clean the shop out, paint the walls and shelving, and put two good coats of paint at the front. I had a new facia made and fitted, painted with my name across it in gold leaf letters which brightened the side of the Corn Exchange facing Shambles Shambles Street. Although I made the shop presentable I hadn't the slightest idea what to stock for trade. After some weeks I began to stock tobacco and other items relating to the tobacco trade, knowing quite well I would be up against severe competition as there were already ten tobacco shops in town but at the ripe old age of nine-teen I was running my own business - much better than handling lumps of meat.

My first weeks takings amounted to just over £20 and £30 in the second week. Mother never charged me board so my expenses were low. Trade continued to increase and I kept open all week, including Sundays. Shambles Street use to be used for the 'Bunny Run' which continued along Huddersfield Road. Scores of teenagers paraded in their Sunday Best and tried to 'get off' with the opposite sex. Many would call and buy cigarettes, usually Woodbines, in packets of five for two old pence. Perhaps it made them feel grown up. As December approached I decided to buy extra stocks of tobacco but a week or so before Christmas, when I was walking along Peel Street at 1.30 in the morning with my dancing partner, we noticed a fire near the Market Hill area. On closer investigation we found that the Corn Exchanged had burnt down. I just stood there, flabbergasted, the entire building gutted, not a sign of my shop which I had worked so hard for. My first business venture was in ruins - after only four months. The insurance did not cover the new Christmas stock, new scales and £5 in loose change ready for the next day's trade but I just managed to pay by debts.

New premises in the Arcade

For many weeks after the fire I just walked about not knowing which way to turn. To pass time I went to the occasional dance with my dancing partner and sometimes would go into the market and listen to the quack doctors selling their 'cure-all' patent medicines. Two friends of the quack doctors, pretending to be customers, would barge their way to the front of the crowd and hand over money for 'purchases'. I was always amazed to find people at the rear then being taken in by this, moving forward to make purchases. But most of my spare time I spent looking for another shop - similar to the one at the Corn Exchange - and at a reasonable rent.

Walking down the Arcade I noticed that foundations had been laid for some new shops so I inquired about them at the Arcade office where the man already knew about my burnt down shop. The annual rent was £60, along with about £40 rates. I agreed to lease the bottom shop - which was next to Benjamin Harral's - as soon as they were completed. I then bought two counters, shelving and other oddments from a sale and fitted out the shop myself. The wholesalers that had supplied me previously let me have the stock I required despite my shortage of cash. During the first few weeks I managed to make a surplus to cover expenses and the business kept improving. After a year's trading I just managed to scratch a living after opening seven days a week, from nine in the morning to eight at night. This was during 1928 when I was 21 years old.

Travellers began calling, offering their wares. I began to introduce other kinds of goods in order to help boost trade. These were chocolates, boiled sweets and biscuits. After alteration to the window display trade began to increase, leaving me with a better margin of profit. Although I continued for another two years, until about 1930, the profits were not sufficient to warrant my opening for seven days a week.

Life as a Cheese Factor, trading from Britannia Street

My brother Bruce who lived in Nantwich was an agent in Cheshire selling milking machines for Messrs Gascoignes of Reading. He was over in Barnsley for a day or two and called to see me at the shop, offering me a partnership with his business – as a Cheese Factor. At first I wondered if he was serious but I quickly agreed to his offer. The system we adopted was to bypass the wholesale provision merchants and sell direct to the to the grocers, therefore saving about three pence per pound. I let it be known that I would be leaving the shop and looked forward to a change.

The question now arose as to where we could store the cheese. I looked around and noticed two large warehouses in Britannia Street, one already occupied but the other suitable for our purposes (Figures 8-10). We decided to take it at a reasonable rent. The interior was in

Figures 8-10. Dick Bedford and the Bedford warehouse, Britannia Street, Barnsley.

a decent condition so didn't need much alteration. We had the front painted with our name on the facia. A ten hundred-weight van was then purchased which was painted in cream and with BEDFORDS, CHEESE FACTORS, BRITANNIA STREET, BARNSLEY. Our agreement was that I was to receive a wage each week with both of us sharing the profit at the year end, my brother being a sleeping partner only.

I had to get ready to purchase cheese from the fairs and farms in Cheshire. Fairs were held at Nantwich, Whitchurch, Wem and Chester at various dates. The first batch I bought was from Nantwich. After testing and friendly arguing about price I had purchased about two tons of first class Cheshire cheese which was delivered to our warehouse the next day by an haulage firm used to handling cheese as great care had to be taken not to damage the edges of the cheeses.

My first selling route was planned for Lincolnshire, calling at shops that were able to purchase at least a whole cheese. After testing with a cheese iron, and tasting the price which was two-and-a-half pence per pound less than they had paid the wholesaler was agreed. I made sales at Thorne, Goole, Crowle and Scunthorpe. Distance was no object as petrol was only one shilling [5p] a gallon.

Cheshire cheese fairs were held in a large hall with the floor covered with clean straw. Each side of the hall the farmers could be seen aside their cheese, waiting for the clang of the bell at ten o'clock when selling and buying began. The amount of cheese at different fairs varied from 50 to 100 tons. You haven't to be in a hurry to buy. The practice was usually to go around boring and testing for texture and asking their price. I always kept my eyes on the cheese which had been graded, although lots of cheese unstamped was of good quality. The cheese we required had not to be too old but rather on the new side so as to be ripened in our warehouse to prime condition. I had to watch carefully for when a bit of straw was placed on one of the lots, it was a sign a sale had been made and buying began. Then I would make a move and argue the price with the farmer for different lots until I had bought sufficient for our needs which would amount to four or five tons. When a sale has been made it is a gentleman's agreement not to give back-word to a sale or argue the price. After paying the farmer I would make my way home to be clear of the moors by 4.30 so as to avoid any fog.

The weight of each cheese we bought was between 40 and 60 pounds, wrapped in white muslin material standing on clean straw, and varied in lots of five to about fifteen. The cheese had to be handled with great care. When it arrived at out warehouse it had to be turned each week to get it in prime condition and also to check for any cracks, so as to avoid the cheese-fly laying any eggs which, if not noticed, would turn into maggots and ruin the valuable cheese.

7. Buns but no Beer: Barnsley's Coffee Taverns

by Kate Taylor

DRINKING REACHED ITS PEAK in 1875. In that year the average consumption per head nationally was over thirty-four gallons of beer and one gallon of spirits. But for working men and women who sought a social life there was little alternative then but the public house, with or without its music hall. Drinking places could be much warmer and cosier than people's homes. Single men living in lodgings (and there were many of these in Barnsley) needed somewhere to find companionship. Beer was cheap, safe to drink, and regarded as both manly and health-giving. But strong drink led also to debt, theft and violence, and it could result in time taken off work.

The Cocoa and Coffee Tavern movement, which began in the 1870s in ports such as Liverpool (Figure 1) and Hull, was an effort largely promoted by the philanthropic middle class. Its aim was to provide premises similar to public houses but without their intoxicants. There was to be the same light, comfort and conviviality and the same opportunity to read newspapers or hear them read. But fruit cordials, mineral waters, tea, coffee and cocoa and cheap food were to be the only refreshments. It was made possible by the drop in price of tea and coffee themselves.

In different towns public meetings were called, local clergy and other prominent men made speeches, funds were pledged and companies were formed to establish a local Cocoa and Coffee Tavern. The first of Sheffield's taverns, which was both purpose-built and sizable, was funded entirely by Frederick Thorpe Mappin and was opened on 9 April 1877.[1] Wakefield's first tavern was founded in March 1878 after a public meeting in the Music Saloon there.[2]

In Barnsley, however, such local efforts as there were achieved nothing. Edward Newman (1898-79) wrote to the *Barnsley Chronicle* in December 1878 offering £25 plus an annual sum of £1 towards setting up a Tavern.[3] Offers of further sums came from Alderman Brady and William Moore.4 It was, however, left to private enterprise in the form of a Mr Pilcher from Liverpool to provide what public concern failed to support.

Barnsley's first Cocoa and Coffee Tavern was opened on 13 March 1879 in a suite of rooms in the recently opened Chronicle Buildings

EXTERIOR

INTERIOR, UPPER FLOOR

Figure 1. The new Coffee Tavern at Liverpool as it appeared in *The Graphic*, 12 January 1876.

in Peel Square (Figure 2).[5] The 'great and the good' were present at the formal proceedings in the Temperance Hall, including councillors, ministers from the Church of England and the Congregational, Baptist and Wesleyan Methodist denominations, members of the Board of Guardians and W Watson from the Miners' Permanent Fund. The Mayor, Councillor B Marshall, referred to the success of the Tavern in Sheffield, 'notorious as an intemperate town', and claimed that such establishments were likely to improve society 'religiously, socially, morally and even physically'. Mr J J Dunne reported that the Wakefield Cocoa and Coffee Tavern had made £200 profit in its first six months' operation and that on Saturdays it sold 120 gallons of tea, coffee and cocoa. Whilst such places could not reclaim drunkards, he suggested, they could at least stop people turning to drink. The Rector of St Mary's, Reverend W W Kirby, particularly welcomed the provision of a ladies' room and hoped that working people coming into Barnsley from rural areas for the markets would patronise it. The Congregational minister, Reverend J F T Hallowes, described the working class as 'pre-eminently a social people, not able to enjoy intellectual recreation but liking to meet socially and talk'. Mr Pilcher referred to the helpful advice he had had from his landlord, Charles

Figure 2. Peel Square looking towards Chronicle Buildings (now Tommy Wallocks pub), where the Cocoa and Coffee Tavern had its premises.
By kind permission of the Tasker Trust

Lingard, the proprietor of the *Barnsley Chronicle*.[6] The party then moved across to Chronicle Buildings and the Mayor opened the premises.

Edward Newman was unable, because of poor health, to be present at the opening. He had come to Barnsley in 1823 to practise as a solicitor, initially in partnership with his brother William. In 1853 he had become the first chairman of Barnsley Board of Health and was known for his readiness to 'take an active part in public movements'.[7]

The Cocoa and Coffee Tavern occupied a part of two floors of the Chronicle offices. A large shop fronting on to Peel Square was to serve as a general bar and a shop on the Pitt Street side of the building was the smoking room. Upstairs on the first floor was an 'elegantly furnished' reading room cum refreshment bar and there was a ladies' room facing Pitt Street. The manager's flat and kitchen were on the second floor. Communication with these was effected via speaking tubes. Lighting was by gas. The overall air 'of comfort and elegance' was provided by mirrors, ottomans, chairs, marble-topped tables and greenhouse plants.

Benefactors could buy penny tokens to distribute to the poor which would entitle them to a bun and a small cup of cocoa or coffee. A coffee cart, provided from the Tavern, was regularly sited on May Day Green.

A second, more modest, Cocoa and Coffee Tavern with just two rooms, was opened by Mr Pilcher in premises at the junction of Pontefract Road and Sheffield Road on 13 May 1880 under the management of Mr H Vaux.[8] At least from 1880, and probably from the outset, the Peel Square tavern was managed by George Boycott.

For a period in the 1890s middle-class philanthropy became involved with the Barnsley taverns when the Barnsley Coffee Tavern Company was formed. This was registered on 6 June 1890 with a nominal capital of £2,000 in 400 shares of £5 each. The original shareholders, each holding only a single share, included Boycott himself – now described as 'proprietor' – Harry Johnson (chemist, of Queen Street), Lewis Cooke (cashier, of 9 Victoria Crescent), James Herbert Wilkinson (accountant, 14 Eldon Street), George Alfred Bond (solicitor, Cockerham Grove), W J F Davidson (gentleman, Hall Bank), and Charles Lingard (gentleman, Cockerham Hall). Lingard, Johnson and Cooke were directors.[9]

Charles Lingard (1847-1900) was the youngest son of Thomas Lingard, the Barnsley stationer who had acquired the *Barnsley Chronicle*. He had for some years, initially in partnership with one of his brothers, run the printing and publishing business himself and had been in control when the Peel Street Chronicle Buildings were erected. A member of the Friendly Lodge of Freemasons, he became director of Barnsley Gas Company in 1891 and of Clarkson's Brewery in 1893. He was also a member for a time of Barnsley Board of Guardians.[10]

By 3 July 1890 only the seven shares as allocated above had been taken up and a later report shows that only 280 shares had been subscribed by 20 September 1895. George Boycott now held forty of these and Johnson, Lingard, Cooke, Bond and Davidson held twenty each. Philip Darnall, another accountant, had replaced Wilkinson and he, too, had twenty shares.

The major subscribers, however, were two of Barnsley's 'great and good', Edith Guest of Victoria Road, and Thomas Frederick Charles Vernon Wentworth of Wentworth Castle, each of whom had subscribed to 60 shares. Edith Guest (1804-51) was not untypical of the Victorian well-to-do spinster in her support of the established church and her commitment to good works. She had inherited property in Cudworth from her father, Richard Bayldon Guest. When a move was afoot to make Cudworth a parish in its own right, independent of Monk Bretton, she subscribed £1,000 towards the endowment and church building. Later she paid for a stained glass window and gave £500 for a parsonage house. In Barnsley she supported the Society for the Care of Friendless Girls and the Home of Hope.[11]

Thomas Wentworth (1831-1902) was, it seems, known for being 'nervous and bashful' as well as philanthropic. His obituary in the *Barnsley Chronicle* observed that 'probably his only public appearance in Barnsley was when he was prevailed upon to preside over the annual meeting of Barnsley Ragged and Industrial School' in 1866. However, he provided £300 towards clearing the debt on Barnsley Drill Hall, gave generously to St Peter's Church building fund and the Beckett Hospital and always took a large party to charity balls. At Aldburgh, Suffolk, where he had a shooting lodge and where he died, he was a benefactor of the lifeboat and after a disaster in 1900 gave £200 to the fund for the widows and orphans.[12]

No further shares were taken up and in December 1898 the company went into voluntary liquidation. It never owned any property.[13]

At some point the company opened a Tavern in May Day Green. This managed initially by G Brailsford and is described in trade directories variously as a coffee tavern and restaurant or a temperance and commercial hotel.

The coffee taverns have left few traces. According to Christine Otto, the Peel Square Tavern became renowned as a place where election candidates could give their addresses.[14] However, in the last decades of the nineteenth century political and other public meetings in Barnsley were regularly held, not at the Coffee Tavern but in the Temperance Hall, the Public Hall in Eldon Street, the Co-operative Hall, the Queen's Hotel and even the Circus at Townend.[15]

Drunkenness was less of an issue by the early 1900s. Other forms of popular entertainment, including the Circus, which in 1903 became the Hippodrome, provided rival attractions to the public house. The Peel Square Coffee Tavern ceased trading in or about 1903. The May Day Green Tavern is still listed in the *Barnsley Red Book and Almanack* for 1907 but is not there in the 1908 edition.

Notes and References

1. The *Sheffield Daily Telegraph,* 10 April 1877.
2. Research by the author.
3. *Barnsley Chronicle*, 29 December 1877.
4. *Barnsley Chronicle*, 5 January 1878.
5. *Barnsley Chronicle*, 15 March 1879.
6. Paterson, A *A History of Barnsley Journalism*, n.d. (Barnsley Local Studies & Archives Library)
7. *Barnsley Chronicle*, 18 December 1879.
8. *Barnsley Chronicle*, 15 May 1880.
9. Company papers in the Public Record Office, Kew.
10. *Barnsley Chronicle*, 27 October 1900.
11. *Barnsley Chronicle*, 3 December 1904.
12. *Barnsley Chronicle*, 4 January 1902.
13. Search made at the West Riding Registry of Deeds, Wakefield.
14. Otto, Christine, 'Barnsley Chronicle and South Yorkshire News', unpub.thesis, 1977, Barnsley Local Studies and Archives.
15. Where the Liberals held a meeting, *Barnsley Chronicle*, 4 March 1889.

8. MEMORIES OF BARNSLEY'S THEATRE ROYAL

by Pamela Watford

BARNSLEY'S THEATRE ROYAL has seen many changes over the years, and during its hey day as a working theatre long queues formed in Wellington Street for variety shows and dramas. Today, *The Theatre* (Figure 1) is alive to the sounds of pop bands and people still flock there amid a surrounded by nostalgia, but it remains very much a place of the 1990s. The traditional Theatre Royal, in common with many other provincial theatres, has long gone, closing its doors in 1957. Apart from re-opening for Bingo, in 1961, it lay dusty and in decay until awakened briefly for the filming of the Robert Lindsey film *Bert Rigby – You're a Fool*, when local people were used as extras.

If theatre lovers had had their way, Barnsley would have had its own theatre back, and transformed to its former glory in time its centenary in December 1998. A brave battle by Friends of the Theatre Royal Trust ended in failure in 1995. Hard work which included fund raising concerts at Keresforth Hall, plus support from German school children, and many stars such as Roy Hudd and Ian Lavender did not pay off. The task of raising money to buy the theatre was too much, and the vendors' price was too high. The building was, however, restored and refurbished, opening as a popular live band venue in 1995.

Figure 1. The Wellington Street theatre remains one of Barnsley's most attractive late Victorian buildings.

Barnsley's Theatre Royal was built in 1898, although an earlier was damaged by fire, replaced by the present structure which has been rightly acclaimed as a gem of Victorian theatre architecture. The designer was Walter Emden who also designed the Garrick in London. The first performance was by Morrell & Moillot's Number One Geisha Company. Originally, it appealed to a more 'cultured' audience but of course went on to stage popular

Figure 2. Ken Dodd who worked at the Theatre Royal in his teens.

musical hall, variety and pantomime shows.

Music hall stars included George Elliott who was described at the time as 'the Chocolate Coloured Coon', Syd Field, Vesta Tilley, Hetty King, George Formby senior and Gracie Fields. A fifteen year old Charles Chaplin appeared in the play *Sherlock Holmes,* and a young Ken Dodd (Figure 2) played one of his early dates there, as did young Julie Andrews with her parents Ted and Barbara. The Andrews' act was called the Laughing Troubadours of Song. They stayed at Mrs Mitchell's theatrical boarding house, just across the road from the theatre. The name 'Mitchell' , as Kate Taylor has shown in the previous *Aspects of Barnsley* volume (4), was prominent in the theatre's history, the first association being with manager W H Mitchell who died in 1901. He was succeeded by his son, Albert Arthur, who started his theatrical career as violinist in the orchestra at the age of thirteen.

Amongst the famous comedians appearing at the Theatre Royal were Norman Evans, Dave Morris, Jimmy Clithero and Barnsley's own Albert Modley (Figure 3). Older readers will remember his catch phrase which was 'in't it grand when yer daft?'. When Albert played the theatre on one date, after being away from the

Figure 3. As a young man Albert Modley worked as a railway porter and started telling jokes to irate passengers who had missed their connection. His famous railway sketch was therefore based on actual working experience.

Figure 4. Frank Randle as 'The Old Hiker', his most famous character comedy role. *Courtesy of Roger Walton*

Figure 5. Frank Randle (1901-57), one the most popular comedy acts to appear at the theatre *Courtesy of Roger Walton*

Barnsley for a long time, he was said to have had to refresh himself with the names of the pubs which he had forgotten.

One comedian who did not forget the name of the pubs of Barnsley was Frank Randle (Figures 4-5), who spent much of his time in the nearby *Shakespeare Inn* which was a popular rendezvous for stars and patrons alike. Occasionally Frank would spend so much time in the pub that he would miss a performance (Figure 6). He regularly had crates of beer delivered to his dressing room. In contrast, comic Jimmy James, who did

Figure 6. Extract from *The Star*, 21 December 1953

MR RANDLE'S SHOW DID NOT GO ON

Discord in the Interval

An angry crowd of theatregoers filled the street outside the Theatre Royal, Barnsley, on Saturday night, after the second house of " Randle's Scandals for 1953 " had failed to continue at the end of the interval. The audience, growing restless as the interval went on, had been told by a member of Mr Randle's company that there had been a disagreement between Mr Randle and the theatre management, and that money would be refunded at the box office.

Immediately afterwards a member of the staff of the theatre announced on behalf of the management that there was no reason why the show should not continue, and that while they were waiting there would be music by the orchestra. The show did not continue, and eventually the audience left the theatre, and gathered around the box-office asking for the cost of the seats to be refunded.

The management referred the theatregoers to Mr Randle, saying that he had no authority for the announcement made on his behalf. The crowd then formed in the street outside to wait for him, but eight policemen, were on duty there and in the end the crowd was dispersed without any money being returned.

a brilliant impersonation of a drunk as part of his stand up routine, never drank off stage.

Many well known Barnsley people have fond memories of the Theatre Royal, but sadly, some of them are no longer with us, including the celebrity actor Brian Glover. Brian supported the campaign to re-open the venue, in fact his own career began there as a young boy when he was a dresser for Frank Randle. Brian's main duty was to collect Frank from whichever pub he was in, and get him to the theatre in time for the show.

The late Councillor and former Mayor of Barnsley, Gerald Hadfield and his family had strong connections with the Theatre Royal. His mother and grandmother worked there, and he worked on the lights as as a boy. Gerald had fond memories of those days, including the performances of top comedy duo Jewel and Warris (Figure 7) – they generously tipped him five shillings. He also recalled a character called 'Willy', who was not too hot on hygiene yet used to fetch pies and peas from a local vender to sell to the chorus girls, often letting his thumb overlap into the basins!

The name 'Tommy Wallocks' is famous in Barnsley, now commem-

Figure 7. Top comedy duo Jimmy Jewel and Ben Warris.

orated in the pub of that name in Peel Square. But yet another local character, whose real name was Sutherland, was also nicknamed 'Tommy Wallocks', and renown for removing furniture etc on a hand cart. He was often in the audience at the theatre, exchanging banter with the comics on stage. 'Tommy' had to be restrained one night, whilst sitting in the gallery, when he was the butt of a comic's jokes.

Councillor Len Picken has fond memories of evenings at the Theatre, as a youngster and later every Friday evening with his wife to be, Margaret, when they enjoyed many a good variety show. He remembers the Silver Songsters in the 1930s, and acts in the war who raised money for the forces. Len recalls one night when a magician asked for a volunteer from the audience which resulted in an enthusiastic character named Jackie Monks, from Cudworth, offering his services. The only problem was he was sitting in the box by the stage, yet that didn't stop him participating. He leapt forward, breaking his leg in the process!

From the 1930s Barnsley celebrity Stan Richards, famous for his many appearances on Yorkshire Television's *Emmerdale*, but from a strong musical and comedy background, visited the theatre on a regular basis. Before he became famous, Stan played piano in local pubs and clubs and was influenced by the variety acts that he saw at the theatre.

My own memories of the Theatre Royal where I used to visit as a child with my parents are vague, but I do remember in the 1950s seeing several plays, including a performance of *Jane Eyre*. At that time Charles and Lily Denville were presenting plays, as they had in previous years. I recall being taken back stage by the manager to meet the Denville Players and obtained some of my first autographs.

On another occasion I was watching the show when my dad started chatting to his former headmaster, Mr Frost of Gawber who was sitting in the row in front of us. In the interval he asked what we thought of the young singer who had given a good performance, and asked us if we would like to meet him backstage. We hadn't the time, but I do remember that the singer, Gary Miller, became quite famous though he died at a young age.

Coronation Street stars also trod the boards of the Theatre in their early careers as variety acts. Betty Driver (Betty Turpin) did a music hall act, as a singer, also featuring three poodles who pulled off items of her clothing, leaving her clad in just underwear. Bill Waddington (Figure 8), who played Percy Sugden, did a stand up routine.

In 1949, comedienne Hylda Baker, famous for her double act with male stooge 'she knows yer know' Cynthia, and later in the television

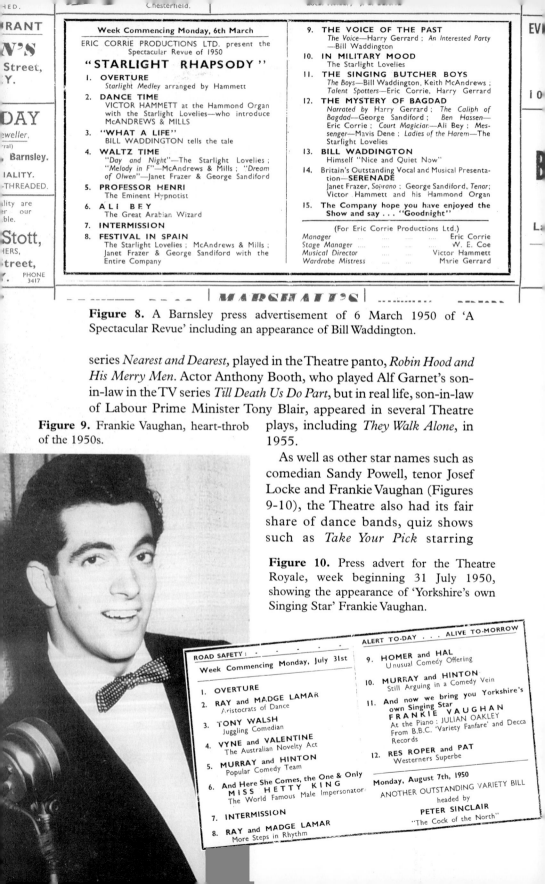

Week Commencing Monday, 6th March

ERIC CORRIE PRODUCTIONS LTD. present the
Spectacular Revue of 1950

"STARLIGHT RHAPSODY"

1. **OVERTURE**
   Starlight Medley arranged by Hammett
2. **DANCE TIME**
   VICTOR HAMMETT at the Hammond Organ
   with the Starlight Lovelies—who introduce
   McANDREWS & MILLS
3. **"WHAT A LIFE"**
   BILL WADDINGTON tells the tale
4. **WALTZ TIME**
   "Day and Night"—The Starlight Lovelies ;
   "Melody in F"—McAndrews & Mills ; "Dream
   of Olwen"—Janet Frazer & George Sandiford
5. **PROFESSOR HENRI**
   The Eminent Hypnotist
6. **ALI BEY**
   The Great Arabian Wizard
7. **INTERMISSION**
8. **FESTIVAL IN SPAIN**
   The Starlight Lovelies ; McAndrews & Mills ;
   Janet Frazer & George Sandiford with the
   Entire Company

9. **THE VOICE OF THE PAST**
   The Voice—Harry Gerrard ; An Interested Party
   —Bill Waddington
10. **IN MILITARY MOOD**
    The Starlight Lovelies
11. **THE SINGING BUTCHER BOYS**
    The Boys—Bill Waddington, Keith McAndrews ;
    Talent Spotters—Eric Corrie, Harry Gerrard
12. **THE MYSTERY OF BAGDAD**
    Narrated by Harry Gerrard ; The Caliph of
    Bagdad—George Sandiford ; Ben Hassen—
    Eric Corrie ; Court Magiciar—Ali Bey ; Mes-
    senger—Mavis Dene ; Ladies of the Harem—The
    Starlight Lovelies
13. **BILL WADDINGTON**
    Himself "Nice and Quiet Now"
14. Britain's Outstanding Vocal and Musical Presenta-
    tion—**SERENADE**
    Janet Frazer, Soprano ; George Sandiford, Tenor ;
    Victor Hammett and his Hammond Organ
15. **The Company hope you have enjoyed the
    Show and say . . . "Goodnight"**

(For Eric Corrie Productions Ltd.)

Manager	Eric Corrie
Stage Manager	W. E. Coe
Musical Director	Victor Hammett
Wardrobe Mistress	Marie Gerrard

MARSHALL'S

Figure 8. A Barnsley press advertisement of 6 March 1950 of 'A Spectacular Revue' including an appearance of Bill Waddington.

series *Nearest and Dearest,* played in the Theatre panto, *Robin Hood and His Merry Men.* Actor Anthony Booth, who played Alf Garnet's son-in-law in the TV series *Till Death Us Do Part,* but in real life, son-in-law of Labour Prime Minister Tony Blair, appeared in several Theatre plays, including *They Walk Alone,* in 1955.

Figure 9. Frankie Vaughan, heart-throb of the 1950s.

As well as other star names such as comedian Sandy Powell, tenor Josef Locke and Frankie Vaughan (Figures 9-10), the Theatre also had its fair share of dance bands, quiz shows such as *Take Your Pick* starring

Figure 10. Press advert for the Theatre Royale, week beginning 31 July 1950, showing the appearance of 'Yorkshire's own Singing Star' Frankie Vaughan.

ALERT TO-DAY . . . ALIVE TO-MORROW

ROAD SAFETY :

Week Commencing Monday, July 31st

1. **OVERTURE**
2. **RAY and MADGE LAMAR**
   Aristocrats of Dance
3. **TONY WALSH**
   Juggling Comedian
4. **VYNE and VALENTINE**
   The Australian Novelty Act
5. **MURRAY and HINTON**
   Popular Comedy Team
6. **And Here She Comes, the One & Only
   MISS HETTY KING**
   The World Famous Male Impersonator
7. **INTERMISSION**
8. **RAY and MADGE LAMAR**
   More Steps in Rhythm

9. **HOMER and HAL**
   Unusual Comedy Offering
10. **MURRAY and HINTON**
    Still Arguing in a Comedy Vein
11. **And now we bring you Yorkshire's
    own Singing Star
    FRANKIE VAUGHAN**
    At the Piano : JULIAN OAKLEY
    From B.B.C. 'Variety Fanfare' and Decca
    Records
12. **RES ROPER and PAT**
    Westerners Superbe

Monday, August 7th, 1950
ANOTHER OUTSTANDING VARIETY BILL
headed by
PETER SINCLAIR
"The Cock of the North"

Michael Miles and the Carol Levis 'Discoveries' talent show, *Stars of Tomorrow*, hosted by Barry Took. Many of us will also remember the popular Morton Fraser Harmonica Gang which included the young comedian and singer Dave King (Figure 11). Speciality acts included a variety of performers ranging from knife throwers, animal and circus 'turns' to a complete Wild West Show. A magician, The Great Carmo, made lions and elephants disappear. Animals ranged from snakes to elephants, one of which made regular visits to the Box Office, attracted by buns from the clerk.

The Theatre remains in the heart of Barnsley's pub land. In the 1950s it was only a short walk away to the *Wine Shades* pub where landlord Tommy Fisher was host and entertainment billed as a *Jovial Evening at the Wine Shades*. Back in the 1900s the Theatre had problems in the renewal of its drink licence which was persistent refused, so patrons had to pop across to local pubs. A Reverend Dawson claimed that young people were being served at the bar in the theatre in large numbers, and believed that these bars were used as a

Figure 11. Entertainer Dave King who appeared at the Theatre in the Morton Fraser Harmonica Gang.

means of demoralising and degrading a lot of young people.

Nowadays alcoholic refreshment is not a problem in the thriving Theatre-pub, which comprises several bars, including the *Ticket Office* next door, with furnishings strong on Barnsley nostalgia, and provides a popular lunch-time venue for meals, as well as catering for evening drinkers.

Many theatres have suffered the fate of Barnsley's own theatre, although some have struggle through, and continue to bring top professional entertainment to the provinces. Although we have the Civic Hall (but currently closed), Barnsley people rarely have the chance to experience live local theatre.

Even in its time the Theatre Royal suffered lean patches, and problems such as fires didn't help matters. It was after a series variety 'flops' staged by the Denville Company, that the curtain finally came down, following a performance of *Peg O' My Heart*. Several years previously it had had a £10,000 renovation, but to no avail.

In December 1998, theatre lovers will be sad that Barnsley's Theatre Royal did not survive to enjoy its centenary, but we can at least be thankful that it has not been demolished. It still 'swings' today, although its young customers will not remember the golden years of its existence. There remain very many happy memories, and in that majestic building the spirit of the old now mingles with the new.

9. A Sponsored Migration from Staffordshire to Hoyland in the Mid-Nineteenth Century

by Melvyn Jones

BY THE MID-NINTEENTH CENTURY the population of England and Wales was growing rapidly. When the first census was taken in 1801 the population was nearly nine million. By 1851 it was 18 million and by 1901 it was over 32 million.[1] Not only was the population growing rapidly, it was becoming increasingly concentrated in urban and industrial districts, the result of high birth rates and large-scale population movement. Out of 3.3 million people aged 20 years and above living in London and 61 other towns and cities in England and Wales in 1851, only 40 per cent had been born in the town or city of their residence. The percentages varied from place to place depending upon the degree of industrialisation or other development (e.g., resort development). In Leeds about 42 per cent of the adult population were in-migrants, but this figure rose to just under 75 per cent in Manchester-Salford and Bradford, and in Liverpool it was more than 75 per cent.[2] A number of regional studies of migration in Victorian Britain undertaken during the last 50 years have shown that, apart from the Irish, who by 1851 numbered 727,000 in England alone, most in-migrants to the urban and industrial districts travelled relatively short distances from the regions immediately surrounding the centres of rapid growth.

These earlier findings have been borne out by the most recently published research on migration in Great Britain which was based on information provided by family historians and genealogists to a team of researchers at Lancaster University.[3] This information, in the form of the migration histories of 16,091 individuals born between 1750 and 1930, who between them made 78,864 migrational moves in their lifetimes, has shown that for most of the period in question the vast majority of migrations were short-distance within a well-defined region, with long-distance movements being unusual; until 1880 the average migration distance was only 35 km (just under 22 miles). Only London had a truly nation-wide 'migration field'. The research also showed that most movement was within settlements or between settlements of similar size and that the most common migrational experience was as part of a family migration. It was also found that single migrants were more likely than family groups to move longer distances and go from a small settlement to a larger one.

In the six registration districts that made up the exposed coalfield of South Yorkshire[4] in 1851, many migrants had moved short distances from unindustrialised parishes and townships into rapidly industrialising ones. Added to these, were many others from the rest of (mainly rural) Yorkshire and from surrounding counties. With the exception of the 6003 Irish immigrants, by far the largest numbers of residents born outside Yorkshire were from Derbyshire (13,965), Nottinghamshire (5,704), Lancashire (3,292) and Lincolnshire (2,849).[5] However, migrants from more distant English counties were present in substantial numbers: 1777 Londoners, 1405 from Warwickshire and 1434 from Staffordshire.[6] It is with migrants into South Yorkshire from one of these more distant counties that this study is concerned.

Elsecar and Milton Ironworks and the Staffordshire connection

For a large part of the nineteenth century there were two ironworks in Hoyland. The Milton Ironworks, situated to the south of Hoyland village, had been established sometime between 1799 and 1802. It was leased by the Walkers of Masbrough until 1821, and then by Hartop, Sorby and Littlewood from 1821 to 1824. Hartop was Henry Hartop from Sheffield, where his father operated the Park Ironworks. After Hartop's partners withdrew in 1824, he went into partnership with the Graham brothers, London iron merchants, who invested £30,000 in the business. Hartop withdrew from the partnership in 1829 and the Graham brothers operated alone until 1848, when they decided to give up the works. The nearby Elsecar Ironworks, which was in fact located just over the township boundary in Brampton, had been established in 1795. It was leased until 1827 by John Darwin and Co., but from that date until the end of the 1840s it was run by managers directly on behalf of Earl Fitzwilliam. From 1829 until about 1844 it was managed by Henry Hartop, and then by his son, John. It employed 74 men in 1846.[7]

In June 1848, following the failure of the Graham brothers' partnership, the Milton Ironworks was advertised for sale (Figure 1). Earl Fitzwilliam decided to lease both the the Milton and Elsecar Ironworks and in 1849 a tenancy agreement was signed with George and William Henry Dawes, the sons of John Dawes, an ironmaster who

To IRONMASTERS, and Manufacturers of Steam-Engines, Boilers, Castings, Rails, Bar Iron, &c., &c.

MILTON IRON WORKS

TO BE LET, for a term of 21 Years, and may be entered upon the First of October next, all those Old-established Iron-Works, called "THE MILTON IRON-WORKS", situate near to the Elsecar Coal-Field and the Tankersley Park Ironstone Grounds, and at a convenient distance from the Manufacturing Towns of Sheffield, Rotherham and Barnsley in the County of York, The Works consist of:-

TWO BLAST FURNACES, with every requisite Appendage:-

FORGE and MILL, with Puddling and other Furnaces, Chafery for Drawing Uses, Rolling and Slitting Mills, &c, capable of manufacturing from 90 to 100 Tons of Finished Iron per week:-

FOUNDRY, with Pits, Drying Stoves, and every requisite Apparatus for making Engine Work, and Castings of every description, to the extent of 100 Tons per Week:-

ENGINE-FITTING SHOPS, with Lathes, Boring and Planing Machines, Boiler Makers' and Smiths' Shops, and every requisite for carrying on Engine and Railway Work to a large extent:-

Together with an ample supply of ELSECAR COALS and TANKERSLEY PARK and SWALLOW-WOOD IRON-STONE, on terms to be agreed upon.

The Works possess at present excellent Canal and River Communications, and will shortly have the advantage of the South Yorkshire Railway.

N.B. --Although the Owner of the Works would not absolutely restrain the Lessees from making and Manufacturing Hot Blast Iron, yet he would prefer treating with parties who would undertake to make and manufacture Cold Blast Iron only.

For further Particulars apply to **Mr. NEWMAN**, of Darley Hall, near Barnsley; or Mr. Woodhouse, of Overseal, near Ashby-de-la-Zouch.

Darley Hall, near Barnsley, 15th June, 1848.

Figure 1. Newspaper advertisement inviting bids for a new tenant at Milton Ironworks, June 1848.

ran the Bromford Ironworks in West Bromwich in the 'Black Country' of Staffordshire. George Dawes (Figure 2) was to manage the two ironworks for more than 30 years.[8]

Benjamin Biram, the Earl's colliery agent, recorded in his diary the negotiations leading to the setting of the new leases:

2 February, 1849

Met Mr Woodhouse [lawyer], *with Mr Dawes & Mr Marshall* [probably Dawes' lawyer] *about Milton & Elsecar Ironworks*

Figure 2. George Dawes. Detail from an oil painting by Richard Smith, 1880. It was presented to George Dawes at a meeting held at Elsecar Market Hall. Funds for its commission were subscribed by more than 500 people including friends, local inhabitants and members of the workforce at Milton and Elsecar Ironworks.
North Lincolnshire Museum and Art Gallery, Scunthorpe

Thursday, 15 March, 1849

Met Mr Dawes with Mr Newman [the Earl's legal representative in South Yorkshire] *at the Midland Hotel Derby afterwards accompanied Mr Newman & Mr Woodhouse to London*

Friday, 16 March, 1849

Conference at Earl Fitzwilliam's in Halkin Street respecting the letting of Milton & Elsecar Iron Works when his lordship agreed to let Elsecar along with Milton

Saturday, 17 March, 1849

Mr Woodhouse & myself waited upon Mr Dawes at Handsworth to arrange terms for his taking the Iron Works [9]

In April, 1849, John Hartop, manager of the Elsecar Ironworks for the Earl and who had also been responsible for sinking deep ironstone pits at Skiers Spring, wrote letters to the Earl about his own future. He also wrote to the Earl about the fact that George Dawes intended to bring workmen with him from the Black Country, and the impact that this might have on local employment:

23 April, 1849
…When last I saw Mr Dawes he told me that the greater part of his

workmen out of Staffordshire would come with him, in that case
perhaps only a part of those now working here [Elsecar Ironworks]
will be able to get employment under him, in which case it might be
as well that they should [be] *under proper notice* [so as] *not* [to] *miss*
a chance of finding work elsewhere, for they are to a man very steady
and reliable & it would be a pity to replace them with strangers
coming into the neighbourhood...[10]

Hartop's letter raises a number of interesting questions. Did key
workers accompany George Dawes from Staffordshire to Hoyland? If
so, how many? Were they family men or young, single men? If they
came, where did they live? Did they simply intermingle with the
existing population or did they, in the early stages at least, form segre-
gated populations living near the two works?

Fortunately, the gap between the date from which the new leases
for the two ironworks took effect and the next census (the night of
30/31 March 1851) was less than two years. At that census, the census
enumerators for the enumeration districts into which Hoyland township was divided (there were three enumeration districts in Hoyland
in 1851) entered the information they had collected on to special
forms in what were called Enumerators' Books. In 1851 the information for each household comprised the names of all persons in the
household, their gender, age, marital status, occupation and place of
birth (village, town, and county). In addition the head of household
was identified and the relationship of all other persons in the household to the head was given.

Enumerators' Books are made available to the public after 100
years. It is therefore possible to scrutinise the Hoyland 1851 returns
and to attempt to answer the questions posed above.

The migrant population of Hoyland in 1851

The population of Hoyland Nether township in 1851 was 2,892
(excluding the 20 people on barges in the canal basin at Elsecar).[11]
The three enumeration districts into which the township was divided
were Hoyland Village (including the houses around Milton
Ironworks) with a total population of 1,046; Stubbin, Skiers Hall,
Elsecar and Lower Jump with a combined population of 1,080; and
Upper Hoyland, Hoyland Lane End, and Hoyland Common with a
combined population of 766. The numbers and percentages of those
born within the township and those who had migrated to Hoyland are
shown in Figure 3.

Figure 3 shows that the population of Hoyland township in 1851

	Hoyland -born	Migrants					Totals
		born in rest of S.Yks	born in rest of Yks	born in bordering counties	born in rest of Engl. & Wales	born in Scotland, Ireland or overseas	
Hoyland village + Milton	525	303	25	31	160	2	1046
Stubbin-Elsecar	573	360	33	30	78	6	1080
Upper Hoyland, Lane End + Common	354	276	66	46	20	4	766
Hoyland Nether township as a whole	1452 (50.2%)	939 (32.5%)	124 (4.3%)	107 (3.7%)	258 (8.9%)	12 (0.4%)	2892

Figure 3. 'Native-born' and migrants living in Hoyland Nether in 1851 by enumeration district. *Census enumerators' books, H.O. 107/23333*

was overwhelmingly Yorkshire-born (87 per cent), with just over half of the population born in Hoyland township itself. It was usual in the nineteenth century, as we have already seen, for most migrants to be short-distance migrants, largely because of lack of information about job opportunities at long distances, and because employment opportunities would have been available for most would-be migrants at relatively short distances from their existing place of residence in the many rapidly growing cities, towns and industrial villages which were characteristic of early Victorian Britain.[12] This generalisation is borne out by closer examination of Figure 3. Almost a third of those living in Hoyland township in 1851 were short-distance migrants from places in the rest of South Yorkshire. These short-distance migrants constituted 65 per cent of all the migrants living in Hoyland township in 1851. A further 8 per cent of Hoyland township's population in 1851 (16 per cent of all migrants) were medium-distance migrants from the rest of Yorkshire (mostly from West Yorkshire) and from counties bordering South Yorkshire – Lancashire, Cheshire, Derbyshire, Nottinghamshire and Lincolnshire. This means that only 270 of the township's population (9.3 per cent of the population and nearly 19 per cent of all migrants) were what could be called long-distance migrants from the rest of England and Wales, from Scotland, from Ireland and from beyond the British Isles.

Further examination of Figure 3 shows that whereas there is a continuous steep falling-off of migrants with distance in Upper Hoyland/Hoyland Lane End/Hoyland Common (276 short-distance

	Hoyland-born	Born in rest of S.Yks	Born in rest of Yks	Born in bordering counties	Born in rest of Engl. & Wales	Born in Scotland, Ireland or overseas	Totals
Hoyland village	484	260	24	26	39	1	834
Milton Ironworks	41	43	1	5	121	1	212
Stubbin Lane/Stubbin	180	127	18	23	65	6	419
Elsecar	363	224	13	7	12	0	619
Lower Jump	30	9	1	0	2	0	42

Figure 4. 'Native-born' and migrants living in the various parts of Hoyland Village/Milton and Stubbin/Elsecar/Jump enumeration districts in 1851. *Census enumerators' books, H.O.107/23333*

migrants, 112 medium-distance migrants, 24 long-distance migrants), this is not the case in the Hoyland Village/Milton enumeration district or in Stubbin/Skiers Hall/Elsecar/Lower Jump. In these two enumeration districts there were more long-distance migrants from the rest of England and Wales than medium-distance migrants from the rest of Yorkshire and counties bordering South Yorkshire - 160 against 56 in Hoyland Village/Milton and 78 against 63 in Stubbin/Skiers Hall/Elsecar/Lower Jump. In Figure 4 these two enumeration districts have been sub-divided into their component parts so that the exact locations of these long-distance migrants can be pin-pointed. It is clear from Figure 4 that the greatest concentrations of migrants originating beyond the boundaries of Yorkshire, Lancashire, Cheshire, Derbyshire, Nottinghamshire and Lincolnshire resided in Hoyland Village, Milton Ironworks and Stubbin (this latter area coincides with housing on either side of the present King Street, Hill Street and Fitzwilliam Street between the eastern end of Hoyland Village and Elsecar). If George Dawes had recruited Staffordshire ironworkers to come to Hoyland to work in the Milton and Elsecar Ironworks, these are the places in Hoyland where they and their families were most likely to be found.

Before going on to analyse the birthplaces of the long-distance migrants living in Hoyland township in 1851, it is important to turn our attention briefly to the location of the Bromford Ironworks from which the migrant workers would be recruited. This ironworks was located on the western edge of West Bromwich in the extreme south

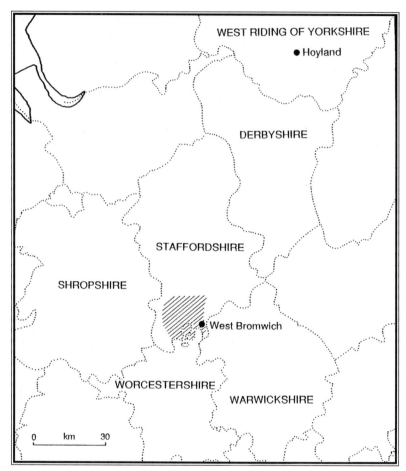

Figure 5. The location of West Bromwich in Staffordshire and the Black Country (shown by diagonal shading).

of the county of Staffordshire (Figure 5). There are a number of highly significant features of its location which need to be taken into account in deciding whether any long-distance migrants living in Hoyland in 1851 had recently been living in South Staffordshire and probably working at the Bromford Ironworks.

First, knowing that half of Hoyland's residents in 1851 were born in Hoyland township, we must expect a substantial proportion of any migrants who had worked at the Bromford Ironworks to have been born in West Bromwich. Secondly, knowing that nearly a third of the residents of Hoyland in 1851 were from neighbouring places in South

Yorkshire, we must expect the same in South Staffordshire; we must therefore consider anybody who had been born in the industrial district to the west of West Bromwich, the so-called Black Country, containing industrial settlements such as Bilston, Darlaston, Sedgley, Tipton, Wednesbury and Wolverhampton.[13] Thirdly, account must be taken of the fact that for historical reasons a small 'island' of Worcestershire containing Dudley lay within Staffordshire very close to the Bromford Ironworks. Fourthly, because West Bromwich was near the boundaries with Warwickshire, Worcestershire and Shropshire, individuals born in those counties with some connection with South Staffordshire should also be carefully considered.

Staffordshire migrants in Hoyland township in 1851

Before embarking on an identification of Staffordshire migrants, it may be useful to reconsider what evidence the census enumerators' books provide. Of critical importance in tracking down migrants are family names, occupations, ages and birthplaces. Family names are important for tracing family connections. For example, an unmarried female, aged 20, a servant to a Yorkshire-born family, but born in Tipton, may, without other evidence, have moved to Hoyland one day, one year or one decade ago. But if in another part of Hoyland township there is an ironworker and his wife with the same family name, both aged about 45, and born in Tipton or a neighbouring settlement, then we can probably safely assume that the female servant is a member (daughter) of an ironworker's family recruited by George Dawes.

Occupations are also obviously a basic clue. We would expect most of the migrant workers from Staffordshire to be ironworkers.

Ages are important in two respects. Migration is generally age-selective. Once settled in a secure occupation and with no major career ambitions, unless there are major over-riding factors, established families with the parents approaching or past middle age will be loathe to move. People with most of their adult life ahead of them and with prospects of advancement are the ones most likely to react positively to a new opportunity. Except for senior positions, therefore, we are likely to be looking for heads of households under 45 years of age and for young, single men. Because the migrant population is likely to be young there may have been a significant number of recent births among them, which may throw some light on the precise time at which the migration occurred.

Birth-places are crucial in two ways. First, they enable us to iden-

	Migrants born in:					Migrants born in rest of Engl. & Wales but migrating from Staffs	Infants born in Hoyland o₁ parents migrating from Staffs
	Staffs	*Worcs*	*Warks*	*Shrops*	*Sub-total*		
Hoyland village	25	5	1	3	34	0	0
Milton Ironworks	90	20	3	0	113	4	6
Upper Hoyland	0	0	0	0	0	0	0
Hoyland Lane End/Common	2	0	2	0	4	0	0
Stubbin	43	11	1	2	57	7	3
Elsecar/Lower Jump	3	0	0	1	4	0	0
	163	36	7	6	212	11	9

Figure 6. The migrant community from South Staffordshire living in Hoyland Nether in 1851. *Census enumerators' books, H.O. 107/23333*

tify very precisely a large number of the South Staffordshire migrants: they will have been born in the Black Country. Secondly, if a migrant from South Staffordshire to Hoyland was himself a migrant to the Black Country from elsewhere at an earlier date, then the birthplaces of his wife and/or children may confirm that he has recently moved to Hoyland from South Staffordshire.

Bearing these points in mind we can now consider the census information. Figure 6 shows the number and distribution of recent migrants from Staffordshire, Worcestershire, Warwickshire and Shropshire living in the various parts of Hoyland township in 1851. Altogether there were 212 men, women and children, mostly from Staffordshire and mostly living – as suggested above – around Milton Ironworks and in Stubbin. The table also shows that there were eleven infants born in Hoyland of migrant parents. These ranged in age from one month to eleven months. The fact that there were two other infants in migrant families, both aged one, and both born in West Bromwich, suggests that the main migration had taken place in the spring of 1850. Figure 6 also shows the number of migrants who had moved from South Staffordshire in 1850, but who had been born beyond the boundaries of Staffordshire, Shropshire, Warwickshire or Worcestershire. How some of these were identified is dealt with below.

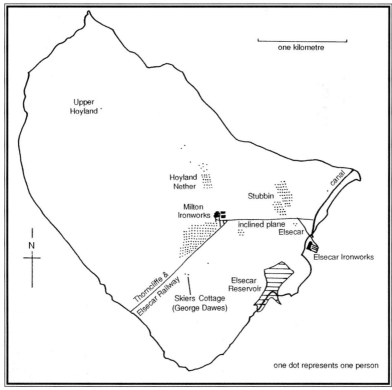

Figure 7. Generalised residential location in Hoyland township of the South Staffordshire migrant community.

Altogether, then, the migrant community from Staffordshire was a substantial 232 – only 8 per cent of the total population, but 86 per cent of all long-distance migrants. The generalised residential locations of these Staffordshire migrants within Hoyland, and in relation to the two ironworks, is shown in Figure 7.

Figure 8 shows the birthplaces of the 212 migrants from Staffordshire, Shropshire, Warwickshire and Worcestershire. Not surprisingly, 75 per cent of these migrants had been born in South Staffordshire, with 71 (a third) born in West Bromwich where the Bromford Ironworks was situated. The closeness of most of the birthplaces to West Bromwich emphasises the importance of short-distance migration, a phenomenon already referred to. The attraction of employment at the Bromford Ironworks had created its own local migration field, like a magnet attracting iron filings. Another feature of interest is the fact that a number of the migrants from West

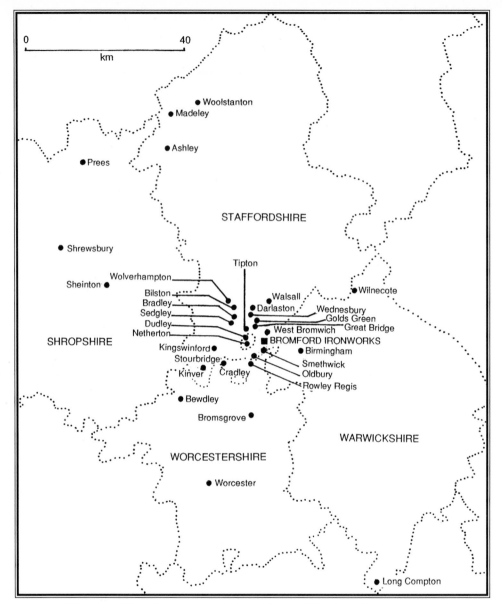

Figure 8. Birthplaces of the 212 residents of Hoyland Nether who had moved from South Staffordshire in early 1850.

Bromwich to Hoyland, had earlier made medium-distance moves from the smaller towns and rural parts of the West Midlands to find employment in the Black Country – the migrants from Prees and Sheinton in Shropshire, Bewdley and Bromsgrove in Worcestershire and Wilnecote and Long Compton in Warwickshire come into this category.

Greenside, Hoyland Village

Name & Surname	Relation	Condition	Age Male	Age Female	Rank, Profession or Occupation	Where Born
William Vaines	Head	Mar	60		Nailmaker	Yorkshire, Hoyland
Ann D^o	Wife	Mar		57		D^o D^o
Frances D^o	Daur	U		13	Scholar	D^o D^o
Elizabeth D^o	D in Law	Mar		25		D^o D^o
Thomas Lowe	Lodger	Mar	24		Furnace Heater	Staffordshire, Sedgeley
Ann D^o	D^o	Mar		24		D^o D^o

Hoyland Village

Name & Surname	Relation	Condition	Age Male	Age Female	Rank, Profession or Occupation	Where Born
Benjamin Skidmore	Head	Mar	28		Iron Pudler	Staffordshire, West Bromwich
Phoebe D^o	Wife	D^o		27		D^o D^o
Ann D^o	Daur			7		D^o D^o
Benjamin D^o	Son		5			D^o D^o
Louisa D^o	Mother	Widow		67		D^o D^o

Milton Ironworks

Name & Surname	Relation	Condition	Age Male	Age Female	Rank, Profession or Occupation	Where Born
Thomas James	Head	Widowed	60		Moulder	Monmouthshire, Newport
George D^o	Son	U	20		Moulder	Staffordshire, Tipton
Jane Whittingham	Servt	Mar		23	Housekeeper	Warwickshire, Long Compton

Milton Ironworks

Name & Surname	Relation	Condition	Age Male	Age Female	Rank, Profession or Occupation	Where Born
William Smith	Head	Mar	31		Mill Furnaceman	Staffordshire, West Bromwich
Olivia D^o	Wife	Mar		31		Worcester, Cradley
Mary Ann D^o	Daur			6		Stafford, Smethwick
Thomas D^o	Son		4			D^o D^o
Emma S D^o	Daur			11m		Yorkshire, Hoyland

Brick Row, Milton

Name & Surname	Relation	Condition	Age Male	Age Female	Rank, Profession or Occupation	Where Born
Thomas Roberts	Head	Mar	32		Iron Pudler	Herefordshire, Hereford
Catharine D^o	Wife	Mar		31		Stafford, Oldbury
Mary D^o	Daur			8		D^o Oldbury
John D^o	Son		4			D^o Oldbury
Thomas D^o	Do		2			D^o Oldbury
Samuel D^o	Do		1m			Yorkshire, Hoyland

Skiers Cottage

Name & Surname	Relation	Condition	Age Male	Age Female	Rank, Profession or Occupation	Where Born
George Dawes	Head	Mar	33		Iron Master	Staffordshire, West Bromwich
Mary Ann Bantnor	Serv	Widow		35	House Keeper	Warwick, Birmingham
Samuel White	Serv	Serv	19		Groom	York, Wentworth

Figure 9. Extracts from the census enumerators' books, showing examples of different kinds of migrant households. *Census enumerators' books, H.O.107/23333*

Figure 9 shows extracts from the Hoyland census enumerators' books, giving examples of different kinds of migrant households in Hoyland in 1851. Example A shows two young migrants, a furnace heater and his wife, lodging with a long established Hoyland family. The second example, B, shows a migrant family occupying their own cottage. All had been born in West Bromwich, including the head of the household's widowed mother. Extract C is an example of a migrant who some time earlier in the century had migrated from South Wales to the Black Country where his twenty year old son had been born. Their domestic needs were taken care of by a housekeeper, who herself had migrated to South Staffordshire at some time in the past from South Warwickshire, about 40 miles south-west of West Bromwich. Example D shows a nuclear family headed by a mill furnaceman born in West Bromwich. His wife had been born about ten miles away in Cradley in Worcestershire and his eldest two children in Smethwick, just two miles from West Bromwich. His infant daughter, aged eleven months, confirms that the family were recent migrants to Hoyland. Extract E again provides an example of a head of household who had been born in Oldbury, just two miles from the Bromford Works (Oldbury was in Worcestershire not Staffordshire as recorded by the enumerator). The different birthplaces of their third and fourth children – the two year old in Oldbury and the one month old in Hoyland – indicate that they were recent migrants to Milton. The last extract, F, shows the household of George Dawes, ironmaster, the new tenant of Milton and Elsecar Ironworks, inhabiting a secluded cottage, next to Skiers Spring Wood, about a quarter of a mile south of Milton Ironworks. His groom was locally born, but his housekeeper, a widow, had been born in Birmingham, about six miles from West Bromwich; she must have been a short-distance migrant to the Black Country before moving to Hoyland.

It was pointed out earlier that migration tends to be age-selective and in the case of economic migration, i.e., migration connected with the loss of jobs at the place of residence or with the prospect of good employment elsewhere, this normally results in the movement of younger rather than older people. The migration of the South Staffordshire ironworkers and their families to Hoyland in 1850 bears out this generalisation. Figure 10 shows the age-sex structure of Hoyland as a whole (top diagram) and the migrant community from Staffordshire, including children born in Hoyland of migrant mothers (bottom diagram) in the form of age-sex (population) pyramids. The difference between the two pyramids is striking. In Hoyland as a whole in 1851, the structure of the population was not markedly different

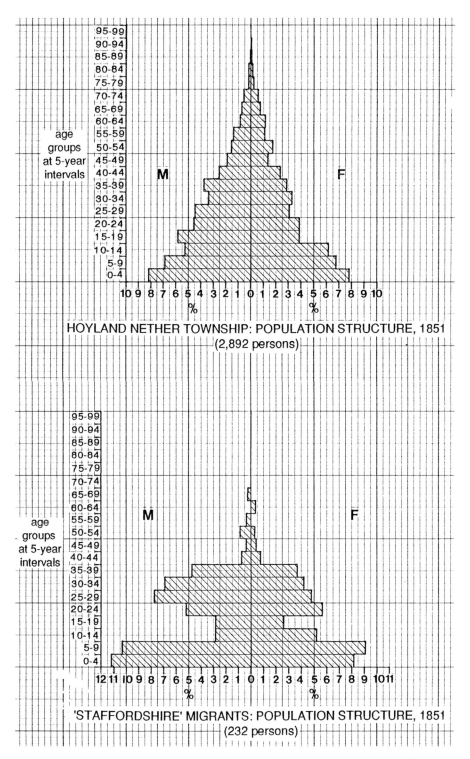

Figure 10. Population structure of Hoyland Nether as a whole in 1851 (top) and the recently-arrived Staffordshire migrant community in 1851 (bottom).

from England and Wales as a whole with 41.02 per cent of the population aged 0-14 (England and Wales in 1851, 35.25 per cent), 44.47 per cent aged 15-44 (England and Wales, 46.25 per cent) and 14.5 per cent over 45 (England and Wales, 18.5 per cent). The small difference between Hoyland and England and Wales in those aged under 15 and over 45 is to be expected as Hoyland was an expanding industrial community attracting economic migrants from near and far; it would, therefore, be expected that it would have a larger proportion of children and a smaller proportion of older people than the country as a whole.

However, when we turn to the migrant community from Staffordshire, the differences in population structure from those of both England and Wales and Hoyland township are enormous. Nearly 47 per cent of the Staffordshire migrants were under the age of fifteen, 50 per cent were aged between 15 and 44 and only 3.4 per cent were aged over 45. The pyramid shows quite clearly that the bulk of the adult migrant population was between the ages of 20 and 40, with a large number of children under 10. Only seven persons out of 232 were over 50 years of age, and only three over 60. Two of the latter were widows who had moved with their married sons.

Conclusions

As was pointed out at the beginning of the study, long-distance migrations in early Victorian Britain were the exception rather than the rule. This makes the South Staffordshire-Hoyland migration worthy of attention. It was an uncommon but by no means unique migrational phenomenon.[14] What was more unusual were the circumstances in which the migration took place: recruitment by a single employer who was himself one of the migrants.

The 1851 census, the main source of information for this study, provides only a snapshot of a continually changing picture, and the study raises a number of additional interesting questions:

~ To what extent, in the following decades, did the male children of the Staffordshire migrants follow their fathers and elder brothers into employment at the two ironworks? Already by 1851 a ten year-old boy from Staffordshire had become an apprentice cordwainer (boot and shoe maker).

~ How quickly did the distinctiveness of the Staffordshire community disappear as younger Staffordshire migrants married into long-standing local families or those of migrants from elsewhere?

~ And how long did the residential concentration continue to exist in the face of continued in-and out-migration, changing family circumstances and occupational change.

Continuity of employment at the two ironworks by members of the families of the Staffordshire migrants is likely to have been significant, but it is equally likely that other distinctive features of the community – including speech patterns among the young – would have been quickly eroded as assimilation with the rest of the Hoyland population took place. No doubt a close study of later census enumerators' books and access to individual family histories would answer these questions.

Notes and References

1. D Mills and K Schurer (eds), *Local Communities in the Victorian Census Enumerators' Books,* Oxford, Leopard's Head Press, 1996, p.73.
2. J H Clapham, *An Economic History of Modern Britain: the early Railway Age,* Cambridge, Cambridge University Press, 1926, pp.536-37.
3. C G Pooley and J Turnbull, 'Migration and mobility in Britain from the eighteenth to the twentieth centuries', *Local Population Studies,* No 57, Autumn 1996, pp.50-71.
4. The exposed coalfield of South Yorkshire extends from the village of Woolley in the north-west to Thurnscoe in the north-east, and from the western suburbs of Sheffield in the south-west to Harthill in the south-east. Geologically it is bounded on the west by the Millstone Grit Series and on the east by a Magnesian Limestone escarpment.
5. M Jones, 'Changes in Industry, Population and Settlement on the Exposed Coalfield of South Yorkshire, 1841-1908', (unpublished MA thesis, University of Nottingham, 1966), pp.155-56.
6. Jones, thesis, pp.155-56.
7. A K Clayton, 'Henry Hartop at Elsecar Ironworks', in *Hoyland Nether*, Hoyland Nether UDC, 1973, Chapter X, pp.52-53.
8. A K Clayton, 'The Dawes Brothers at Milton and Elsecar', *Hoyland Nether,* pp.64-69.
9. Sheffield Archives, Wentworth Woodhouse Muniments: the diaries of Benjamin Biram, Stewards Papers 16X (1849).
10. Sheffield Archives, Wentworth Woodhouse Muniments, G45/10a.
11. Census Enumerators' books for Hoyland Nether (three enumeration districts), 1851. Public Record Office, call number H.O. 107/23333.
12. See, for example, R Lawton, 'Population Movements in the West Midlands 1841-1861', *Geography,* 48, 1958, pp.164-77 and W F Hornby and M Jones, 'Regional and local migration in Britain since 1851' in *An Introduction to Population Geography,* 2nd edition, Cambridge, Cambridge University Press, 1993, pp. 118-23.
13. Compared with the industrial towns and villages of the Black Country, Hoyland Nether must have seemed to be semi-rural, especially to the east and south-east in the direction of Earl Fitzwilliam's Wentworth estate. In 1843, in the introduction to the Midland Mining Commission, Thomas Tancred described the Black Country thus: 'The traveller appears never to get out of an interminable village, composed of cottages and very ordinary houses. In some directions he may travel for miles, and never be out of sight of numerous two-storied houses, so that the area covered by brick and mortar must be immense. These houses, for the most part, are not arranged in continuous streets, but are interspersed with blazing furnaces, heaps of burning coal in process of coking, piles of ironstone calcining, forges, pit-banks, and engine chimneys; the country being

besides intersected with canals, crossing each other at different levels; and the small remaining patches of surface soil occupied with irregular fields of grass or corn, intermingled with heaps of the refuse of mines or of the slag from the blast furnaces. Sometimes the road passes between mounds of refuse from the pits, like a deep cutting on a railway; at others it runs like a causeway, raised some feet above the fields on either side, which have subsided by the excavation of the minerals beneath...The whole country might be compared to a vast rabbit warren.'

14. For another example of long-distance group migration to South Yorkshire and the establishment of a substantial migrant community see Melvyn Jones, 'A Welsh Diaspora and a Yorkshire Colony: The Establishment and Development of a Welsh Community in Carlton and Smithies', in *Aspects of Barnsley 2*, ed. Brian Elliott, Wharncliffe Publishing, Barnsley, 1994, pp.49-71.

Acknowledgements

I am grateful to Olive, Countess Fitzwilliam's Wentworth Settlement Trustees and the Director of Sheffield City Libraries for permission to quote from the Wentworth Woodhouse Muniments in Sheffield Archives.

10. George Orwell and the Road to Pogmoor Sands

by Rose Johnston

THE REST OF THE WORLD remembers George Orwell (Figure 1) as the author of *Animal Farm* and *Nineteen Eighty Four*. But to some of Barnsley's poor in the 1930s he was the six foot four stranger with size twelve feet who marched through their front doors, armed with a tape measure to inspect their houses.

Orwell had come to Barnsley in March 1936, to collect material for the book published a year later as *The Road to Wigan Pier*. This volume, half documentary, half an account of Orwell's personal brand of Socialism, brought Barnsley and the writer to national attention. So why did Orwell come here? What did he do here? How true a picture did he paint? And what effect did the experience have on him – and on the town?

The publisher Victor Gollancz commissioned the book in January 1936. He had already published in 1933 Orwell's *Down and Out in London and Paris*, a graphic account of Orwell's life as a tramp, which had been a modest success. Now he wanted something similar, set among the unemployed in the north of England.

Encouraged by the offer of a £500 advance, which would enable him to marry his fiancee Eileen O'Shaughnessy, Orwell left his job in a Hampstead bookshop and headed North. He took the train to Coventry, then travelled on foot and by bus through the Black Country to Manchester, in a doss house. From Manchester, he went to Wigan, Sheffield and Barnsley to research his book.

Figure 1. George Orwell on Southwold Beach, 1934. *Courtesy of the George Orwell Archive, University College, London.*

Why Barnsley?

The worst long term unemployment in 1936 was in coalmining, ship-building, iron and steel and cotton industries. Before Barnsley, Orwell had already spent time in Wigan, another mining town of a similar size. More logical planning would surely have taken him to a textile town or a port. Quite simply, Orwell went where his network of contacts led him. He had set off with letters of introduction from Independent Labour Party members in London and from Richard Rees and Middleton Murry, who owned and edited *The Adelphi*, a left wing peri-odical, which had printed some of Orwell's early work. *The Adelphi* connection led him to Manchester and to Frank Meade, a trade union official in charge of printing the magazine. Meade directed Orwell to Wigan and to Joe Kennan, an electrician who had worked in the pits.

Through the mining community, there were strong links between Wigan and Barnsley. In Wigan, Orwell met Paddy Grady, secretary of the National Unemployed Workers' Movement. Grady, an unem-ployed miner, provided him with contacts in Barnsley.

The Lodgings

Orwell arrived in Barnsley on 11 March 1936, after a week in Sheffield. Mr Wilde, secretary of the local branch of the Working Men's Clubs and Institute Union, found Orwell lodgings at 4 Agnes Terrace, off Day Street. This was the home of a miner, Albert Gray, his wife Minnie and their two girls Irene and Doreen (Figure 2). Although he arrived amid the chaos of washday, Orwell was quick to note that the room was the best he had up here, clean and decent with flannelette sheets.

Orwell lodged in the downstairs front room, which was self-contained, the front door opening into a corridor. Also staying in the house were a joiner who was working on the construction of the new dog track nearby – the Dillington – his young son and a professional pub singer. All the larger pubs in town at the time employed singers and dancers, some of them very immoral, Mrs Gray told Orwell. At other times the lodgers were a similar mixture to those in Orwell's digs in Wigan – many of them

Figure 2. The Gray family. Albert is standing, on right; Minnie seated with children Irene & Doreen.
Courtesy of Mr K Goodlife

commercial travellers and newspaper canvassers. The latter were set on by papers such as *John Bull*, to work an area selling subscriptions, usually with a free gift or bargain offer to entice customers.

Albert Gray, then aged fifty, had been a miner since before Orwell was born. He was used to meeting a colourful mixture of people through his small boarding house and readily chatted to Orwell about mining and his war experiences. probably he was more of a novelty to Orwell than the writer was to him.

Orwell and the Fascists

One of the names given to Orwell by Paddy Grady was that of Tommy Degnan, a miner and Communist, but Orwell met him by chance and in extraordinary circumstances.

On Sunday 15 March, Oswald Mosley, leader of the British Union of Fascists, marched along Eldon Street leading a column of Blackshirts.[2] A police escort separated them from the jeering crowds lining the street. They entered the Public Hall (Figure 3), now known as the Civic Hall, where Mosley addressed an audience of about 700, including Orwell. A hundred or so Blackshirts were 'on duty', throwing out anyone who tried to ask awkward questions at the beginning of the meeting. As Orwell noted in his diary, Mosley said at the start that anyone ejected would be charged under the *Public Meetings Act*. No police were inside the hall, leaving the stewards, on Mosley's say-so, to throw out those causing 'interruption'. Anyone asking a question Mosley found difficult to answer was liable to get both a hammering from the Blackshirts and a fine from the courts. A group of lads too young to be admitted gathered in the foyer and found it enter-

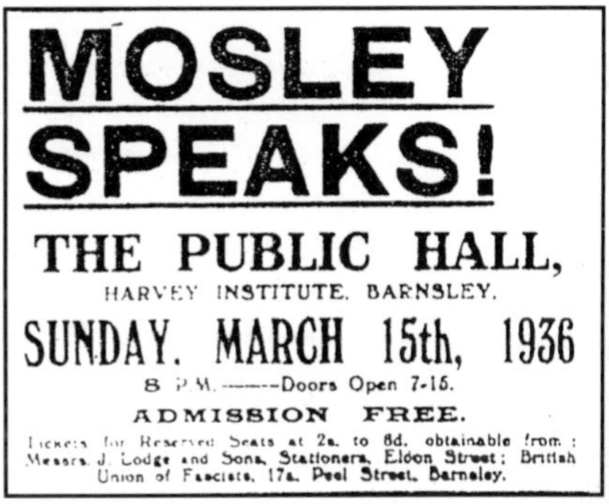

MOSLEY SPEAKS!

THE PUBLIC HALL,
HARVEY INSTITUTE, BARNSLEY.

SUNDAY. MARCH 15th, 1936

8 P.M.——Doors Open 7-15.

ADMISSION FREE.

Tickets for Reserved Seats at 2s. to 8d. obtainable from: Messrs. J. Lodge and Sons, Stationers, Eldon Street; British Union of Fascists, 17a, Peel Street, Barnsley.

Figure 3. Notice of Mosley's meeting at the Public Hall, Barnsley. *Barnsley Chronicle*, Saturday 24 March 1936.

taining to watch the ejections, some of whom had been beaten up by the Fascists.

After the meeting a large indignant crowd gathered outside the Hall. Orwell waited with them but Mosley did not appear. Police dispersed them and Mosley was spirited away through a back door. One of those Orwell saw thrown out of the Fascist meeting turned out to be Tommy Degnan. Later, in the *Three Cranes Hotel* (Figure 4), the two men had a strong argument about the heckling that had gone on

Figure 4. The *Three Cranes Hotel* (1930-63), Queen Street, Barnsley, where Orwell and Tommy Degnan met and argued. *Barnsley Archives.*

at the meeting.[3] Orwell , while fiercely opposed to Mosley's views, defended his right to speak. Degnan felt that Orwell underestimated the danger posed by Mosley and the British Union of Fascists, and by Hitler. However, they had more in common than separated them and by the time Orwell's book was published in March 1937, both men were fighting as volunteers in the Spanish Civil War.

It was a debate echoed soon afterwards in the Council Chamber. In April, the manager of the Public Hall reported to the Library and Harvey Institute Committee that twelve shillings worth of damage had been done to the seating at the Fascist meeting. The Committee recommended that this be claimed from the organisers. Councillor G Mason JP moved that the premises should not be left to this organisation in future, sparking off a row about free speech. Alderman Walton pointed out that other towns had banned the Fascists. Ninety-five percent of their supporters were imported by bus, he said, 'If Sir Oswald Mosley is so keen on free speech, we will give him May Day

Green and I will guarantee to get order for him'. The motion was carried and the Fascists had held their third and last meeting at the Public Hall.

May Day Green, the open market area in the town centre, was commonly used for political meetings as was Market Hill, where on 22 March Orwell went to a Communist meeting. The visiting speaker was verbose and disappointing but Tommy Degnan was much more effective – 'very broad Lancashire and though he can talk like a leading article if he wants to he doesn't choose.' About 150 attended and six shillings was collected for the defence of those arrested at the Fascist meeting. As a finale, an effigy of a Blackshirt was burned on a bonfire.

Orwell wrote to both *The Times* and the *Manchester Guardian* about Mosley but noted in the diary for 20 March that neither had printed his letter. He would have done better to write to the *Barnsley Chronicle* and *South Yorkshire Times* where the arguments raged on for weeks in the letters page.

Around the Houses

Orwell was keen to inspect working class housing for himself, reckoning that he visited between one and two hundred houses in various mining towns and villages. One example, a two up and two down in Wortley Street, had a stone sink worn almost flat and overflowing, cracked walls, rotten window frames and let rain in. One child had suspected T B. The house was infested by bugs. There was no electricity supply, and gas mantles were fed from a penny slot meter. The weekly rent was 5s. 3d. This was typical of the worst in town, but Orwell described some houses in Mapplewell, including some in Spring Gardens, as about the worst he had seen. Bugs were a menace, and once in, were there as Orwell put it, 'until the crack of doom'. They lurked in cracked walls under wallpaper and inside tubular bed frames. People would remove the bed knobs and pour in Naphalene to kill them, or more likely, drive them next door.

Orwell saw the cheapness of fuel in the mining areas as the one great mitigation of unemployment. In the South, a hundredweight of coal cost 2s.6d. but only 1s. 6d. in coal areas. Miners could buy coal at 8s. or 9s. a ton, and would sell or give it to unemployed neighbours. Even among the poorest, an empty fire grate was unusual. People would bank up the fire at night, then damp it down with the dregs from the teapot to keep it going until morning. Pans and kettles were boiled on the open fire, which heated the oven alongside, and in the newer houses, the hot water boiler.

Figure 5. *The Gardeners Arms*, Castlereagh Street. *Brian Elliott*

Orwell went to see Tommy Degnan at Garden House, 'a dreadful barn of a place...an almost ruinous old house' where he was more or less squatting with a group of single men who were on the dole and 'living in the extreme of misery.' This was in Castlereagh Street near the *Gardeners Arms* (Figure 5).

Ellis Firth lived in Albert Street East, paying 9s. 0d. rent out of his public assistance of 32 shillings a week. He was the 'unemployed miner' whose weekly budget featured in Orwell's chapter on food.

Mercifully, a series of Compulsory Purchase and Clearance Orders made in 1937 later swept away most of these slums and their residents were rehoused in new corporation estates such as Kendray and Cundy Cross. Such was the sense of occasion that the Council painstakingly photographed these areas before demolishing them and the results can be seen in the Barnsley Archives at the Central Library (Figures 6, 7 & 8).

Orwell was critical at the slow rate of building new houses. Famously, he criticised Barnsley Council for spending nearly £150,000 on a new Town Hall ahead of housing, in a borough of

Figure 6. Nos 2, 4, 6, 7 Court 2 Wortley Street, 1937. Back-to-back houses. *Barnsley Archives.*

Figure 7. No. 7, Court 1, Baker Street, 1937. Rabbit Hutches and Hen Houses were not allowed in the new council estates. *Barnsley Archives*

Figure 8. Interior of one-roomed dwelling at No.9 Blucher Street. *Barnsley Archives.*

70,000 inhabitants, largely miners, 'not one of whom has a bath in his house!'

Orwell had a talent for provoking outrage. Gilbert Langstaff, editor of the *Barnsley Chronicle*, reviewed the book on its publication in March 1937, with a volley of facts and figures: actually 9287 males in Barnsley worked in mines and quarries and all 3200 council houses had baths, as well as at least some of the 11,298 other working class houses. And the old Town Hall had been a disgrace, with offices scattered all over town, and the assembly chamber near the police cells.

Of course, Orwell was shown only the worst housing. For the better off, Barnsley had its share of the 1930s boom in suburban semi's. In 1936, houses on the new Limes Estate on Gawber Road (Figure 9) were advertised at £395, those on the Cockerham Estate at £550-800. Many of the town centre terraces were sound, and modernised and still provide good homes today. Some, like the Grays' home, already had electricity.

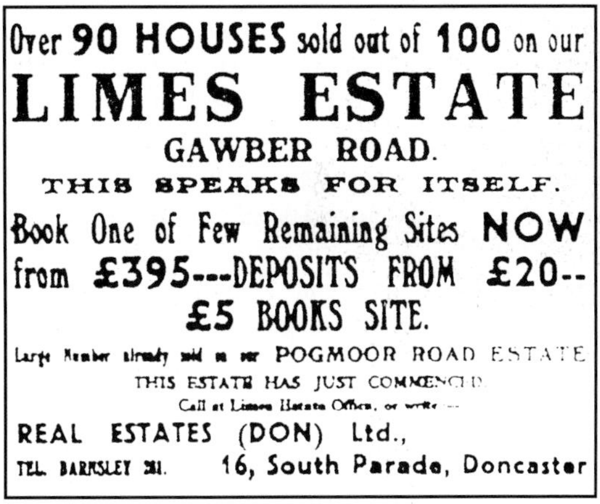

Orwell remarked in his book on the courtesy and patience with which he was received into people's homes. Ellis Firth, however, recalled many years later that he had been uncomfortable at the way Orwell had used a tape measure to record room sizes. He reminded him of a policeman (Ellis had worked as a bookie's runner so had a nose for policemen). In Wigan, Orwell had been mistaken for a 'dole snoop'. As an Eton-educated, former Burma police inspector, it is perhaps not surprising that Orwell lacked the common touch. No-one who reads *The Road to Wigan Pier* could, however, doubt his compassion for the poor and his anger at their situation.

Over **90 HOUSES** sold out of **100** on our

LIMES ESTATE

GAWBER ROAD.
THIS SPEAKS FOR ITSELF.

Book One of Few Remaining Sites **NOW** from **£395---DEPOSITS FROM £20--£5 BOOKS SITE.**

Large Number already sold on our POGMOOR ROAD ESTATE
THIS ESTATE HAS JUST COMMENCED
Call at Limes Estate Office, or write --

REAL ESTATES (DON) Ltd.,
TEL BARNSLEY 211.   16, South Parade, Doncaster

Figure 9. Advertisement for the remaining ten houses for sale from the Limes Estate, Gawber Road, Barnsley, March, 1936. *Barnsley Chronicle.*

Down the Pits

On 19 March, Orwell went down a 'day hole', the Wentworth Pit, with the deputy, Mr Lawson, who lived in Dodworth. It was an old, very wet pit, where he described the conditions as 'like hell.' Two days later he went down Grimethorpe Pit, then one of the most modern in Europe. Its advanced mechanisation was unique in England, though the system was in use in Germany and the USA. It was then turning out about 500 tons of coal a day. Grimethorpe also had electric lighting, Davy lamps being used only for gas testing.

Orwell was particularly impressed by the excellent pit baths, with their 1000 showers and separate lockers for each man's clean and dirty clothes. Maybe it was seeing these facilities, in contrast to other pits where miners went home black with coal dust to bathless houses, that inspired Orwell's outburst against the new Town Hall. Tommy Degnan, who had been taken prisoner in 1918 and sent to work in the Polish mines, told him that all Polish mines as well as French ones had pit baths. Accurate or not, this also impressed Orwell.

No-one has described the working lives of coal miners as powerfully as Orwell. Critics from Gilbert Langstaff to Walter Greenwood (author of *Love on the Dole*, 1933), however infuriated they were by other parts of the book, had nothing but praise for his vivid pictures (Figure 10) of coalmining, such as this example:

> *You cannot see very far, because the fog of coal dust throws*
> *back the beam of your lamp, but you can see...the line of half-*
> *naked kneeling men...driving their shovels under the fallen*
> *coal and flinging it swiftly over their left shoulders...It*
> *is a dreadful job they do, an almost superhuman job...For*
> *they are not only shifting monstrous quantities of coal, they*

Figure 10. Hand-got coal mining.

are also doing it in a position that doubles or trebles the work.

All of us really owe the comparative decency of our lives to poor drudges underground, blackened to the eyes, with their throats full of coal dust, driving their shovels forward with arms and belly muscles of steel.

Afterwards

In 1946, in *Why I Write* Orwell said that up to the end of 1935 he had still lacked political orientation. It was the Spanish war and other events of 1936-37 that changed him. On a personal level his journey through the north of England must have been a major factor. His friend Richard Rees many years later said that both Orwell's attitude and writing were transformed by his time in the north, as if something smouldering inside him had burst into flame.[4] The poverty and injustice he saw then made Orwell into a political writer, rather than the novelist he had seen himself earlier.

Before Orwell set foot outside Hampstead, *The Road to Wigan Pier* was destined to be a grim read. He came to see the worst effects of the Depression and did not have to look far. At the fag end of winter, he saw life in the mining areas at its dreariest.

In the two weeks he spent here, he captured a series of images of Barnsley, like black and white photos taken on a rainy day, which have haunted the town ever since. It is a tribute to the power of his writing that the book has carried an influence beyond its authority. The cliches it produced in the national press, the Barnsley of cobbled streets and back-to-back houses, lasted for decades after the demolition squads had moved in.

Many were hurt and offended by the bleak portrait Orwell drew. What he missed were the things his tape measure could not size-up - the strong bonds between family, friends and neighbours, the comradeship of the miners, the warmth and humour which made life tolerable.

For his earlier book he had lived as a tramp. He had become part of the down and out world. But he could never become part of the working class community he had come to experience. He seemed to sense this himself. At the end of Part One of the book, he describes the coziness of the more prosperous working class home where the father is in work and the family gathers round the open fire on a winter's evening – 'a good place to be provided that you can not only be in it but sufficiently of it to be taken for granted.'

For all that, *The Road to Wigan Pier* ensured that the superhuman efforts of the miners and the deprivations of the poorest in Barnsley in the 1930s will never be forgotten. Whatever you think of Orwell, his politics or his tape measure, we can all be grateful for that.

Notes and References

1.George Orwell, 1903-50. Born Eric Arthur Blair, India. Educated Eton. Inspector, Indian Imperial Police, Burma 1922-27. Novelist and journalist. Pogmoor Sands and Gawber Lighthouse were imaginary holiday resorts. Being able to afford a real holiday, often Blackpool at Barnsley Feast, was a sign that you were doing alright.
2.Sir Oswald Ernald Mosley 1896-1980. MP - Conservative, Independent, then Labour. Resign from 1929 Labour Government and became leader of the British Union of Fascists.
3.Orwell also visited the Radical and Liberal Club at least twice, once with Mr Wilde. It was then the Co-op building at the corner of Market Street and Wellington Street.
4.Rees interviewed in 1970 on *Omnibus*, BBC.

Books and Acknowledgements

The Road to Wigan Pier; The Road to Wigan Pier Diary; Collected Essays. Penguin Books and Harcourt Brace Jovanovich, USA.
Bernard Crick, *George Orwell: A Life,* Penguin Books, 1980.
Joseph Jones, *The Coal Scuttle,* 1936. Jones was Mayor of Barnsley 1935-37 and President of the Miners' Federation of Great Britain 1934-38. Orwell quotes from this work.
Edna Forrest, 'Memories of a Barnsley Childhood' in Brian Elliott (ed), *Aspects of Barnsley 3,* Barnsley,1995. Edna describes life in the 1930s in Silver Street, halfway between Agnes Terrace and the housing Orwell visited.
Thanks to the staff of Barnsley Archives and Local Studies; The Orwell Archive, University College, London; Mr K Goodliffe; Mr D Stead.

11. ELSECAR: THE MAKING OF AN INDUSTRIAL COMMUNITY, 1750-1830

by Ian R Medlicott

DURING THE EARLY NINETEENTH CENTURY Elsecar was an industrial community set within a rural environment. The relative tranquillity of the village today stands in marked contrast to the scene which met the eyes in 1815. Adjacent to the canal lay the Elsecar New Colliery, dominated by its Newcomen-type pumping engine and two steam-winding engines that hauled the coal to the pit top. Waggon-ways ran to the pit stack and down to the canal where the coal was emptied, with the aid of tiplers, directly into the waiting boats. In close proximity to the Colliery was the Elsecar Coal Tar Works and the Elsecar Ironworks. A short distance up the valley a similar scene was repeated with the siting of the Milton Ironworks and the Elsecar Old Colliery. The area was a vibrant hub of activity lit, after dark, by flames from the blast furnaces and coke ovens and through this smoke laden environment, engine sounds and pungent smells penetrated the air. From this scene came the materials of the industrial revolution produced by workers who lived nearby in the newly built houses and terraces (Figure 1).

Figure 1. Elsecar and the sites mentioned in the text. *The Author*

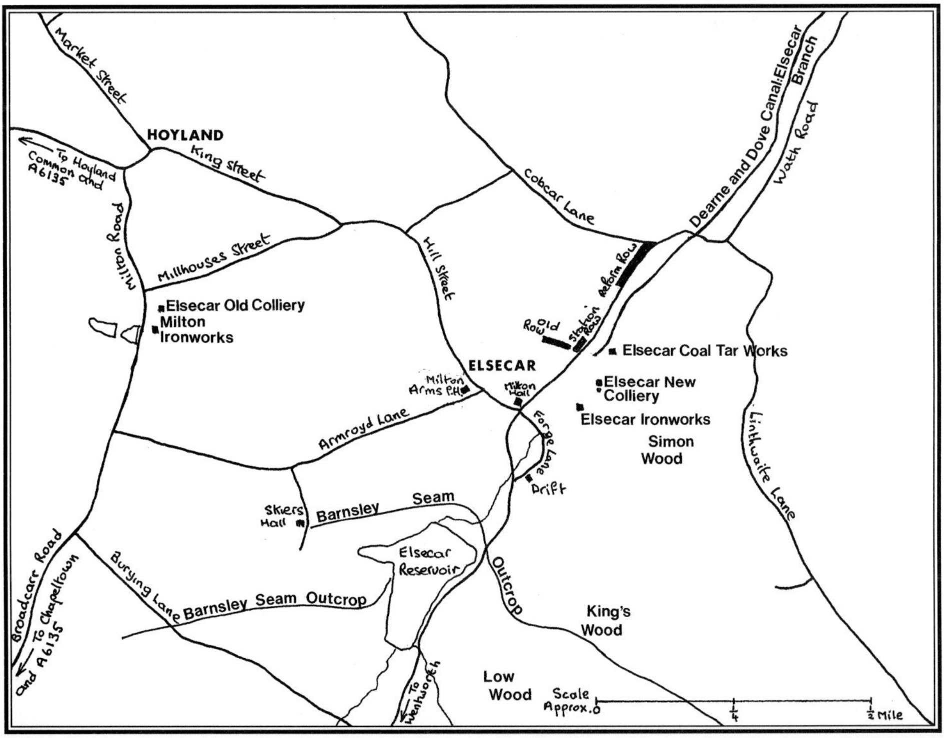

It is from 1750 that this study intends to trace the economic development of the Elsecar valley, with coal mining in particular, from a small isolated rural backwater on the edge of the Wentworth estate. Across the Elsecar valley lay the nine feet thick Barnsley seam that outcropped in a line through Hoyland Lane End, Stead Farm, Skiers Hall, across the north-east corner of the Elsecar reservoir, and on to Low Wood, King's Wood, and Nether Haugh near Greasbrough. During the nineteenth century the seam was particularly valuable for its use in locomotives, steamers, iron-smelting, gas production, and domestic applications.

It is only after 1750 that any substantive documentary coal mining evidence exists, although coal had been worked in the area for a long time. In 1750 the Ist Marquis of Rockingham started negotiations with Richard Bingley to lease the Elsecar Colliery. Bingley was to work the mine for eleven years at £35-14-0 per annum, employing no more than two 'colliers'. However, the rent would be foregone for two years:

> ... *in Consideration of the Said Rich:d Bingleys under-taking at his own Expense to Cleanse, Feigh and Repair the Level formerly made and Driven by one M:r Monckton ...*[1]

The level was to be cleared to Elsecar Green, where it had been discontinued by Monckton, and then driven to the foot of the coal being worked at a close called the 'great Arm-royd'. Bingley would be allowed to lease the Colliery after the level had been cleaned and repaired or failing this to pay a fine of £200.

If Bingley took out the lease it was soon surrendered for on 1 September 1752 Thomas Smith was instructed to commence working the Colliery the next day. Thomas Smith supervised the Colliery and submitted fortnightly reports to Rockingham, with the Estate Account Book for 1755/56 showing the mine was now 'In Hand' and run by 'managers'. However, by 1757 the Colliery was in the hands of tenants, according to Fairbank's survey of the same year which referred to Rockingham as the owner and 'John Hall, Thomas Smith & Jones' as tenants. In 1757/58 the Estate Account Book recorded, for the first time, under 'Colliery rents', 'John Hall & Co., Elsecar, Kilnhurst &c, half a yrs. rent' of £170. This continued until 1764/65 when 'Hall Mr Jnn & Co only entd for Year, being then taken into hand'. Throughout the period 1752 to 1764/65 Thomas Smith continued to oversee the Colliery for Rockingham.

The instructions given to Thomas Smith in September 1752 was to employ two 'Getters', one 'Filler', one 'Hurrier', two men above ground, and a 'stacker' to keep an account of all coal got and sold. The men were to be paid fortnightly, with Thomas Smith to receive a wage as a 'Workman', plus £20 per annum as 'Overseer' of the Colliery. Men were set to work clearing and driving the level and sinking a new pit, for which Thomas Hoyland and George Smith were paid £3-16-0 at 5s per yard for 15 yards 1 foot plus 2s for 'Earnest and Drink at Bargain making'. By 2 December 1752 the new pit was complete, with materials transferred from the old pit to where 'The Coal is Exceeding good in ye new pit'.[2]

The poor state of the roads, shortage of carters, especially at harvest time, and the fluctuating demand for coal resulted in mining being an irregular or seasonal activity at the Elsecar Colliery. An account for 21 April to 19 May 1753 stated that although coal sales had improved from the previous week:

> *...we Expect no Extraordinary Sale till most of the Law Wood Coals be gone for they are very Busy Everyday and their Roads both Level and Better repaired than some of our Roads are.* [3]

Later that year Thomas Smith wrote:

> *October 6th 1753*
>
> *This is to give your Hon:ble Lordship an Account that from August 11th to October 6th we have pull:d No Coals by Reason of being Over Stock.d.*[4]

While prior to 20 October 1770 the workers had been laid off for 20 weeks. Some of the colliers appear to have cultivated smallholdings that would have supplemented their income. Edward Dickinson rented 3a. 1r. 31p., Michael Hague 5a. 1r. 34p., and Joseph Hague 3r. 2p. of land, and in Fairbank's 1757 survey an 'Ed. Dickinson' held land near Elsecar Green. The extensive Wentworth estate, with its numerous agricultural and industrial activities did enable employees to be redeployed elsewhere on the estate. There was a marked reluctance to dismiss workers. This was not only an example of landed paternalism towards the employees but it also enabled a pool of skilled labour to be drawn upon when market conditions improved. During the 1760s the Elsecar colliers were employed ditching, hay-making, hedging, and thatching and in 1771 some were transferred to the Lowwood Colliery to meet the demand for coal at the mine. In December 1812, to avoid throwing men out of work Fitzwilliam suggested, transferring colliers from the Elsecar New Colliery to a pit

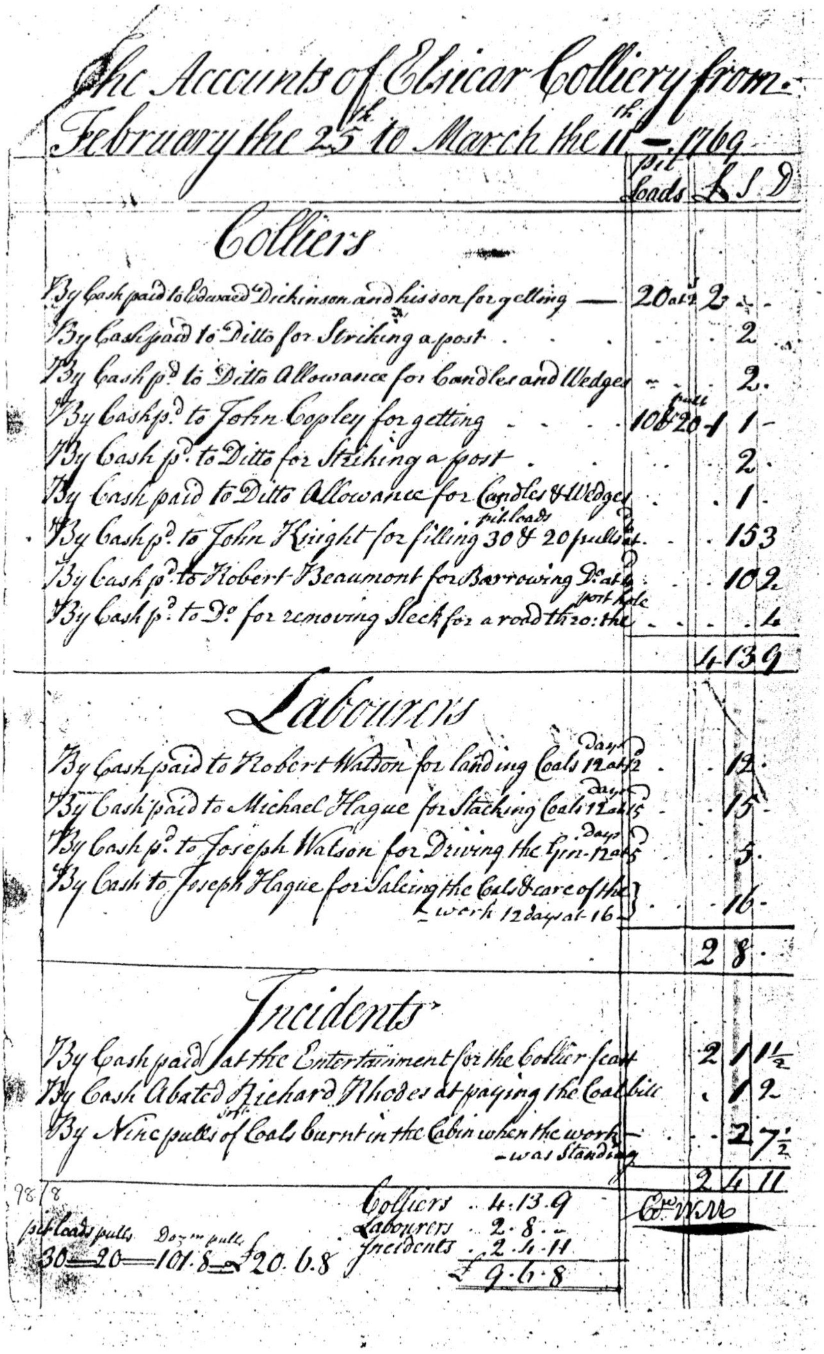

The Accounts of Elsicar Colliery from February the 25th to March the 11th — 1769

	Pit Loads	£	s	d
Colliers				
By Cash paid to Edward Dickinson and his son for getting —	20 at 2s	2	-	-
By Cash paid to Ditto for Striking a post . . .	-	-	2	
By Cash pd. to Ditto Allowance for Candles and Wedges	-	-	2	
By Cash pd. to John Copley for getting . . .	10 & 20 pulls	1	1	-
By Cash pd. to Ditto for Striking a post .	.	.	2	
By Cash paid to Ditto Allowance for Candles & Wedges	.	.	1	
By Cash pd. to John Knight for filling 30 pit loads & 20 pulls at .	.	.	15	3
By Cash pd. to Robert Beaumont for Barrowing Do. at	.	.	10	2
By Cash pd. to Do. for removing Sleck for a road thro: the post hole	.	.	.	4
		4	13	9
Labourers				
By Cash paid to Robert Watson for landing Coals 12 days at 12	.	.	12	
By Cash paid to Michael Hague for Stacking Coals 12 days at 15	.	.	15	
By Cash pd. to Joseph Watson for Driving the Gin 12 days at 5	.	.	5	
By Cash to Joseph Hague for Saleing the Coals & care of the work 12 days at 16	.	.	16	
		2	8	
Incidents				
By Cash paid at the Entertainment for the Collier feast		2	1	1½
By Cash Abated Richard Rhodes at paying the Coal bill		.	1	2
By Nine pulls of Coals burnt in the Cabin when the work was Standing		.	2	7½
		2	4	11

98/8

pit loads	pulls	Dozen pulls	£
30	20	101.8	20.6.8

Colliers	4.13.9
Labourers	2.8.–
Incidents	2.4.11
	£ 9.6.8

Cr. W.M.

Figure 2. The Accounts of the Elsecar Colliery from 25 February to 11 March 1769. *Sheffield Archives, Wentworth Woodhouse Muniments, F98/8* (presumably the Elsecar Old Colliery) to provide coal for the new furnace at the Milton Ironworks, driving new 'winnings' and 'levels', although none may be required, and employing men on a new road, or on any other work until the demand for coal had increased. However, Fitzwilliam's actions may not have been entirely altruistic, as these measures could also have been designed to prevent the social unrest prevalent elsewhere in South Yorkshire, from affecting the Wentworth estate.

In 1752 the Elsecar Colliery employed seven workers, not including Thomas Smith, with payment calculated by the load (6 tons 16 cwt). Two 'Colliers' were paid at 1s 8d per load, one 'Filling' 5d, one 'Barrowing' 5d, two 'pulling' 4 d, the 'Horse' 2d, and Joseph Hague at 7s per week for 'Stacking and Keeping the acct'. However, by 1769 all the surface workers received daily wage rates with only the underground workers paid according to output (Figure 2). The thickness of the Barnsley seam enabled a high output per man to be achieved. Between 19 May and 16 June 1753, 64 pit loads (436 tons 16 cwt) was worked, and for the year 30 December 1752 to 29 December 1753 output amounted to 603 pit loads (4,115 tons 9 cwt).

A watershed in the development of coal mining in Elsecar was marked by the opening of the Elsecar New Colliery in September 1795. The stimulus for such an enterprise was almost certainly the royal assent given on 3 June 1793 to the Dearne and Dove Canal Bill, with its proposed branch into Elsecar. This promised, along with Darwin and Co. intention to establish an ironworks in Elsecar, to open up new markets for Elsecar coal. The original intention was for the canal branch to go only as far as Cobcar Ing, some 600 yards short of the new Colliery, but after protracted negotiations Fitzwilliam persuaded the Canal Company to extend the branch, at a cost of £3497-10-6.

Direct supervision of the Elsecar New Colliery was given to John Deakin, colliery viewer, assisted by Michael Hague, overlooker, of the Elsecar Old Colliery:

> *Mr John Deakin for three Year's Salary for inspecting and directing the working and management of the Collieries to Christmas 1796. ..£189-0-0.* 5

Materials for the Elsecar New Colliery came mainly from the Wentworth estate and included, wood for corves, pit props, and whim gins, stone for the buildings, and bricks to line the shafts. A new brick kiln was built at Elsecar to supplement supplies from the Low Wood brickworks, with stone extracted from a quarry in Simon Wood, and

Figure 3. The Newcomen Engine and bye-pit at Elsecar. *The Author*

from a new one opened in Low Wood.

The first item of expenditure for the Elsecar Colliery New Works was entered on 12 April 1794, for boring in Simon Wood to ascertain the direction of a fault that threw the coal down 25 yards. In July the pumping engine pit and the bye-pit were being sunk with the coal reached at a depth of 35 yards, by December 1794. There followed the erection of the Newcomen-type pumping engine, under the supervision of John Bargh, an engineer from the Chesterfield area (Figure 3). The Elsecar engine was probably pumping water by the end of July 1795 and by December it had almost drained the Lowwood level through about 400 yards of coal. Limited coal production started in September 1795 and Fitzwilliam must have gained some satisfaction and relief when Charles Bowns, land agent, wrote on 24 November 1795:

> *It is with great pleasure that I inform Your Lordship that the Elsecar Colliery promises to be the best Mr Deakin ever saw, he has examined the Roof of the Coal &c and finds every thing as good as can be – the Carpenters are at work with the Machine for Drawing Coals, and the greatest part of the Cast Metal materials are upon the place.*

Mefr.rs Darwin & Co have begun their Blast and find the metal Extraordinary good, and to answer their fullest expectations. [6]

Initially the coal was wound to the surface by a whim gin rather than the more technologically advanced steam-winding engine or whimsey. This may have reflected a desire to commence production as soon as possible, to obtain a return on capital, and to install further high cost capital equipment when justified by the market. Capital expenditure did rise after the Elsecar Ironworks started production in 1795, and in 1798 when the Canal opened as far as Elsecar. A whimsey was built in 1796 under Jonathan Woodhouse, senior, from Ashby-de-la-Zouch, a prominent Leicestershire civil and mining engineer, and land agent to the Earl of Moira. Cast metal goods were supplied by Jarratt, Dawson, and Hardy, of the Low Moor Ironworks, Bradford, with a steam boiler from Darwin & Co. In the same year conductors were installed in the bye-pit, a tramroad laid, patterns for a 'Rail Road' and two tiplers purchased from Phipps, Clay, and Deakin, and waggon patterns sent from Flocton. Towards the end of 1798 anther bye-pit was sunk and a steam-winding engine installed, which coincided with the opening of the canal into Elsecar. There followed further expenditure on iron rails, and in March 1799 orders were given for:

The Pit Top at Elsecar New Colliery to be raised 12 feet and a double Rail Road laid from thence in to the Bottom of Simon Wood about 10 yards to the East of the Engine Tenters House and from there a single Road upon Tiplers for putting Coals into a Battery according to a Plan delivered to John Falding by Mr Deakin. [7]

The interdependence of the coal and iron industries was reflected in Elsecar, where the collieries supplied coal to the Elsecar and Milton ironworks, and they in turn produced corf wheels, engine parts, iron rails, and other castings for the mines. Although the majority of iron goods were supplied by the Elsecar, Milton, and Thorncliffe ironworks on the Wentworth estate, outside suppliers often provided the more precision or specialist castings. These included the Low Moor Ironworks, Bradford, the Butterley Works, Derbyshire, and the Coalbrookdale Company in Shropshire.

In areas of sparse population the limited supply of labour, especially of skilled workers, could cause recruitment problems. As a consequence, colliery proprietors were often obliged to provide accommodation at subsidised rents to attract the necessary labour.

This was undoubtedly the case in Elsecar as the demand for workers rose rapidly between 1795 and 1802 as labour was required for the Elsecar New Colliery, Elsecar Old Colliery, and the Elsecar and Milton ironworks. As early as 27 May 1792 Bowns wrote:

> As Colliers are now scarce, and we are in want of them at Elsecar we must put ourselves to some inconvenience to procure them . . .

He went on to relate that a John Lindley, who had previously worked at Lowwood, was prepared to leave his present employment at Attercliffe to work at Elsecar, if a house could be provided, and that 'Michael Hague says that one man at present will be sufficient, & he knows not where to find another'.[8] To provide accommodation for colliers from the Elsecar New Colliery, four houses, including one for the manager, was ordered to be built in Cobcar Ing in July 1796 and between 1796 and 1798 Fitzwilliam built, converted, or repaired at least forty-two dwellings for the Colliery. It was around this time that Old Row and Station Row were built in Elsecar and as the labour force expanded in the nineteenth century many more dwellings were built (Figures 4, 5, and 9).

The increase in capital expenditure from 1796 and the development of new markets brought about a significant rise in output. At the Elsecar New Colliery output rose from 12,710 tons in 1798 to 48,567 tons in 1825 and at the Elsecar Old Colliery from 5,631 tons in 1788 to 27,692 tons in 1825. The workforce increased to cater for the demand for coal, and by July 1808 there were 95 miners at the Elsecar

Figure 4. Elsecar:Old Row. *The Author*

Figure 5. Elsecar:Station Row. *The Author*

New Colliery and 20 at the Elsecar Old Colliery rising by 1825 to 103 and 46, respectively. The Elsecar collieries remained profitable concerns, based on the accounting criteria of the time, which gives some insight into why Fitzwilliam continued as a colliery proprietor rather than revert to the position of lessor, as was increasingly common among the landed classes during the eighteenth century.

The Technological Development of the Collieries

During the 1750s the Elsecar Colliery employed the minimum of capital equipment with shaft sinking the largest single item of capital expenditure. The shafts were some fifteen yards deep and with the low output and the shallowness of the seam, it was more cost effective to sink new shafts than to extend the workings. Shafts at the Elsecar Colliery lasted, on average, for twenty four months with three sunk every two years. The whim gin and other materials could be easily dismantled and then reassembled in a new shaft. This compares with the 35 yards depth of the engine pit and bye-pits at the Elsecar New

Colliery in 1798. It was not only the depth of the pits, but also the capital cost and complexity of the Newcomen engine and the steam-winding engines which made it uneconomic for them to be moved regularly. Therefore, by the end of the eighteenth century fewer shafts were being sunk with the workings extended greater distances from the shaft bottom.

Fairbank's 1757 survey of the Elsecar Colliery showed a deep level running from the 'Old Gin Pit' on Elsecar Green to the 'Old Sough & Pit on the Throw', branching off this level was the 'New Deep Level Sough' and the 'New Sough Pit', the line of the deep level went on to the 'Great Arm Royd'. There was also a basset level running parallel at some 154 to 220 yards distant with three air pits, two open pits, a working pit, and a sinking pit.[9] The coal was worked from the drainage level towards the basset, with pits used for haulage and ventilation. By the early nineteenth century the Colliery was working the coal nearer Hoyland centre at the Milton Ironworks adjacent to Milton Road. However, as collieries became more extensive, and worked at greater depths, it necessitated the introduction of more advanced technology and mining expertise to facilitate the movement of increased quantities of coal, and to overcome the possibility of bottlenecks at the various stages of production. In addition, the difficulties associated with drainage and ventilation had to be overcome.

Shaft sinking

Prior to sinking the Elsecar New Colliery bore holes were taken to ascertain the depth, extent, and thickness of the coal seam, and the presence of any faults. On sinking a shaft, a horse-driven whim gin was positioned over the pit mouth to haul up the waste materials, ventilation was provided by air pipes worked by pumps, and gunpowder was used to blast the hard rock. Boring and shaft sinking was generally paid at rates that varied according to depth. An oval pit measuring nine feet by seven feet at the Elsecar Old Colliery in 1799, was sunk at 16s per yard for the initial 16 yards, 22s per yard for the next 16 yards, and 28s per yard the remainder.[10] When shafts only lasted some two years the sides were shored up by wood, in later years when they became more permanent features they were lined by bricks. Drifts were sometimes sunk to allow easier access to the workings. A drift or 'footrill' sunk in 1820, may have been the one that can still be seen on Forge Lane, and it was from such entrances that Fitzwilliam escorted guests into the collieries (Figure 6).[11]

Figure 6. The entrance to the drift or footrill on Forge Lane, Elsecar. *The Author*

Drainage

The Elsecar collieries were drained by stone lined soughs driven at a slight upward gradient into the deep of the mine to allow the water to discharge into the Knoll Beck, Elsecar (Figure 7). To prevent the workings being flooded it was vital the soughs be kept clear of any blockage. This was particularly uncomfortable and dangerous work with risks from roof falls and gas. The Lowwood Colliery sough, that

Figure 7. 'Early Mode of Getting Coal'. Rev A Gatty,D.D., *Sheffield:Past and Present,* Sheffield 1873 p.183

also drained into the Knoll Beck, had been cleared for a distance of 400 yards by 29 October 1793, when the men were driven out by gas 'from which the old works are not likely to be clear till Frosty weather'. By 29 January 1794 some 700 yards had been cleared from the new pit at Elsecar. It was 'clogged' with mud and 'oker' and had to be removed by a man and three boys who worked in a headroom of only 27 inches, stirring up the sediment with water and allowing the stream to wash it away. As a consequence, the work was long and tedious, carried out daily as long as they are able to bear.[12]

The Newcomen-type pumping engine installed at the Elsecar New Colliery in 1795 was to drain an area of coal below the existing soughs. Although a Watt steam-pumping engine could have provided a two-third saving on fuel over the Newcomen engine, fuel costs were not a major item of expenditure at a colliery. The Newcomen engine had the advantage of a proven record of reliability, it was relatively simple to maintain and work, and was able to use the mainly unsaleable small coal. The original Elsecar engine had a wooden beam and a forty-two inch cylinder that raised water from a depth of 35 yards. On 2 September 1797 Joshua Biram, clerk, (in 1805 he became the house steward) calculated that it could raise 386 gallons per minute and take 9 hours 49 minutes per day to keep the mine free from water.[13] During the early decades of its operation, serious problems were encountered with the considerable inflow of water from their own and neigh-bouring collieries. This resulted in lost production and additional expenditure on pumping equipment and new soughs. In 1801 the cylinder was replaced with one of forty- eight inches, supplied by the Butterley Ironworks, and in March 1811 the engine was having to work sixteen hours per day, although the average for that time of year was twelve hours. In 1812 further equipment was installed with an account for 31 August, 'The Coalbrookdale Company for castings &c for the Engine 192-3-3', and by November 1812 the engine worked three pumps, one of thirteen inches, and two of eight inches raising water at a rate of 604 gallons per minute.[14]

Ventilation and Lighting

Colliers faced the risk of explosions from 'fire-damp' or methane gas, or suffocation from 'choke-damp' or carbonic acid. Gas could be expelled from the workings by changes in atmospheric pressure, especially where an air shaft was positioned at a considerable elevation from the deep level. During the winter months fresh air entered the sough, passed through the workings and left via a shaft, with the air flow reversed during the summer months. This method of natural ventilation may have been used to assist the movement of air in the Elsecar collieries, as it was in the Lowwood Colliery old workings. A more reliable method of ventilation was to place a fire at the bottom or part way down a shaft so the upward movement of hot air from the furnace would force fresh air down a nearby downcast shaft. This may have been the system used in the Elsecar Colliery in 1752 when a brazier was purchased for the pit. While an account for the 2 September 1752 to 24 February 1753 recorded, 'fire pan Coals 17 pulls 00-4-11 1/2'. In July/August 1769 Michael Hague received 1s 3d for fetching a 'fire-pan' and 'gearing' a pit when it was full of damp.[15] A fire pan was a receptacle for the furnace that was placed in the upcast shaft.

The greater depth and more extensive workings of the Elsecar New Colliery increased the danger from gas. Even so, the basic method of ventilation remained the same until the introduction of ventilation fans in the 1850s. Fire pans continued to be used with the air coursed around the workings by trap doors but there was not a sufficient number of boys employed to work all the doors. Therefore, some of the trap doors were operated by the colliers who sometimes succumbed to the temptation to prop them open. In June 1832 Viscount Milton wrote to Joshua Biram asking him to rebuke the man responsible for leaving open a trap door, as only a few months earlier he had spoken 'strongly' when a similar incident had occurred.

In such a combustible environment fire posed a constant threat, with the risk of explosions and the possible loss of life, equipment, and production. During May 1805 a fire in the Elsecar New Colliery held up production for several weeks and even when the fire had been extinguished the workings could not be entered until the heat had abated. The ease at which a fire could start is illustrated at the Elsecar New Colliery when it was thought that as a collier was going to his work place, with a lighted rope, a spark ignited some hay or straw at the stables. Although the fire was soon extinguished, one of the horses was singed with the others affected by smoke.[16]

Colliers worked by the light of candles or lamps and later by safety lamps, but the latter could only produce about one-quarter the light of a candle. As colliers were paid according to output they sometimes removed the protective gauze of the lamp to obtain a brighter light. The evidence suggests that the Fitzwilliam colliers did not always use the safety lamps provided, for in Viscount Milton's letter of June 1832 he wrote not only of his annoyance of a trap door being left open but also that no accident need occur if the colliers would use their lamps.

Twenty years later the propping open of a trap door and the removal of a safety lamp gauze was the cause of an explosion which led to the loss of ten miners. There was sometimes a lack of self discipline by the miners and an insufficient enforcement of the safety rules by the management.[17]

Haulage and Winding the Coal

In 1752 coal was hauled manually from the work face to the shaft bottom but what receptacle/receptacles were used at each stage of conveyance or how the coal was moved it is not possible, with accu-

Figure 8. A plan of Elsecar Colliery by Joshua Biram 27 September 1793. *Sheffield Archives, Wentworth Woodhouse Muniments, MP55*

racy, to state. However, coal baskets were used with several entries, for example, on 6 March 1753 'Matthew Swift 8 Dozn Coal Baskets 2/6'. Corves made of wooden planks were also employed at the Colliery, with payments made to Thomas Vickers for carpenters work between October 1752 and January 1753 for sawing planks for corf sides, mending and making corves. The corves may have been hauled on runners or wooden rails or placed on a sledge and dragged by the 'Barrower' to the bottom of the shaft. The coal was wound to the surface by a windlass and then taken by horse-drawn sledge to the 'pit hill' ready for sale. In July 1754 the windlass was replaced by a horse-driven whim gin and in January 1769 a 'Brown Mare Risng Six Years Old for the pit Bottom as pr Receipt 5-15-0' was set to work. The whim gin was still at work 26 years later, with shafts by then 33 yards deep. The improvements in haulage and winding enabled heavier loads to be moved more quickly, the substitution of men for boys, and a subsequent reduction in wage rates. The introduction of a horse for underground haulage allowed the coal to be moved greater distances, and reduced the frequency of sinking pits. Winding coal to the surface by a windlass involved the employment of two men each paid at 4 d per load, but following the erection of a whim gin one man received 4d per load with a 'Gin Driver' at 1 d per load. Likewise, 'Barrowing' was paid at 5 d per load which fell to 4d per load after the 'Mare' had been introduced for underground haulage. The low output of the Elsecar Colliery did not justify the installation of steam-driven whim-seys and even by 1793, according to a plan by Joshua Biram, a whim gin still wound the coal to the surface, with one corf or basket descending as a loaded corf was raised, while a horse-drawn sledge pulled the coal to the pit stack (Figure 8).[18]

The opening of the Elsecar New Colliery required a greater quantity of coal to be raised from the pit more quickly and from greater distances, and therefore, a more efficient method of conveyance was needed. Horse-drawn wheeled corves and waggon-ways were installed, with steam-driven whimseys to wind the coal to the surface. Within the shaft, conductors were positioned to prevent collisions either with the shaft side or between the corves as they passed each other. By 1818 flat ropes had been introduced to wind heavier loads, from greater depths, and to ease the loading on the winding drum axle. On the surface waggon-ways moved the coal to the pit stack or down to the canal where it was loaded, with the aid of tiplers, directly into the boats.

The Method of Working the Coal

By the late eighteenth century the Elsecar Colliery was worked under a systematic method of mining. A variant of the bord and pillar system was used as it was thought that longwall mining was unsuitable for the Barnsley seam, due to the brittleness of the roof. The Colliery had a deep level measuring two yards wide by five feet high, with a counter level lying parallel to act as a filter to reduce the possibility of a blockage in the main water course. The banks or work places were nine yards wide by seven and a half feet high, except where the roof was 'tender' which then reduced the banks to eight yards in width. To enable a bank to be used as a roadway two rows of props were placed to support the roof, providing a passage six feet in width. The roof was supported by ribs of coal three feet wide and up to 100 yards in length, widened at the ends for added support. The ends of the ribs and the props were later removed as the roadways were abandoned. Post holes were driven diagonally across the ribs towards the pit shafts to provide easier movement of the corves and to assist ventilation. This work was difficult as the grain or laminations within the coal worked against the collier, as compared to working in the banks, and for this an additional payment was given of 2s for 'striking a post'. The removal of pit props was an hazardous operation as the roof was liable to collapse, and a rate of 12d per dozen props retrieved was paid. The top one and a half feet of the seam was left to help support the roof and as this fell down when the props were withdrawn, it could then be collected.

The Elsecar New Colliery worked the coal under a similar system in banks 400 yards in length. A plan of the proposed method for working the Elsecar New Colliery by Michael Hague, on the 21 July 1794, was for banks ten yards wide, but John Deakin's plan dated 25 October 1796 called for banks of eight yards wide with posts ten yards in width either side of the boardgate. The reduction in the banks would have been due to the fragility of the roof. This method of working the coal enabled a greater quantity of coal to be extracted than the 50 per cent or less that was often the case underbord and pillar mining. At the Elsecar New Colliery, from 26 September 1795 to 5 July 1808, of 57.37084 acres of coal 'Broken Into' some 38.3459 acres were 'Clean Got' or 67 per cent, and of the remainder between 20 and 25 per cent was later worked.[19]

The coal industry was among the first to experience the economic advantages of the division of labour. Although the Elsecar Colliery employed only eight miners in 1769, the coal was hewn from the coal face by 'Colliers' who undercut the seam with a pick to a depth of 2 feet 6 inches to 3 feet 6 inches, with the undercut coal supported by sprags or short props. Large pieces of coal were split off the coal face with the aid of metal wedges. After these had been cut into the appropriate sizes, a 'Filler' loaded the corf or basket ready for the 'Barrower' to haul it to the pit bottom. The 'Gin Driver' wound the coal to the surface where it was unhooked and taken to the pit stack. The 'Overseer', by this date, was responsible for coal sales and 'care' of the 'work'.

The Market for Coal

The Elsecar Colliery was typical of a small inland mine remote from a navigable waterway and serving an essentially local market. The isolated position of the Colliery restricted the majority of coal sales to within a radius of three miles from the mine. In the 1760s coal was sold to the local brickyard, hospital, ironworks, smithies, farmers, lime kilns, maltsters, domestic consumers, and for direct estate use at Wentworth. However, a considerable amount of coal was carried by cart a distance of 5.25 miles to the estate's wharf at Kilnhurst on the Don Navigation. From there it was taken by boat and then overland to markets on the magnesian limestone to the east, returning with limestone for the lime kilns on the estate. Fairbank's 1757 survey of the Elsecar Colliery shows two lime kilns in the vicinity of Armroyd Lane, Elsecar. Out of a total of 525 pit loads 15 pulls (3,585 tons 15 cwt) of coal sold between 2 February 1754 and 6 January 1755, some 108 pit loads 2 pulls (737 tons 9 cwt), or nearly one-fifth, was carried by cart to Kilnhurst. A further 60 pit loads 9 pulls (411 tons 1 cwt) was sent for Rockinghams use at Wentworth.[20]

The major single consumer of Elsecar coal was Young, Clay, & Co. of the Chapel Furnace, Chapeltown, a distance of 2.75 miles from the Colliery. In 1767 they purchased 595 dozen (1,260 tons), of coal out of total sales of approximately 1,807 dozen pull (3,794 tons 15 cwt), or 33 per cent. The introduction of coke in the blast furnaces of the Chapel Furnace in 1778 and the surrender of the Company's Westwood Colliery lease in 1791 may account for the increase in purchases from the Elsecar Colliery by the 1790s. In 1798, for example, the Elsecar Colliery supplied 3,067 dozen 8 corves (6,442 tons 16 cwt) to the Chapel Ironworks, out of total sales of 7,396 tons. The opening of the Elsecar branch of the Dearne and Dove Canal reduced the cost of transport at the Elsecar collieries and enabled the penetration of more distant markets. Several attempts were made to enter the lucrative London market. In 1792 Fitzwilliam had considered sending coal to London, but while the pit head price was 4s 6d its carriage into London raised this to £1-9-2. A further enquiry was made in 1802 on whether any:

> *...coal vessels want to venture to the London market...it will be an opportunity for trying, how either the Elsecar or Parkgate coal will sell in London. 21*

None of the attempts made before 1830 achieved any long term success, as the proprietors of the 'Great Northern Coalfield' could usually undercut coal from the inland coalfields, before the introduction of the railways.

The cheap bulk movement of coal along the canal system did enable the Elsecar collieries to consolidate their markets to the east and south-east, as far as Gainsborough, Lincoln, and Wisbech. This is reflected in the quantity of Elsecar coal sent down the Dearne and Dove Canal. In 1800 this amounted to 720 tons per week, and out of 73,384 tons shipped down the Canal in 1810, Elsecar accounted for 26,462 tons or 39 per cent of the total combined sales of 67,186 tons from the collieries. Even so, within a relatively short distance the cost of transport could more than double the price of coal. Although the price of a waggon of Elsecar coal in 1823 was 12s 6d at the pit head, it rose to £1-11-6 at Lincoln, and to £1-13-8 at Malton, North Yorkshire.[22] As a consequence, their markets remained local, with the fortunes of the Elsecar collieries being closely linked to those of the Elsecar and Milton Ironworks. In 1810, for example, the Elsecar Ironworks purchased 13,503 dozen (28,356 tons 6 cwt), or 58 per cent of the total sales of the Elsecar New Colliery whilst the Milton Ironworks purchased 6,615 dozen 11 pulls (13,893 tons 8 cwt), or 77 per cent of the total sales of the Elsecar Old Colliery. With such dependence on the ironworks any slump in demand for castings was immediately reflected in a decline in coal sales. The economic depression of 1812 saw only one furnace in blast at Elsecar, with at least 2,500 dozen (5,250 tons) of coal in hand. Coal sales to the Milton Ironworks fell to 5,302 dozen 5 pulls (11,135 tons 3 cwt) from the Elsecar Old Colliery, and at the Elsecar Ironworks to 5,665 dozen 2 pulls (11,897 tons 2 cwt), from the Elsecar New Colliery. However, by 1814 the demand for coal and iron had revived with sales from the Elsecar Old Colliery rising from 15,941 tons in 1814 to 28,161 tons in 1815.

The alternating periods of boom and slump continued with the economic depression of 1816 followed by a recovery in 1819. In a letter to Fitzwilliam on 31 May 1819, Joshua Biram wrote that boats for the Elsecar New Colliery were having to wait from ten days to a fortnight to load, and that at the time of writing there were between ten and twelve boats waiting at the Elsecar wharf. By 1827 the economic depression resulted in the bankruptcy of the Elsecar Ironworks and to financial difficulty at the Milton Ironworks. The possibility of closure of the ironworks was averted by the intervention of Fitzwilliam, as the concerns were so vital to the continuation of the collieries and employment on the estate. Accordingly, Fitzwilliam purchased the Elsecar Ironworks for £4,194-11-0 and took the works under direct estate management for the next twenty years. The Milton Ironworks were purchased by Fitzwilliam for £27,000 and leased back to Graham & Co at six per cent interest per annum.[23]

A determined attempt to break into the market for coal by-products came with the erection of the Elsecar Coal Tar Works on land adjacent to the Elsecar New Colliery, known today as 'Distillery Side'. The production of coke for the South Yorkshire ironworks promised to be a lucrative venture, and the reduction of tar imports following the Napoleonic blockade and the increased demand from the ship-building industry, would have provided a ready market for the sale of tar. Thomas M Parker was employed to conduct experiments in a barn at Skiers Hall in 1813, and later that year construction was started on the Elsecar Coal Tar Works. On 18 July 1815 the accounts record, for the first time, 'Thomas Scholey for Freight & Dues on 20 Barrels of Tar to Hull 2-0-0'. There followed shipments of coke to places such as Ripon, York, and London, and sales of tar, spirit, varnish, and lamp black. However, production was of short duration with the works closing on 31 January 1818. There had been serious technical problems that had resulted in several explosions, management difficulties, and opposition from the local ironmasters.[24]

Social Conditions of Miners

Coal mining was one of the most physically demanding and dangerous occupations, carried out in uncomfortable conditions. Colliers served a long apprenticeship starting as trap boys, horse lads, or ginney lads and progressing, as they became stronger, to trammers and hewers at the coal face. It was common for whole families to be employed, but unlike many other South Yorkshire collieries no females or boys under nine years of age were taken on in the Elsecar mines. Fitzwilliam appeared reluctant to employ workers from outside the estate who were not familiar with the accepted work practices and whose personal qualities were unknown. Once employees had proved their honesty, trustworthiness, and competence, their relatives were often employed. Such nepotism had the additional advantage, for the landowner, of facilitating the transference of skills and knowledge, and assisting in the promotion of work discipline. As a consequence, employment in the collieries was often carried on from one generation to the next with many family members working in the mines at any one period of time.

Certain customary practices that were common in agrarian societies, such as payments for tools and the provision of food and drink at certain times of the year, were introduced into the collieries. At the Elsecar collieries allowances were given for candles, shovels, and wedges, with flannels provided for wet work. Christmas boxes were given, and in February each year the colliers were treated to a 'Coal Feast'. An account for the Elsecar Colliery in 1769 states: 'The Charge of the Coal Feast' malt and hops £1-0-4 , beef 14s 3d, veal 3s 1d, bread 1s 2d, butter 1s 4d, tobacco and pipes 11d, total £2-1-1.25

Shortly after taking the Elsecar Colliery in hand Thomas Smith wrote to Rockingham

Feb 24 1753

May it pleafe your Hon r. ble Lordship

It has Been a Cuftom for the Colliers & other pit men: to have A weekpull or fire Coals paying Sixteen pence p. Doz.n the price of Getting they Humbly desire yo:r Lordship wo.d Comply with ye above Cuftom.[26]

Rockingham duly accepted the custom. Food, drink, and entertainment was provided when contracts were entered into, buildings erected, or a colliery opened. On 15 December 1794, the Household Account Book recorded for the Elsecar New Colliery, 'John Fallding & Samuel Sykes for Meal &c. &c. for an entertainment for Masons, Carpenters &c at rearing the Engine House 4-10-4'.[27] In large collieries frequent injuries called for medical treatment on a regular basis. A memorandum in 1797 for the Elsecar New Colliery stated:

Question to ask Earl Fitzwilliam if a surgeon is to be allowed to the main'd Colliers, – Mr Deakin says it is customary to provide surgeons at other Collieries.[28]

A surgeon was employed to attend the colliers and by 1806 William Lunn was retained on an annual fee of £50.

The very nature of coal mining produced a variety of injuries, with accidents from roof falls being the most common in the Elsecar collieries, but familiarity with danger could breed carelessness and indifference to the potential hazards. Fitzwilliam provided allowances and pensions that varied according to income and family circumstances. Although he showed a genuine interest in the welfare of his employees it was important that miners return to work as soon as possible for it was sometimes difficult to recruit skilled labour. When William Evans was hurt by a fall of coal in January 1810, Joshua Biram recommended an allowance of 9s a week 'for relief and assistance'. Such allowances could be carried on over a long period of time, beyond what would normally be necessary on grounds of self interest. Edward Dickinson, collier, at the Elsecar Old Colliery, for example, received 5s per week for at least 194 2/7 weeks from 1804 to 1808.

Injured colliers were given donations of a guinea with weekly allowances for long periods off work and widows' pensions, usually of 2s 6d per week. George Boid, collier, was hurt by a 'great fall of Coals upon him', in February 1806, he was poor, had a wife and four children and had been ill prior to the accident. He received a guinea donation. Two years later, following another accident, Boid's wife received 13s per week for six weeks during his stay at the Leeds Infirmary, and in December 1811 he was killed by another fall of coal, leaving a widow, and by this time, seven children. His widow was given a pension of 2s 6d per week. Accidents also occurred as men rode in the shafts. In January 1809 Samuel Fallding, carpenter at the Elsecar New Colliery, was severely hurt when the rope broke that supported the crosspiece upon which the colliers rode. He fell about eighteen yards onto a stage, breaking his shoulder. A dangerous practice was riding in the shaft as materials were being lowered. In January 1807 Joseph Kay and his brother decided to come up as 'puncheon wood' was being lowered, a piece of wood slipped striking Joseph who fell fifteen yards to the bottom, broke his skull and died, leaving a wife and three children. Richard Jessop was killed by a fall of stone in December 1808 while collecting roof coal that was allowed to fall down in the banks when the pit props were removed.29 A combination of good ventilation practice and the shallow depth of the workings would account for the few recorded injuries from gas. Therefore, the incident at the Elsecar New Colliery in November 1808 when Thomas and George Harrison were slightly burnt by fire-damp was uncommon:

Figure 9. Elsecar : Reform Row. *The Author*

> *. . . which, by its explosion put their candles out and set their*
> *waistcoats on Fire, which men laying at a little Distance from them,*
> *one of them had two or three small places on his back burnt so much*
> *as to cause the skin to come off.*[30]

A brief word must be written about the quality of accommodation for
the colliers. According to Tremenheere, Mines Commissioner, writing
in 1845, the Fitzwilliam dwellings were, 'of a class superior in size and
arrangement, and in conveniences attached, to those belonging to the
working classes'.[31] They comprised of four rooms, a pantry, a small
back yard, an ash pit, garden, and conveniences for every six or seven
houses. The houses described were probably those of Reform Row
(Figure 9). The high rents of 2s per week may well have reflected the
quality of the houses and the length of the gardens. However, the
accommodation was tied to the continued employment at the colliery

and if a collier moved or was dismissed he lost his house, and the threat of losing their jobs was used to discourage the employees from taking industrial action or joining a trades union.

Even so, Fitzwilliam had a paternalistic attitude towards his employees, performing many of the functions of the welfare state, with the provision of sickness and injury allowances, widows' pensions, free medical treatment, schools and good housing. In addition, colliers were eligible for the St Thomas Day Donation, and the Collop Monday Charity. During times of scarcity and high prices, Fitzwilliam gave out food and blankets. In January 1801 blankets were distributed and herrings and rice were sold at greatly reduced prices, and in August, Fitzwilliam suggested buying more rice as prices appeared to have fallen, and that it 'may be worth while to get some more for the Labourers & Colliers ...'[32]

Conclusion

The direct involvement by the owners of the Wentworth estate in the exploitation of coal in the Elsecar valley, was of prime importance to its development into an industrial community. Fitzwilliam provided the capital, political influence, and determination to work the coal and ironstone reserves by opening and developing the Elsecar New and Old collieries, encouraging the establishment of the Elsecar and Milton ironworks, and promoting the extension of the Elsecar branch of the Dearne and Dove Canal. The experience acquired in the direct management of the Elsecar collieries led to Fitzwilliam exploiting the coal reserves elsewhere on the Wentworth estate, to become one of the major coal producers in South Yorkshire.

Acknowledgements

I am grateful to Olive, Countess Fitzwilliams Wentworth Settlement Trustees and the Director of Sheffield City Libraries for permission to quote from the Wentworth Woodhouse Muniments in the Sheffield Archives.

Notes and References

Abbreviations : WWM-Wentworth Woodhouse Muniments; F.B.-Fairbank Collection.
1. The 1st Marquis of Rockingham was succeeded by his son, the 2nd Marquis in 1750, who in turn was succeeded in 1782 by his nephew, William, the 4th Earl Fitzwilliam. WWM, F96/1. Richard Bingley leased the nearby Lowwood Colliery that was taken into direct estate management in 1763.
2. WWM, F95/5; F96/1/8; F.B.12; A228; A231; A241. Apart from the Elsecar Colliery, Thomas Smith supervised other collieries at least from 1757/58, such as a mine at Westwood, still at £20 per annum. Thomas Smith was probably one of the partners in John Hall & Co, and it may have been their property Smith supervised for Rockingham. In the 1750s 39pulls=1pit load, 1pull=3cwt, 1pit load=136cwt. By 1770 40pulls=1pit load=140cwt. At the Elsecar New Colliery

23 corves=1pit load=138cwt.. 1 corf=6cwt.. For both collieries 1dozen=42cwt, 1 waggon=48cwt..

3. WWM, F95/11.

4. WWM, F95/6.

5. WWM, A54. After the Elsecar New Colliery opened in 1795, the Elsecar Colliery became known as the Elsecar Old Colliery.

6. WWM, F71-13-1. For a more detailed study of the Elsecar Newcomen engine, see A K Clayton, 'The Newcomen-Type Engine at Elsecar, West Riding', *Transactions of the Newcomen Society*, Volume XXXV (1962-1963).

7. WWM, Stw.P. 13a

8. WWM, Stw.P. 6(iv).

9. F.B., 12; The deep level ran in a line from approximately the Milton Hall to the *Milton Arms* Public House. It has been suggested that the deep level sough that branched off this was never driven along the line of the survey, see A K Clayton, 'Coal Mining at Hoyland', *Transactions of the Hunter Archaeological Society*, Volume 1X, Part 2, (1966)pp.77, 81.

10. WWM, F98; Stw.P. 13a.

11. WWM, F97/9; A101.

12. WWM, F106 (b).

13. WWM, F70/91.Converted from ale gallons to Imperial Standard gallons at the rate of 1=0965 gallons.

14, WWM, A86; Stw.P. 5 (iii).

15. WWM, F97/8; A223; F98/19.

16. WWM, Stw.P. 5(ii).

17. WWM, Stw.P. 4(vi); G. Mee, *Aristocratic Enterprise* (Glasgow,1975),pp.124-128.

18. WWM, F97/11; A223; F97/11; F95/8/24; MP55. It has been suggested that the corves may have been sledges, see Clayton, *Coal Mining at Hoyland*,p.85.

19. WWM, MP55,56; F100/14. The boardgate from the engine pit to the bye-pit was reduced from 30 yards to 20 yards in length.

20. WWM, F96/30.

21. WWM, Stw.P. 3(ix).

22. C. Hadfield, *The Canals of Yorkshire and North- East England* (Newton Abbot, 1972)pp.74,286; Mee, *op.cit.*pp.29-31.

23. WWM, A115; A348; F100/33; F107(f). Walker & Co gave up the Milton Ironworks in 1821.

24. WWM, A91; Mee, *op.cit.*p.74.

25. WWM, F98/8.

26. WWM, F95/8.

27. WWM, A50.

28. WWM, A50; Stw. P.13a.

29. WWM, Stw.P. 5(ii).

30. WWM, Stw.P. 5(ii).

31. Mee, *op.cit.* p.141.

32. WWM, Stw.P. 3(ix).

12. Penistone Market and Cloth Hall

by David Hey

ON THURSDAYS THE MOORLAND TOWN of Penistone takes on a different character from that which it assumes during the rest of the week. Thursday is market day and the central streets are busy. A decision taken three hundred years ago has had lasting effects. But Thursday was not the first choice when Penistone market was founded in the 1690s. Another four hundred years previously a local market had been held on a Tuesday, so this was the day that was favoured for the revival. It soon became clear, however, that Penistone market would never get off the ground unless that day was changed. A market would undoubtedly benefit the people of Penistone, but others feared that it might well harm the market that was held each Wednesday only seven miles away at Barnsley. The Penistoners had to change their day if they were to have any chance of getting their market started.

Penisale

When Godfrey Bosville of Gunthwaite Hall led the first attempts to found a market at Penistone in 1698, he claimed that the parishioners had long possessed the right to hold a weekly market and an annual fair under a charter that had been granted in 1290 to Elias of Midhope, the lord of the manor of Penisale. His claim was rejected by the government on the grounds that the rights had lapsed and that, strictly speaking, they did not apply to Penistone, but it is interesting to find that in the late seventeenth century local people remembered the old market and fair, which had been founded four hundred years earlier but which had long since been discontinued. It is interesting, too, to find that they were familiar with the name Penisale, which by then had long since fallen out of use except as an alternative name of an old moorland manor. Perhaps Bosville had access to the original charter, or a copy, for he knew the exact days on which the market and fair had been held centuries earlier?

Local historians have long puzzled over the exact site of Penisale. The earliest references to the place date from 1190-1208, which is as early as one might reasonably expect records to survive for a manor that was not named in the Domesday Book of 1086. In the earliest documents Penisale was variously spelt Penigheshal, Penighalg, Peningsale, and so on.[1] The first element of the name is obviously the same as that in the name of Penistone, which was recorded in the Domesday Book as Pengeston and Pangeston, and in the late twelfth century as Peningeston. While it is possible that this element was derived from an Anglo-Saxon personal name, it is more likely to have come from the Celtic word pen, meaning a prominent hill, as in Pen-y-Ghent (Yorkshire) or Pendle Hill (Lancashire). The second element, halgh, is another which occurs elsewhere in England; it means a nook of land on the edge of an estate. Both elements of the name help us in our attempt to locate the site of the manor. Although Penisale appears under various spellings in later charters, it is not listed in the various tax returns – the poll taxes and lay subsidies – of the fourteenth century. We may wonder therefore whether Penisale was not an actual village but the name of a district. A parallel can be drawn with Ecclesall (now a Sheffield suburb), which was not a settlement but a district on the boundary of the estate served by the Celtic church at Ecclesfield. Indeed, the various spellings of Penisale indicate that the name was probably pronounced as if written – sall, as in Ecclesall. The pen to which the name refers was perhaps the great ridge which separates Penistone from Midhope and which ends in a prominent head at Hartcliffe. The tun, or central settlement where the parish church was built, lay on the northern side of this ridge; Penisale lay at the southern side, close to the parish boundary formed by the Little Don. But we cannot be certain about such matters. Another possibility is that the pen was the hill that rises above the river Don on which Penistone is built.

The approximate location of Penisale was known to the later inhabitants of the parish of Penistone. Legends grew up about its disappearance. John Ness Dransfield, who wrote a long-winded history of the parish in 1906, quoted a tradition that an old yew tree in the grounds of Alderman's Head, near the river, had been the site of the court of the manor of Penisale and the focal point of the market and fair, and he printed the text of a poem, *The Yew Tree of Penisale,* which had been written anonymously.[2] John Wilson, the eighteenth-century antiquary of Broomhead Hall, had measured this notable yew and had found it to be twenty-five feet in circumference. Wilson recorded in his notebook that the tree had been set on fire by a Bradfield man in 1758 and that it had burnt for five days.[3] According to Joseph Kenworthy, the historian of Stocksbridge and Midhope, the yew tree was said to have stood in a field on the north side of the road from Stocksbridge to Langsett. Kenworthy discovered the foundations of buildings on the opposite side of the road, on the bank of the river, where oral tradition pointed to the site of an old corn mill.[4] It is worth noting that this valley road was not there when Penisale had a market and fair; the route was created in 1805 as part of the new Wadsley-Langsett turnpike road. The old highway from east to west followed the top of the ridge, high above the valley. The tradition of the yew tree is a dubious one that can neither be proved nor disproved, but the site seems too far from the highway to be a credible choice for a market place.

We need to return to the surviving documentary records in order to establish the extent of the manor of Penisale. Amongst the medieval sources are some references to the possessions of the monks of Kirkstead Abbey, a Cistercian house in Lincolnshire. These date back to at least the late twelfth century when William, the son of John, lord of Peningeston, granted land to the Kirkstead monks and his 'right in the moor next to their grange of Peningeshalg'.[5] The site of this grange, from which the lay brothers of the monastery farmed this moorland estate, is not known, but perhaps the name of Sheephouse Farm points to a likely candidate. When the abbey was dissolved in the 1530s it was said to have possessions in Penynghall, Midhope and Langsett.[6]

Langsett is the name of the moorland township that formed the south-western part of Penistone parish. Townships were the smallest, and probably the earliest, units of local government and Penistone parish was divided into eight of them. The name Langsett is now confined to the small village by the reservoir that was constructed in 1904 at the edge of the moors, but it was once applied to the whole township, which stretched up and over the hillside to the north of the Little Don. The earliest spellings show that the name was originally Langside, the 'long side' of the great ridge or pen which had given its name to Penisale. Langside or Langsett seems, in fact, to have been an alternative name for Penisale. This was certainly the case by 1818, when the 'Manor of Langsett alias Penisale' was offered for sale. In 1871 the *Dog and Partridge* public house was the scene of the meeting of the 'Great Court Baron of Sir Lionel Melbourne-Swinnerton Pilkington, baronet, Lord of the Manor of Pennyshall otherwise Peningesale (sometimes called Langside or Langsett)'. In 1890 particulars of the owners and occupiers within the manor show that properties there extended throughout the township of Langsett, from Sheephouse in the east to Swinden in the west.[7]

The district known as Penisale therefore seems to have been identical with that otherwise called the township of Langside or Langsett.

In 1290 the lord of the manor of Penisale, Elias of Midhope, obtained
two royal charters, one allowing him to hunt throughout his manor,
the other to hold a market each Tuesday and an annual fair on the eve,
day, and morrow of the feast of St Barnabas, that is 10-12 June. In
1307 the next lord of the manor, William of Sheffield, took the precau-
tion of obtaining new charters to confirm these rights.[8] These charters
of 1290 and 1307 are the only pieces of documentary evidence that
we possess concerning the holding of markets and fairs at Penisale,
though, as we have seen, the memory of these open-air marts on the
edge of the moors was long preserved by oral tradition. Elias of
Midhope was following the example of numerous other lords who
founded markets and fairs in thirteenth – and early fourteenth-
century England, at a time when the population was expanding and
commercial opportunities were promising. Many of these enterprises
were soon abandoned, however, for the Black Death of 1348-50 and
other pestilences reduced the national population considerably and
trade contracted severely. Hooton Pagnell, Braithwell, Wortley and
Wath-upon-Dearne were amongst other South Yorkshire villages
which lost their markets and fairs during the late Middle Ages.
Penisale's experience falls into a wider pattern of initiatives that were
unsustainable during a long period of recession.

Penistone Market

In 1698 Godfrey Bosville planned to revive these ancient rights by
holding a Tuesday market and a 10-12 June fair not on the original
site but by the parish church two miles away at Penistone. He immediately ran into firm opposition from the owners of market rights at
Barnsley and Huddersfield, who said that their markets would be
harmed if rival events were set up at Penistone. Barnsley lay just seven
miles away, and Huddersfield twelve, so the threat of competition
naturally caused them concern. On 10 June 1698, the proposed first
day of the fair, an order was signed forbidding the holding of markets
and fairs at Penistone.[9] Godfrey Bosville's plan appeared to have
floundered, but he and his fellow parishioners were determined in
their resolve. They attempted to placate the people of Barnsley, whose
market was held on a Wednesday, by moving the suggested date of the
Penistone market from Tuesday to Thursday. Then, petitions drawn
up by Nathan Staniforth, the parish clerk and master of Penistone
Grammar School, were taken to the surrounding towns, villages,
hamlets and isolated farmsteads for signatures that would demon-
strate widespread support for a market at Penistone. These petitions

are preserved in the antiquarian collections of John Wilson of Broomhead Hall at the Brotherton Library, the University of Leeds, and are instantly recognisable as being in the distinctive hand of Nathan Staniforth.[10]

A typical petition reads:

We whose names are hereunto subscribed being the principal Gentlemen and Inhabitants of the several Parishes and Towns of Silkston, Thurgoland, Dodworth, Stainbrough, and Hoylandswain, being near adjacent to the Parish of Peniston in the County of York, Do humbly certifie to whom it may concern, That to have a Market at the Town of Peniston aforesaid on Thursday in every week, and a Fair on the Tenth Eleventh and Twelfth of June yearly, will be very commodious to the whole Countrie thereabouts: That the same will be of very great advantage to several parts of the Counties of Chester, Lancaster, and Derby lying next to Peniston afforesaid: And that no Markets or Fairs near that place are held on the same days. And we further humbly certifie, that we verily believe, that the holding of a Market and Fair at Peniston as afforesaid will be of general advantage to the whole Country, and not prejudicial. In Testimony whereof we have hereunto set our hands this Twenty fourth day of August Anno Domini 1699.

The petition was signed by 150 inhabitants of these townships. Across the Pennines, 171 inhabitants of Manchester and Salford, including the various officers, added their support. Their petition reads:

We whose hands are underput Gentlemen and Inhabitants of the townes of Manchester and Salford in the County of Lancaster Doe hereby certifie whom it may concerne That these townes are very populous and usually are weekly supplyed with wheat and other harde corne out of the West Rideing of the County of York and that Wee Doe believe that if a Weekly Market could be Obtained in the town of Penniston in the said Rideing on the thursday (being a day on which the Market days in the townes next adjoyneing thereunto is not) the same wold be of great service to the townes of Manchester and Salford and parts adjacent and wold save great charges in carrying corne from townes more remote from the said townes of Manchester and Salford And therefore doe humbly desire that a Market Might be granted in the said town of Penniston, Weekly on the said day Witness our hands the fourth day of September Anno dni 1699.

The other petitions were signed as follows:

Stockport and Mottram (125)

[Rural parts of Cheshire] (19)

Glossop, Glossop Dale, Hope Woodlands and Edale (99)

Darton, Kexbrough, High Hoyland, Clayton West, Skelmanthorpe and Cawthorne (105)

Kirkburton, Shepley, Cumberworth, Shelley, Kirkheaton and Emley (224)

Holmfirth and Saddleworth (240)

Wakefield (35)

Sandal Magna (21)

Doncaster (28)

Bolton-upon-Dearne, Barnburgh, Adwick-upon-Dearne and Goldthorpe (30)

Tankersley, Wortley and Pilley (107)

Wentworth, Hoyland, Thorpe Hesley, Scholes, Greasborough, Morley, Haugh, Barrow and Cortworth (72)

The parish of Ecclesfield and the chapelry of Bradfield (308)

Sheffield (72)

Attercliffe, Darnall, Brightside and Tinsley (104)

Penistone parish (230)

In all, 2,140 persons from a wide area around Penistone signed the various documents. For the benefit of the government officials in

Figure 1. William Fairbank's plan of Penistone Market Place, dated 1749

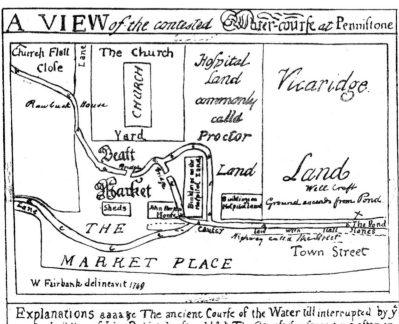

London, to whom the petitions were presented, the exaggerated claim was made that 'such was the state of the country between Penistone and Barnsley, their nearest market, that persons had lost their lives in winter time returning home'.[11] Perhaps this claim was believed, for the application was successful. From 1699 Penistone was able to hold a three-day fair on 10-12 June (the same days as the old medieval fair of St Barnabas at Penisale) and a market every Thursday.

A Market Place was laid out in front of the tower of the medieval church of St John the Baptist, which dominates the hill-top settlement. Was there, one wonders, a village green on this site before 1699, or were some properties cleared away? Our first evidence of the the shape of the new market place comes fifty years after its foundation. A plan drawn up in 1749 by William Fairbank, the Sheffield surveyor, to help resolve a dispute over a water course, shows the 'Beast Market', including 'sheds' and 'John Parkin's house', immediately west of the churchyard (Figure 1).[12] A large stone with the letter P still marks the former north-western corner of this property. On Fairbank's plan, 'The Market Place' lay west of this building, in the present Market Street. Shrewsbury Road did not exist, so the only way to the east was down Church Hill, to the north of the churchyard.

The effect of the market on Penistone was momentous. The various records that survive from the late seventeenth century show that Penistone had been only a small place. Thus, the hearth tax returns of 1672 record only 26 householders in Penistone township (though the poor who were exempt from the tax were not listed).[13] The War Office enquiries of 1686[14] had noted that Penistone had only five guest beds and three stables available for visitors, and a local assessment of 1697[15] named only 33 householders, with no innkeepers and few tradesmen (though with three clothiers). This situation changed when Penistone was turned into a small market town. It is no coincidence that in 1702, three years after the foundation of the market, the old Penistone Grammar School on the north side of the churchyard was placed on a more ambitious footing with the appointment of John Ramsden, of Batley, as master to teach 'all the rudiments of the Latin and Greek Tongues, with the Rhetoric' to the 'Grammar Scholars' and English and Latin to the 'poorer sort'. The new school building, which included accommodation for boarders, was completed by 1716.[16] Inns and shops soon began to appear around the Market Place. *The Spread Eagle, Old Crown, Rose and Crown,* and *Fleece* (closed 1873), and *Horns Coffee House and Tavern* became busy places on market day. By 1770 the sixth edition of William Owen's *Book of Fairs* was advertising four annual fairs for horned cattle and horses at Penistone, all of which were held on market day (the last Thursday in February, the last in March, the Thursday before old May-day, and the one after old May-day). In 1822 Edward Baines's *West Riding Directory* described Penistone as 'a small market town. Thursday is the market day, and a good number of cows, calves and sheep are on that day generally exhibited for sale.' The market and fair established in 1290 had failed, but the hopes of Godfrey Bosville and his fellow parishioners in the 1690s had been fulfilled.

The Cloth Hall

Today, the prime site in the former Market Place is occupied by a building which is fronted by Clark's chemist's shop (Figure 2). The building was not there on William Fairbank's plan of 1749, but, as we shall see, it had a key role in the development of Penistone as a

commercial centre. It was erected as a Cloth Hall in 1763, a couple of generations after the foundation of the market, when confidence in the local economy was still high.

Penistone parish lay on the fringe of the West Riding textile district. It had given its name to a distinctive coarse cloth that tailors turned into cheap, serviceable clothes. 'Penistones' were 12-13 yards long, 1 1/4 yards broad, and weighed 28 pounds. They were similar to other undyed cloths, such as 'Northern Dozens', which were the same length, but half a yard broader, and 33 pounds in weight, and to the more widely-known kerseys, which were only a yard wide, 17-18 yards long, and which weighed just 20 pounds.[17] When Daniel Defoe visited Stourbridge Fair, on the outskirts of Cambridge, in the early eighteenth century, he observed: 'Here are clothiers from Halifax, Leeds, Wakefield and Huthersfield in Yorkshire, and from Rochdale, Bury, etc, in Lancashire, with vast quantities of Yorkshire cloths, kerseyes, pennistons, cottons, etc.'[18] The merchants of the West Riding textile towns included Penistones among their stock. For example, Mr Francis Kellam, a Pontefract mercer and draper who died in 1688, owned '9 yards of Penestone', worth 12s.0d.[19] Further back in time, 'Ordinary Penistones' or 'Forest Whites' and 'Sorting Penistones' were mentioned in Acts of Parliament in 1553, 1554, 1597 and 1607, and a survey of the West Riding textile industry in 1595 noted that 'at Penistone near Barnsley and some villages thereabouts are made about one thousand pieces of White Peny Stones'. These were counted only as half cloths for assize purposes, thus some 500 pieces were made annually.[20] Further information about the

Figure 2. The church of St John the Baptist and Clark's chemist shop, formerly the Cloth Hall. *Courtesy of Old Barnsley*

extent of the trade in the sixteenth century is provided by records of the Searchers at the cloth market held at Blackwell Hall, London, in 1561-62. Lists of fines for defective pieces included the names of 'George Sabell [i.e.Savile], Yorkshire, northern peniston', 'John Blackborne, Yorkshire, peniston' [whom later references show was from Wakefield], and other unnamed Wakefield men who were selling 'penistons', 'peniston dozens' or 'northern penistons'.[21] Finally, a chance piece of evidence from the Elizabethan period comes in a letter written in London in 1587 from Anne Boughton to her father, in which she refers to an acquaintance who would not let his son wear 'a coate of penniston' because it was too hot.[22]

It is clear then that, from at least the sixteenth century, the inhabitants of the parish of Penistone had obtained part of their living through the manufacture of cheap woollen cloth. During the eighteenth century, as the West Riding textile industry grew mightily, the inhabitants of several towns decided to build cloth halls, where pieces of cloth could be brought for sale to the merchants. Halifax (1708), Wakefield (1710) and Leeds (1711) led the way. The finest surviving structure is the Piece Hall that was built at Halifax in 1779, with 315 rooms arranged around a central courtyard. The hall is the major surviving monument from the 'domestic economy' stage of the West Riding textile industry on the eve of the Industrial Revolution.

The growth of trade encouraged the parishioners of Penistone to establish their own cloth market. At first, this was held on market day in the upper part of the Grammar School, close to the Market Place. William Spencer of Cannon Hall, Cawthorne, noted in his pocket book: 'attended first day of Penistone Cloth fair, 30 September 1743'.[23] The previous day an agreement had been drawn up under the direction of Aymor Rich of Bullhouse Hall and George Walker of Hunshelf Hall, two of the leading gentlemen of the parish.[24] This was signed at Penistone on 10 November by 92 cloth makers. It reads:

Whereas All or the Greatest part of the Clothmakers in and about the parish of Penistone have sometime lately brought their Cloth to Penistone to Sell and having had good Encouragement therein by the Mercers for the Sale of their Cloth And the Greatest part of the Trades people (the Clothiers in that Neighbourhood deal with) being desireous that there may be a Meeting at Penistone Established, And we whose hands and Seals are hereunto sett having Agreed to bring our Cloth to Penistone instead of carrying the same to Sheffield for the better encouragement thereof do Severally and for our Severall own Act and Acts only and not one for the other or for the Act or Acts of

the other Covenant promise Grant and Agree to and with Aymor
Rich of Bullhouse in the Parish of Penistone in the County of York
Gentleman and George Walker of Hunshelf in the Parish aforesaid
Gentlemen and either of them or either of their Executors and
Administrators That such of us as shall directly or Indirectly Sell or
expose to Sale by ourselves Servants or Agents any Kersey Cloth or
Plaines at any Markett or Markett to be held at Sheffield by Swatch[25]
or otherways at any time or times on or before the Twenty Ninth day
of September next, that such person or persons as shall so Sell or
Expose to Sale by themselves or any Person or Persons for them or on
their behalf shall well and truly upon demand pay unto the said
Aymor Rich and George Walker or the one of them their or the one of
their Executors or Administrators the Sum of Three Pounds for every
peice of Cloth that such Person or persons shall by themselves or
otherways sell or expose to sale at Sheffield aforesaid or at any
Markett or Marketts to be held there at any time or times on or before
the said Twenty ninth day of September, Witness our Hands and Seals
the Tenth day of November in the Year of our Lord One Thousand
Seven Hundred and Forty three.

A second agreement was made at the same time by the three local
fullers whose mills scoured cloths that had just been woven: John
Wood of Oxspring, and Francis Batty and Thomas Hobson of
Thurlstone township.[26] They agreed not to treat cloth for any manufacturer who had not entered into the first agreement, thereby
effectively preventing anyone from withdrawing their support from
the scheme. The fulling (or 'walk') mill on the river Don at Oxspring
was ancient. As far back as 1306 Robert of Oxspring had granted to
Henry of Rockley two parts of his fulling mill at Oxspring. Later references include one in 1549 to the 'Walke mylne goit' and another in
1729 to 'Oxspring walk miln'.[27] Nineteenth-century maps mark 'Walk
Mill Bank' by the site now occupied by Winterbottom's wire mill. One
of the fulling mills in Thurlstone township was mentioned in the will
of Edward Batty, clothier, which was proved in 1661; its exaction location is uncertain, but may have been at Plumpton. Hobson's mill was
probably on the site which was later converted into the Millhouse
Green Wire Mill, for a fulling mill was recorded here on various occasions between 1598 and 1627,[28] and was marked on the 1854 six-inch
Ordnance Survey map.

The success of the cloth market encouraged the parishioners of
Penistone to build a hall that was more commodious than the upper
room in the Grammar School. John Platt's Journal for March 1763[29]

refers to his making of a 'Plan for a market house or Cloth Hall at Penistone', and to his discussions with Mr John Hatfield (Aymor Rich's brother-in-law, from Laughton-en-le-Morthen) and Mr Josias Wordsworth (the eldest son of the Wordsworths of Water Hall, Penistone, who now lived at Wadworth Hall, near Doncaster). Platt's design was accepted. Penistone Cloth Hall was built that year at the cost of £800, with Josias Wordsworth heading the subscription list.[30]

John Platt was the son of George Platt, who had moved from Disley (Cheshire) to work in South Yorkshire as an architect and master mason. George Platt was responsible for the gentry halls at Cusworth and Hickleton and supervised the building of St Paul's Church, Sheffield. After George's death, at the early age of 43, his son became the leading architect and builder in south Yorkshire. John Platt is known to have designed and built the shambles and butchers' cross at Doncaster (1756) and the Barnsley shambles and market hall (1767). He also worked at Wortley Hall and Wentworth Castle, and was responsible for Thundercliffe Grange, the Feoffees' School at Rotherham, and the rebuilding of Eckington Church.[31] He was the obvious person to turn to for the new Market House and Cloth Hall at Penistone.

It is likely that the large windows of Clark's shop were originally open arches into the Market House and Cloth Hall. We do not know how long the building was used for that purpose. When the Wordsworth estate was sold in 1825 'The Market House' consisted of a dwelling house, a carpenter's shop, two chambers, and several butchers' stalls. By that time, the building may no longer have been used as a Cloth Hall. Penistone lay on the southern edge of the textile district, and the improved communications of recent years had favoured the use of the major Piece Halls further north. Penistone Cloth Hall was gradually converted to other purposes. A room was used by the Barnsley magistrates for meetings of the petty sessions until the 1840s, and during the second half of the nineteenth century the present chemist's shop served as J H Wood's 'Post Office and Printing Office'. In 1861 the eastern part of the Cloth Hall was made into a pub called *The White Bear*; when it closed in the 1920s, it became the local home of the British Legion.[32]

The old cloth makers of Penistone parish had combined their trade with work on a smallholding. This traditional dual occupation continued well into the nineteenth century, but with the growth of population increasing numbers of men had no chance of farming land and were forced to work full-time at their looms. The row of weavers' cottages at Tenter Hill, Thurlstone, is the best surviving local example of early nineteenth-century accommodation for families whose men folk worked on the top floor, in rooms lit by a range of windows. The women and children often worked at the new scribbling and spinning mills, which had been erected alongside the old corn and fulling mills in the river valleys. The increased output of yarn from these mills meant that more weavers were required, but as weaving was not mechanised until well into the nineteenth century, the work was done in cottages built by the mill owners. Lists of men aged between 18 and 45, who were liable for militia service if Napoleon's troops ever landed on the English coast, name only seven weavers, one clothier, one cloth dresser, and one dresser in Penistone township. Thurlstone township, however, had 34 weavers, 20 clothiers, a dyer and a dresser, and Denby township included 62 weavers, 12 clothiers, a dyer and a dresser.[33] The 'clothiers' seem to have been those men who also had a farm, whereas the 'weavers' worked full-time in their chambers. For much of the nineteenth century, the weavers of Thurlstone, Denby and other villages and hamlets south of Huddersfield specialised in the manufacture of fancy waistcoats and were thus known as fancy weavers. My great-great-grandfather, John Hey of Thurlstone, was one of them.

The New Market

Meanwhile, the cattle market continued to be held in the streets around the Cloth Hall. Old photographs (Figure 3) taken by Joshua Biltcliffe show that in the early years of the twentieth century market day was a masculine event. Dairy shorthorns were offered for sale in the old Market Place, up High Street and down St Mary's Street, and sheep pens were placed in front of the *Spread Eagle*.

The old custom of adolescent boys and girls offering themselves for annual hire continued in the Market Place until the early years of the twentieth century. These occasions were known as Statute or 'Stattis' hirings (because they were authorised by statute, or Act of Parliament) and were normally held in the autumn at Martinmas. At Penistone, the hiring day was the Tuesday before New Martinmas Day. An item headed 'Penistone Statute Hirings' in the *Yorkshire Post*, Wednesday, 8 November 1905 reads: 'There was a larger attendance at these statute hirings yesterday than for some years but not many engagements were entered into.' The same paper reported on Wednesday, 9 November 1910 a thin attendance, with very much higher wages sought by all, and on Thursday, 7 November 1918: 'at Penistone statute hirings on

Tuesday, not one male or female servant offered for hire.'[34] The old system had collapsed during the First World War.

By the early 1900s the Thursday market was causing concern over public health. In June 1903 the Ministry of Agriculture and Fisheries ordered that a new site should be found. The members of Penistone Urban District Council responded in a dilatory fashion as various options were discussed, but finally, on 24 November 1910, a new market under covered shedding was opened in Backfields, at the end of a side-street leading from the Market Place, and the adjacent property was made into a recreation ground.

The new site succeeded in attracting business and had to be enlarged in 1933. Its character changed in the 1950s, when new regulations ensured that dairy cows were tuberculin tested. Holmfirth was then the nearest attested market and Penistone became essentially a venue for fat-stock. Since 1994 the market site has been put to further use. As well as the regular Thursday market, sheep, pigs and cattle are sold on Mondays, and store cattle and pigs are sold on Saturdays. A thriving general sales area adjoining the present-day cattle market offers a wide variety of articles and produce.[35] Three hundred years after its foundation, Penistone market continues to thrive.

Notes and References

1. A.H. Smith, *The Place-Names of the West Riding of Yorkshire* (English Place-Name Society: Cambridge University Press, 1961), pp. 332, 336-37.
2. Margaret Gelling, *Place-Names in the Landscape* (London: Dent, 1984), pp. 100-11, 182-83.
3. J.N. Dransfield, *History of Penistone* (1906), p. 267.
4. Leeds University, Brotherton Library, Wilson collection, CLIX, 96.
5. Sheffield Archives, Sp. St. 1154.
6. Bradford Central Library, Spencer-Stanhope collection, 1054; Calendar of Charter Rolls, I (Record Commissioners, 1837), p. 383.
7. List and Index Society, Supplementary Series, III, vol. 2 (1964), p. 261.
8. Calendar of Charter Rolls, II, p.353, III, p. 107. See also W. Farrer, ed., Yorkshire Charters, III (1916), pp. 413-20, and J. Parker, ed., 'Feet of Fines for the County of York from 1246 to 1272', *Yorkshire Archaeological Society Record Series*, LXXXII (1932).
9. Wilson collection, XXXIII, 149d.
10. Wilson collection, VII (78 to 116).
11. Rev. Joseph Hunter, *South Yorkshire: the History and Topography of the Deanery of Doncaster*, II (1831), p. 335.
12. Reproduced in Dransfield, p. 281.
13. David Hey, ed., *The Hearth Tax Returns for South Yorkshire*, Ladyday 1672 (Sheffield University: Division of Adult Continuing Education, 1991), p. 85.
14. Public Record Office, WO 30/48.
15. Nottinghamshire Record Office, Mellish mss, 63-2.
16. John Addy, 'Penistone Grammar School in the Eighteenth Century', *Yorkshire Archaeological Society*, XXXIX (1957), pp. 356-63.
17. H. Heaton, *The Yorkshire Woollen and Worsted Industries* (Oxford: Clarendon Press, 1920), p. 136 note.

Figure 3. Market day in c 1905. *Courtesy of Old Barnsley*

18. Daniel Defoe, *A Tour through the Whole Island of Great Britain* (London: Dent, Everyman edition, 1962), pp. 81-82.

19. Borthwick Institute of Historical Research, York, Pontefract Deanery wills and inventories, proved June 1689. See also G.D. Ramsay, 'The Distribution of the Cloth Industry in 1561-2', *English Historical Review*, LVII (1942), pp. 361-69.

20. Heaton, pp. 79-80.

21. G.D. Ramsay, 'The Distribution of the Cloth Industry in 1561-2', *English Historical Review*, LVII (1942), pp. 361-69.

22. G.E. Dawson and L. Kennedy-Skipton, *Elizabethan Handwriting, 1500-1650* (London: Faber, 1966), p. 66. The original document is in the Folger Library, Washington, USA.

23. Sheffield Archives, Sp. St. 60505.

24. Sheffield Archives, Crewe muniments, 969. Twenty-two of the signatories signed with a mark.

25. i.e. sample.

26. Sheffield Archives, Crewe muniments, 970.

27. Hunter, p. 355; A.H. Smith, p. 335.

28. Sheffield Archives, Crewe muniments, 680, 689, 705, 729.

29. John Platt's journal, for March 1763 (re:Penistone) is available on microfilm in Rotherham Archives and Local Studies Library; and is extensively quoted in J D Pott's booklet *Platt of Rotherham. Mason - Architects,* 1700-1810, Sheffield, 1959.

30. Hunter, p. 335.

31. Platt journal in Potts.

32. J.H. Wood, *Remarkable Occurrences, Interesting Dates and Curious Information* (Local and General), (Penistone, 1890), p. 15; J. Addy, ed., *A Further History of Penistone* (Penistone, 1965), p. 4.

33. Staincross militia returns, J.F. Goodchild Collection, Local History Study Centre, Wakefield.

34. I thank Dr Stephen Caunce for these references.

35. Phyllis Crossland, 'Penistone Market' in Brian Elliott. ed., *Aspects of Barnsley 3,* Barnsley: Wharncliffe Publishing Ltd. 1995, pp. 230-40.

13. John Whitworth, Architect and Surveyor of Barnsley

by Alan Whitworth

IT HAS BEEN SAID BY MANY that it was John Whitworth who was responsible for the face of modern Barnsley. Architect and town planner, it could be argued as Sir Christopher Wren was to London, so was Whitworth to Barnsley. Both enjoyed the fruits of their labours in the same profession, and in some measure, both shared a vision for the future of their towns which they brought to a conclusion and in doing so changed the face of their respective places forever. Yet while it has always been understood by the inhabitants of Barnsley that John Whitworth demolished great areas of the town, laid out new streets and designed a number of public buildings, thereby making radical alterations and paving the way for today's townscape, in fact, a close inspection of the history books of Barnsley reveal little of Whitworth's accomplishments, and compared with other worthies of the town, John Whitworth largely goes unnoticed – however, in fairness for this omission, it should be said that an examination of his life shows that his influence in some areas was not as great as commonly believed.

An obituary in the *Barnsley Chronicle* says that John Whitworth was born about 22 August 1779, to Anne, wife of John Whitworth, saddler and harness-maker.[1] At the time of his birth his father and mother had premises along Shambles Street facing Market Hill (Figure 1), and had been there since 1785, if not before.[2] It is known, however, that John Whitworth, junior, was baptised on 3 October 1779. After this fact, little else is recorded of his early life, except that at a suitable age he took up employment in his father's business in which he continued past the death of his father until 1804, when aged twenty-five, he handed over the business to one of his workmen, George England.[3]

It was then, through patient study and diligent application that John Whitworth set out on a new profession, that of architect and surveyor. What prompted this change of direction is not known, nor is it known with whom he studied, or where, however, it is possible that his new choice of career was inspired by his religious beliefs and possibly his connections with Methodist friends.

John Whitworth from an early period was an ardent supporter of the Wesleyan Methodist Movement, influenced no doubt by his parents. His father was a reasonably devout and possibly pragmatic

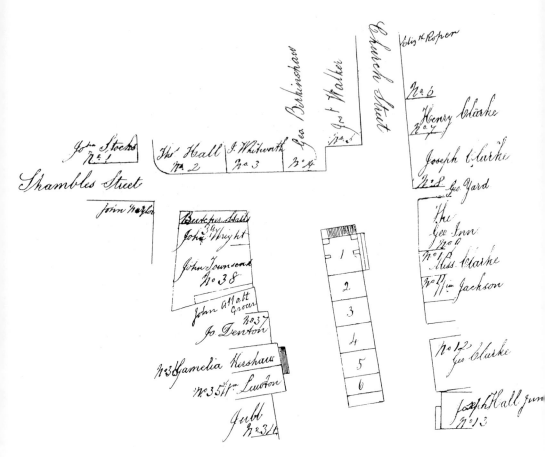

Figure 1. Shambles Street, Church Street and the top of the Market Place in 1785 showing the shop premises of John Whitworth, Snr - No. 3 Shambles Street.

man. He took his family each week to the Methodist Church on Sunday mornings and attended St Mary's Parish Church in the afternoons. Indeed, John's brother, Francis, too, was possibly influenced in some way toward the religious by his father, as in 1793 he was appointed organist at St Mary's, where he played for upwards of thirty years. In turn, Francis Whitworth influenced his own son, George Jagger Whitworth, and in 1824, he became organist at St Mary's, 'the duties of which he discharged with much credit for several years', until his death in 1842 aged thirty-four, following a violent attack of Scarlet

Fever, when his widow undertook the duty of organist until a replacement was appointed in 1845.[4]

John's early connection with architectural practice is obscure, but in 1791 a Wesleyan Methodist Chapel was erected on Pinfold Hill, in which in some way he was associated with its foundation as it is recorded that he was paid 'sundry' expenses in an undated Trustees' document.[5] What is not clear is whether Whitworth had anything to do with its design, or whether the expenses were for other duties as he was already, by this date, a tireless and influential worker in the town's Methodist Movement.

It can, however, be speculated that by the beginning of the nineteenth century, John was probably already undertaking commissions as well as applying himself zealously to his religious principles. For instance, Whitworth, along with William Cooke Mence, of Folly Hall, a solicitor, founded the first Sunday School in Barnsley, opened on Sunday 27 November 1803, and later John was responsible for building the Wesleyan Methodist Sunday School, opened three years later and erected not far from the Chapel. The site was in School Street, which took its title from the building; the north gable end adjoined the Church Field. John Whitworth was superintendent of the girls' school, who were taught in the upper rooms, and W C Mence was master of the boys' school. The site of the school contained 396 square yards, and during the week it was used as a day school. After it ceased being a Sunday School in 1858, the building was converted into four cottages which survived for many years at the top of School Street.[6]

Again, if we are to believe Burland in his date that John Whitworth was still in business as a saddler in 1804, then it could be surmised that he must have begun to dabble in architecture beforehand to be sufficiently competent to design and build this first Sunday School building, and, indeed, such was the confidence that the Chapel Trustees placed in his abilities that 'at a special meeting of the Trustees in 1810 it was agreed that the Chapel should be enlarged, which new erection and enlargement was conducted by the following persons: John Cordeux, George Hill, Joseph Scales and John Whitworth, the architect.'[7] The Chapel was re-opened on 13 January 1811.

In the same year as this 'special meeting', Whitworth was also engaged to lay out and complete all the turnpike roads in the neighbourhood, which he steadily did through a number of years. Again, it can be demonstrated by the importance of this commission, that John must have served his apprenticeship and become established in his chosen profession by the beginning of the century. In his road building he was responsible for 'the Cutting' between Barnsley and Worsbrough Dale, and the then new turnpike roads which also entered the town from Darton, Dodworth, Hoyle Mill and Old Mill, and also the Cockerham road.

Following the passing of the *Act for Lighting, Paving, Cleansing, Watching and Improving the Town of Barnsley* in 1822, John was employed to redesign a new Barnsley town centre. He levelled Shambles Street, and gave Market Hill a new appearance by removing the old Moot Hall, and by raising the lower portion of near Sough

Figure 3. The area between Pitt Street and Croft Ends c.1838 as laid out by John Whitworth showing the principal buildings erected by Whitworth or his contemporaries at the time.

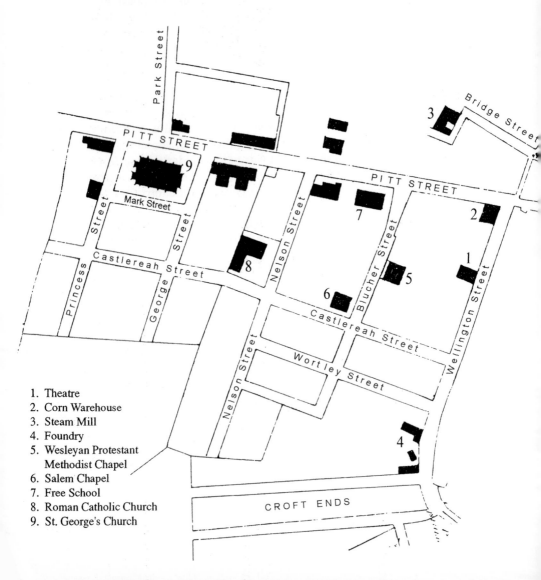

1. Theatre
2. Corn Warehouse
3. Steam Mill
4. Foundry
5. Wesleyan Protestant Methodist Chapel
6. Salem Chapel
7. Free School
8. Roman Catholic Church
9. St. George's Church

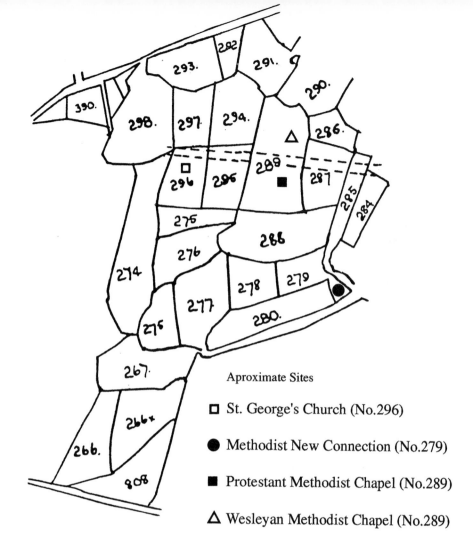

Figure 2. Peashill, Tumbling Hill and The Ing in 1777, later built over and laid out as streets by John Whitworth.

Dyke, and also levelling the higher ground at the top.[8] The Corn Exchange, the Commercial Building (once the Town Clerk's offices), and the old Town Hall were designed and erected under his supervision. John Whitworth obviously was, by this time, an able and competent architect, and by 1823 he was practising from offices in Market Street. [9]

Sir Nikolaus Pevsner, the late eminent architectural historian, in a survey of Barnsley published in his well-known *Buildings of England* series, wrote, 'the best street in Barnsley is Pitt Street. At the corner of Blucher Street the former Free School, dated 1813, [is] pretty with

an elegant handling of the usual elements.'[10] Both Pitt Street and the
Free School were the work of John Whitworth, indeed, it was through
the influence of Whitworth and his interest in education, that the
trustees' of the Ellis Charity School were induced to make a grant of
£700 towards the cost of erecting the school.[11]

Pitt Street was considered a triumph in architectural circles and
well-deserved its accolade as the 'best street in Barnsley'. The land it
was built on was that known as 'Peashills', strictly speaking, the name
properly belonging to four large closes (see Figure 2 - marked 294,

Figure 4. Map of Barnsley c.1777 showing the area (shaded) later
developed and laid out as 'Peasehills Estate' by John Whitworth.

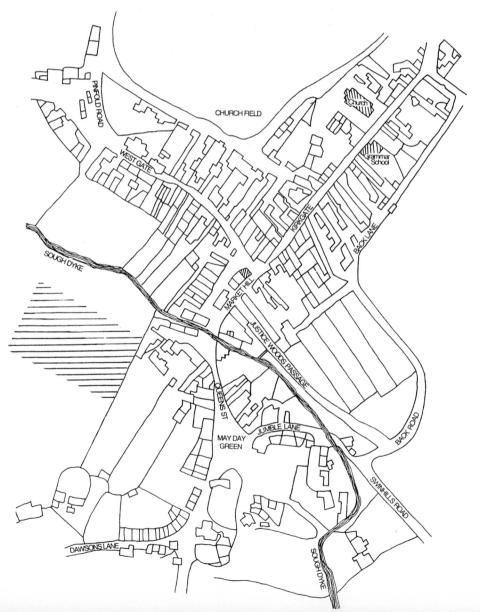

295, 296, 297 and Figure 3) at the summit of the hill, but loosely extended to cover the whole area including and surrounding them and described as,

> *...all that plot, piece or parcel of Land or Ground heretofore part of certain Closes or Parcels of Land, or some of them, lying and being in Barnsley aforesaid commonly called or known by the names or name of the Peasehills, Tumbling Street and the Ing, and containing in length on the Southerly side or end thereof eighty-four feet, on the Westerly side thereof one hundred and seventy-seven feet, on the Northerly side or end thereof eighty feet and on the Easterly side thereof one hundred and seventy-one feet and eight inches and in the whole one thousand five hundred and eighty-eight yards and three feet superficial square [feet] measured...* [12]

In 1815 the whole of this property was purchased by John [Joseph] Hall, an ironmonger, and it was through his exertions in association with Whitworth that the streets were laid out in accordance with the 1838 Plan (Figure 4) and disposed of in plots to suit purchasers shortly afterwards. Already at the corner of Newland and Crofts End was the chapel belonging to the Methodist New Connexion, put up in 1804. As a consequence, Crofts End was carried through to Peashills Nook (afterwards named Queens Square, and now Peel Square) and was renamed Wellington Street in honour of the victor of Waterloo. The first building to be erected in this street was the Theatre in 1819, which remained the only building until Hall had a large seed warehouse built by John Whitworth at the corner of Wellington Street and Pitt Street in 1825. Another plot was bought by John Whitworth himself, who erected upon it a house in which Dr Blackburn and his son, Dr E W Blackburn, successively resided. This was situated in front of the Hall's warehouse.

Other streets progressed in addition to Pitt Street, and in York Street; Princess Street; George Street; Mark Street; Castlereagh Street; Wortley Street; Nelson Street and Blucher Street houses were quickly built and the whole district, so recently nothing but Closes became densely populated as the rapid growth of the linen trade brought about an increase in population.

In 1818 a property had been purchased in Pitt Street by the Methodists, on which a building was erected for the use of the Chapel Minister. Originally designed as two semi-detached houses, it was in later years, converted into one in which sometimes the Superintendent Minister and sometimes his colleague resided; this continued until 1869, from which date a new house was put up in

Dodworth Road.

On Monday 9 February 1829, the first stone of the new chapel in Blucher Street was laid and in due course it was recorded that 'on [the] Sabbath, the 16th day of August [1829] a very handsome and commodious Chapel erected...by the Wesleyan protestant Methodists...was opened for Divine Worship...'.[13]

The land for the chapel was secured initially by lease for one year, on 26 January 1829, by Thomas Marshall, off George Allen, sawyer, of Barnsley. The Trustees of the new chapel, led by Marshall, agreed to start building within ten days and bought the freehold site with borrowed money the next day. John Whitworth did more for them than has ever been recorded. Under certain circumstances he had claim on the land, and doubtless used his influence with Mr Allen to effect the sale. He drew up plans and superintended the building operations gratuitously.

It is from this time that a curious story survives relating to the construction of the Blucher Street Chapel and John Whitworth. The point of it personally escapes me, but I shall nevertheless relate it here as it possibly throws some light on the character of Whitworth hitherto not expressed, and is one of the few anecdotes about the man we have, other than the tale often related of an interview he conducted with two lords and a baronet on the subject of education.[14]

> It is said that the Trustees were poor men, and thought to [compromise on building costs?] by using the same building for a school as well as a Chapel; but John Whitworth, who was a zealous Sunday School teacher at the Westgate Chapel, decided otherwise. Without telling anyone his purpose, he ordered pillars to be put in to support the Chapel floor, and the foundations of the Chapel to be placed so far down that if ever the Trustees asked for a school he could say 'Dig out the earth from under your Chapel and you have your school!' At length he told Thomas Marshall about it, and Marshall, who it was said, could never keep a secret, told the other Trustees about it the same day! What excitement there was! All the teachers volunteered to lend a hand to get the soil out. They worked hard...

and soon all the earth was excavated – the result, presumably, an efficient Sunday School.[15]

It was in that same year, 1829, that John Whitworth married Sarah Parkin, daughter of Reverend Jonathan Parkin. Whitworth had already built a house for himself in Pitt Street in 1822 beside the Pitt Street Chapel, said at the time to be 'more convenient for his work',[16] but by

Figure 5. Barnsley Market Place as developed by John Whitworth. The new Corn Exchange, with it large classical pediment, can be seen at the top of the hill. From Jackson's *History of the Town and Township of Barnsley* (1858) and an original photograph by G Campbell.

1841 he and his family had moved to Regent Street where his nephew, George Jagger Whitworth, a prominent linen manufacturer, also had his residence and warehouse.[17] It is stated that his marriage not only 'greatly increased his domestic comfort, [but] it also promoted both his worldly success and spiritual advancement.' [18]

From this period, Whitworth became increasingly more prominent in the Barnsley Methodist Circuit, 'not merely in the way of his profession, but as a promoter and trustee', and it is said he was concerned with the erection and enlargement of numerous chapels in the villages around Barnsley.[19]

It is often quoted on this subject, that John Whitworth built over forty chapels in the district, however, a study of the histories of the various chapels of the neighbourhood throws up an interesting anomaly. In none of the official histories I read could I find a mention of where John Whitworth was the principal architect, or indeed, where he had any architectural input except to the Pogmoor and Gawber

Sunday School, opened on 2 January 1834, when it is recorded that 'the plan and specifications were made by Mr Whitworth.' If he was involved in the erection of so many chapels as suggested, then his natural modesty is almost beyond belief. Further, I found only the following instances of chapels where Whitworth is documented as being a trustee – Brierley, Dodworth, Royston and Staincross - and it is known that he was also a trustee of the Ministers' house in Pitt Street.

With certainty, the only other building ascribed to John Whitworth than those already mentioned, was the old Corn Exchange and Market House, which was described as a 'useful building, in the Grecian style, situated on Market Hill, at a short distance from the site of the old Moot Hall. The foundation stone was laid by Edward Parker, on 26 May 1851. Mr Whitworth furnished the design for this necessary structure which was erected at a cost of £3,865 12s. 2d., raised partly by subscription and partly by five pound shares.'[20] The upper storey was used on Market Day by farmers and others connected with agricultural purposes, and was also occasionally occupied for concerts and other amusements, for which it was well adapted. The lower part served for the accommodation of vendors selling butter, poultry etc.[21] This building was destroyed by fire in December, 1927.

Whitworth was also involved in the building of the new Congregational Church in Regent Street, opened on 25 September 1856. It was designed by Joseph James, architect, of Furnival's Inn, London, who superintended the works 'assisted by Mr Whitworth' who again, 'gave his professional services gratuitously' although undoubtedly, it was Whitworth who carried out the day to day management of the site over the two years it took to build.[22]

In other areas of construction Burland has written that Whitworth 'projected and brought to a triumphant issue the Dearne and Dove Canal, of which he continued to be the engineer to the time of his death.'[23] This was not so. The Whitworth who was responsible for the waterway was Robert, who surveyed the works in the spring of 1795, under the supervision of William Jessop, following the death of the appointed engineer, John Thompson. Robert Whitworth continued until his death four years later, when one of his sons, Robert or William, finished it.[24] Burland was here in error, no doubt because being familiar with John Whitworth's reputation, when he read the name Whitworth associated with the Dearne and Dove Canal, he automatically thought of John.

It is also said, that Whitworth should be credited with the design and construction of the infamous Barnsley 'obelisk', built as a sign-post in the nineteenth century at the expense of William Cooke-Mence, long-time friend of John Whitworth.

Whatever the truth about the amount of architectural work Whitworth contributed to the town plan of Barnsley, there is no contesting that his contribution to the Methodist cause here was great. He sustained, from time to time, every office in Circuit Methodism open to the laity. He laboured to support the Bible Society, and was for many years the Treasurer of its Barnsley Branch, and its gratuitous Depository in the town. Perhaps in this respect, here was the reason why Whitworth became an original shareholder in the Barnsley Banking Company established in 1832. He was a champion of educa-tion. He lamented the prevalence of drunkenness; and, to check the tide of evil flowing from that source, he became a consistent adherent of total abstinence. And to the Connexion funds, as well as to various charities, both local and general, he was a generous and constant contributor.

Figure 6. A studio photograph of John Whitworth in his old age. *Barnsley Archives.*

An obituary written for the *Methodist Magazine* for 1864, recalls that 'at eighty years of age [Figure 6], his gait and walk were firm and erect, his memory sound, and although he had retired from his profession, yet he would for a charitable purpose plan a school or superintend the erection of a place of worship with all the zeal, attention and care of his earlier days.' It was, apparently, only toward the end of his life that a marked change was observed in his character and posture.

John Whitworth passed away at his home in Regent Street just after the midnight of 26 January 1863, in the eighty-fourth year of his age. The day before his decease, it is recorded that he most affectionately bade his wife farewell, and said, 'Now I have done. Praise the Lord!'[25]

Notes and References

1. *Barnsley Chronicle,* 31 January 1863, p 2.
2. Map of Barnsley dated 1785, showing John Whitworth occupied No 3 Shambles Street.
3. Burland Collection (hereafter BC), Barnsley Local Studies Library.
4. BC, p 193.
5. Whitworth, John. MSS 'Sundries on Wesleyanism in the Barnsley Circuit'.
6. *Pitt Street Methodist Centenary Handbook 1846-1946,* p 8.
7. *ibid.*
8. Alliott, Gerald *The Vanishing Relics of Barnsley,* Barnsley,1996, p 148.
9. *ibid.*
10. Pevsner, Sir Nikolaus, *Buildings of England-Yorkshire:West Riding,* Harmondsworth, 1967, p 94.
11. BC
12. *Pitt Street Methodist Centenary Handbook, 1846-1946,*pp 14-15.
13. *Blucher Street United Methodist Centenary Handbook 1829-1929.*
14. *Barnsley Chronicle,* 31 January 1863, p 2.
15. *Blucher Street United Methodist Centenary Handbook, 1829-1929.*
16. *Pitt Street Methodist Centenary Handbook, 1846-1946* p13.
17. Census, 1841.
18. Beech, John H , *Methodist Magazine,* 1864, p 474-75.
19. *ibid.*
20. Jackson, Rowland, *History of the Town and Township of Barnsley,* London,1858.
21. *ibid.*
22. BC, p 89-90.
23. BC
24. I am indebted to members of the Whitworth One-Name Study Group for information supplied about the life and work of Robert Whitworth.

14. MINERS AND MILER PIGEON RACING

by Jack Wilde

MINERS ALWAYS HAD AN UNDERSTANDABLE need for open air leisure activities such as allotment gardening, freshwater angling and pigeon keeping. A special form of pigeon racing – over a measured mile and via well-known landmarks – was introduced to our local mining communities. It is a sport not widely known but deserves better recognition. Miler Bird Racing has, as we shall see, a number of basic differences to the much more common Homer Bird Racing. It is a sport where spectators as well as participants can experience the thrill of the finish of fast and exciting races; and where birds are purposefully bred for high speed flying.

The present day miler pigeon is the end product of many years of selective breeding by countless pairings of champion male birds with the proven best females. If, after three or four generations the strain has only produced mediocre performing pigeons, then a fresh female is introduced. In the quest for breeding future winners a good sire will be mated many times, mostly with unrelated females of good stock and who have been known to produce winners with some consistency. Champion racers can be of both sex but the majority are males; yet occasionally a female bird can more than hold her own with champion cock birds.

The human involvement with miler bird racing is usually handed on from one generation to another. Most miners or ex-miners who have interest in miler birds own or rent an allotment so as to retain a secure site for the purpose of rearing young pigeons, ideally away from the birds' worst enemy: the domestic cat. The cote, as can be seen in Figure 1, is a sturdy weather-proof wooden hut, not too big but roomy enough to house seven or eight pair of pigeons.

Any novice pigeon fancier who aspires to achieve success would do well to take advice from the elder faction in his group. If he has any real ambitions to own a race-winning cote then his first objective is to purchase a good, well-bred, healthy male pigeon with a proven race record. The next step is to obtain a proven female from the winning line, unrelated to the cock bird. During the pairing up process chemical changes within the female initiate the egg-laying process, so that during the 'chasing' or 'driving' by the male the egg is fertilised and, after nine days, is laid. The hen, with help from her mate, will then

Figure 1. Ken Sheard, veteran pigeon flyer outside his cote at the Royal Arms Paddock. *The Author*

incubate the egg by body heat for a period of nine days, when the chick or 'squeaker' will emerge. At this crucial time an extremely vitamin-rich milk is produced by parent birds for the hungry chicks, crucial to their fledgling development . After the milk has dried up soaked grain can be provided and a very rapid growth rate means that the birds are ready for training in two months.

Fledglings are also identified by means of an irremovable metal ring, attached to one of the feet of the birds. The ring also serves for registration purposes, recorded in the association books, giving the owner the right to compete in officially controlled miler bird races or 'legers' as they are known. If not ringed the bird could only be used for breeding.

During the mating process the 'homing' instincts of the male are intensified and the aim and strategy of the owner is to bring the male bird to 'driving peak', to coincide with the the dates of big prize money legers. Some champion performers appear to have maximum ability whether flying to a sitting hen or a hen that is being ardently 'chased'. Other birds seem to reserve their best when the mating is at its peak.

Figure 2. Ellis Wilde, with watch, 'timing-in'. *The Author*

Training entails flying young pigeons over gradually extended stretches of the same mile course over the same mile course over and over again, so as to allow the bird to recognise landmarks that help to minimise veering from a straight line, as this loses a few valuable seconds.

Miler birds are individually flown, rather than released en masse as in homer racing. The method of timing is also different. In homer races the owner has responsibility of securing the arrival bird, then registering its arrival time with a special timing device that records the ring number, along with the exact time to a split second. Timing clocks are then forwarded to the association headquarters and the owner with the fastest recorded time is the winner. In miler bird racing a synchronised watch system is used, whereby two watches are set to run with a fine degree of accuracy. This enables the timekeeper and the owner operating one mile apart to synchronise the start of the race and the exact time the pigeon commences its run. Before the race begins a start time will have been agreed for the journey time and for the dispatch time of each individual pigeon. On arrival at the mile start the trainer will take his pigeon from the box, and with one eye on the watch will prepare to 'throw' his pigeon at the exact agreed time. 'Throwing' pigeons requires the trainer to grasp the pigeon firmly around the mid-body, with the pigeon's head free to take in its surroundings.

At the mile place, and exactly the same moment, the pigeon will be 'thrown' and the race will have been started; and at two minute intervals the remaining pigeons will be sent on their way. One mile away, in the paddock, the trainer of the expected pigeon will take up a position in the centre of the paddock that gives him a clear view of the field of flight. The trusted timekeeper, watch in hand, will also take up a position of vantage where he can closely observe the touchdown (see Figure 2).

Figure 3. Ellis Wilde, using the hen bird to 'bring-in' the cock. *The Author*

The timing of the race is carried out in stages. First, as the agreed release time is reached, the timer will loudly shout 'Look on', followed by 'Flying'. At the 30 second point he will call out 'Half', followed by 'Fifty', the 'Minute'. As the pigeon could now be reasonably expected to be near at hand the timer starts to chant out the individual passing seconds. When the second pigeon is imminent the timer will calculate the time the oncoming bird has to beat; his calls will now be based on the first pigeon's time and when the timer calls 'Half' he means that there are thirty seconds left for the pigeon to alight and beat the first bird home.

As each pigeon is due the trainer will take up a position in the Ring, which is in the centre of the paddock and is the traditional position to both observe the flight path of her speeding partner, and more importantly to entice the male bird to touchdown. This is accomplished, as we can see in Figure 3, with the aid of the hen bird who is 'dropped' directly in the path of her speeding partner who will be attracted to her and he will alight to resume his courtship.

Legers have been won and lost by poor judgment in this particular exercise;one second too early and the hen could be out of sight of the fast incoming cock bird, causing him to overshoot and lose valuable seconds as he seeks his hen. If the trainer is a little late in 'dropping' then the same calamity may occur. Valuable time can be lost with the incoming pigeon being unable being unable to see his hen and then 'wheeled around', trying to see her. Some trainers prefer to throw the hen high into the air just as the approaching cock bird comes into view and this is the main reason why hens have their wings clipped to prevent them from flying up and away with their mates.

Miler bird racing had been established in Barnsley during the early part of the nineteenth century. In the 1920s and 1930s the sport was certainly going on in central Barnsley, with racing clubs in the Castlereagh Street area, at Kingstone, Worsbrough Common and at Lundwood. The war put at stop to the activity, though stock breeding went on and somehow feed stuff was obtained. Afterwards, when grain became easy to buy the sport was resumed. By the 1950s racing was taking place at the old places, especially Worsbrough Common, and there were two units flying at Kingstone and Lundwood.

At Honeywell in the mid-1950s a meeting took place to look at the feasibility of inaugurating a racing association to be sited at the *Keel Inn* field. Afterwards a group of about twenty enthusiasts began to 'settle' some pigeons on the site and began what was to be the greatest pigeon racing association of the twentieth century.

The business of the next meeting was to set the subscription fees, races and the exact mile places. From the old Ordnance Survey map and from handed down knowledge, it was agreed that the races would be held over the former Honeywell pigeon club mile places. It was also agreed to lease the Keel Field site. The site was next to the *Keel Inn* and was bordered on the eastern side by the Aire & Calder (Barnsley) Canal, whilst the west and south was enclosed by terraced houses. The land covered about an acre of the western slope of the Dearne valley and was free from telephone wires – which would have been deadly hazards to the pigeons.

The eight mile places were the stations used by the previous Honeywell Flying Club. They were all well-known landmarks. Mile place number one lay to the west, near the cricket ground and the old Shaw Lane pumps, adjacent to Barnsley Grammar School. To the east another mile place was known as 'the stump', a reference to a long-forgotten landmark. Northwards, mile place three was the aptly-named Thirty Nine Steps, an old footbridge over the canal. Downstream, the river Dearne flowed underneath another famous site, the old LMS railway viaduct that spanned the river and two canals (Aire & Calder and Dearne & Dove). Not far away was the fourth mile place, Wood Corner. The viaduct was demolished in the 1970s but remnants of the wood survive and what was known as Spring Wood is now Cliff Wood. Older landmark mile places were the Workhouse Gates on Pogmoor Road whilst the site of an old colliery on Wakefield Road – 'Craik's Pit' [See Chapter 4] – served as another mile place. All these old mile places, from the cardinal points of the compass, formed a circle around the Honeywell Paddock.

The birds were raced most weeks of the year, training being a weekly routine. Special sweepstake events took place on Bank Holidays, and every year the important young bird leger was flown in the month of August. Pigeons breed rapidly, ensuring that there were always numbers of youngsters to challenge their elders. Owners would be jubilant about their young birds, only to have hopes dashed as some other speedy novice took the honours and prize monies. Occasionally a super pigeon was produced that dominated the paddock for lengthy periods.

Honeywell was to see a number of outstandingly good birds who could attract hundreds of spectators. In the early days of the Honeywell Association an all-white cock that had been reared at Worsbrough Common was purchased by Ellis Wilde and his partner Ernest Greasley. The white pigeon, known as *Old White Un* had earned a reputation as the most outstanding young pigeon in the Worsbrough area in the early 1950s. He was bred by a veteran pigeon flyer called Arthur Donohoe or 'Ji Dunnoo', a name that was respected in the Barnsley area. Ji had advised Ellis and Ernest to buy the *Old White Un* 'at any price', not only as a money spinner but as a foundation for breeding. This was excellent advice since the bird not only won a tremendous amount of prize money but also bred many winners in a long and distinguished career. *The Old White Un* was then approaching the veteran stage, but he was fast enough to win many legers with amazing consistency. He was exceptionally quick and seemed to possess a thinking brain at the end of a race when his 'daisy cutting' approach was a delight to watch, as also was his habit of flying between the huts and split second wins, providing great thrills for the spectators. His many successes and extraordinary achievements had begun when he was a novice pigeon, quite handsome with white plumage when he had a well earned reputation of beating older and more experienced pigeons.

Ji was born in Union Street, Barnsley, the seventh child of a brewery worker who had an interest in pigeon flying. The small two-up and two-down house, with an enclosed backyard in which Johnny kept a few pullets, along with several pair of milers, was the site of Ji's first pigeon cote. It was in this setting that Ji learned the ropes by being the apprentice trainer with his father's pigeons. Miler bird legers were more difficult to stage in the old built-up parts of central Barnsley as most racing associations did not fly from the central paddock. Because most of the flyers lived in houses with an enclosed backyard, where they kept their pigeon cotes, each pigeon entered in legers had to be trained from the backyard and consequently timed from that spot. The timing between pigeon arrivals had to be increased to allow the timer to be able to get to the different backyard cotes, sometimes in a number of separate streets.

In those days, during the actual leger, groups of spectators could be seen making their way, headed by the timekeeper, watch in hand, going from street to street to time each arrival bird. After the slum clearances this form of racing ceased when pigeon racing associations were reformed in the newer housing areas and paddocks were easier to obtain.

Many tales were related when fanciers got together over a pint in their favourite tap room. One such story still has an airing, usually when drinks are flowing after a Sunday leger. It seemed that one Freddie Williams, a veteran Castlereagh Street flyer, trained a miler bird that developed an unusual twist to its racing. Freddie lived in a small house on Nelson Street with an enclosed yard and unless he went through his back door to the yard he would have to walk into the next street to gain access to his birds. When training his pigeon with the peculiar habit Freddie, rather than walk around the street, took the pigeon through the back door and out on to the street through the front door; and of course the bird became accustomed to this route. One training day, as the pigeon was awaited, Freddie, standing near his back door, watch in hand, and looking up into the sky, was highly surprised to see his pigeon emerge at speed through his back door. At the time Freddie thought little of the incident, yet on the race day he prudently left his front and back doors open. Sunday's leger was to be talked about for years. Freddie's bird was the last to fly, with a time of one minute and ten seconds to beat. All the spectators, the timekeeper and Freddie were in the backyard. As the minute was proclaimed by the timer, and the crowd looking upwards, Freddie, with the hen in his hand, appeared to watching both the sky and his back door. Suddenly, and to everbody's amazement, the pigeon whizzed through the back door, touching down in one minute and nine seconds to win the leger. There were objections, howls of dismay and quite a lot of discourse but Freddie won the day as he maintained that there was nothing in the rules to say a pigeon could not finish in this way.

In later times Ji's *Old White Un* was the chief topic of the tap rooms in the Worsbrough Common pubs. As a novice Ji's pigeon was winning legers with ease, beating older, experienced birds convincingly. He completed his novice year by taking the annual young bird leger of the year title, followed by further successes in his second year. Some of his performances bordered on the unbelievable, especially when he won a leger from a strange paddock from which he had not been 'settled'. It appeared that Ji, having another pigeon more than ready for the Worsbrough leger, decided that the *Old White Un* might just be good enough to win a lucrative 'pot' at Dodworth. Ji was up early on the day and after 'boxing' both his cock and hen set off on the long walk to Dodworth in time to give the *Old White Un* an hour or two to settle in with his hen, and to give him a spin or two over the course and distance. After obtaining the use of an empty cote, Ji placed his pair of pigeons in their nest box. An hour later he gave *Old White Un* a spin over the first half of the mile, then two further flights of the full mile. There was much banter and incredulous looks when Ji wanted to wager his pigeon would beat any named Dodworth bird. The race itself was uneventful, with the second pigeon recording 1:02 which was a good time for this mile, giving the owner a very good chance of winning, this mile never having been won in a time under one minute.

When it came to flying time for the *Old White Un*, Ji took the hen and stood in the centre of the paddock, and insisted on two cleared spaces be left between the cotes that lay in the flight path of his bird. As the 'half' was shouted Ji began whistling and shouting for his now expected pigeon. While the spectators were staring up to the sky, Ji was peering intently at the ground-level of a distant field that lay directly in the expected flight path. At a shout of 'fifty' the *Old White Un* was nowhere in sight but then to the gasps of the crowd, he could be seen, daisey-cutting his way at speed, skimming the grass across the field. At 'fifty-five' he flashed through between two cotes, touching down in exactly 58 seconds. The spectators were astounded that a pigeon from another area could win their leger, and in record time at that. They were also thrilled to witness the incredible performance of a pigeon winning leger in record time without really being 'settled -in'.

Yet for this outstanding pigeon the future was to bring an even greater feat – and that was in defeat. About the time that the Honeywell Association was being inaugurated (and the Worsbrough Association began to wane) Ellis Wilde, with his partner, Ernest Greasley – on Ji's advice – decided to buy the *Old White Un*. The Honeywell Association commenced its programme of competitive racing in the early 1950s and soon became the the the main centre of miler bird racing in the Barnsley district. Some of the most experienced pigeon men and the best mile birds all came together in the Honeywell Paddock. Records tell us that this combination provided the most exciting miler bird racing that had ever been seen in South Yorkshire. The Association lasted for fourteen years during which many champion milers were bred and raced.

Ji Dunnoo joined the Ellis Wilde partnership, as advisor and planner of strategy throughout the racing year, especially where the *Old White Un* was concerned. This bird was then approaching the veteran stage but still a force to be reckoned with. In his first year at Honeywell he won a number of races but perhaps it was not the prizes he won but the style he displayed in his racing that brought acclaim and recognition. With the aid of a pair of high-powered binoculars, I once had the pleasure of observing him from the 'throw' to the finish at Honeywell paddock. The fly that Sunday morning was from the old Craik's pit, Wakefield Road. The morning was unusually warm, sunny and bright, with a strong easterly breeze that would help the pigeons on the touchdown run. At one minute intervals the competing milers were launched on the run for home. As the *Old White Un* was 'thrown' I focused my binoculars on the expected course of flight and could see the pigeon, flying at roof-top height, southwards and exactly over the main Wakefield Road. As he approached the quarter mile, at a point near to the *Sportsman Inn,* he shifted his course slightly to the west. I could see him clearly as he crossed the Fleets Dam, low and at speed, sharply outlined against the darkened water. He climbed to clear the engineering shed of the paper mill and for a moment he disappeared from my view. Glancing at my watch I noted that exactly one minute had passed. I picked him up again just as he flashed between the paddock cotes to touch down, according to my reckoning in 1:12. My time was out by a second, as the old pigeon won the race by two seconds in 1:10.

The *Old White Un,* despite his age, was still able to dominate the Honeywell paddock. This situation continued for most seasons, right up to 1956 when a young pigeon hatched in January of that year was making his mark; he had been bred by Bert Stretton, a local resident. The young *Blue White Feather* had won several legers in which he comfortably beat older birds, including the *Old White Un*. This good young novice won the prestigious young bird leger of the year and had all the makings of a future champion. Ji could not comprehend that his *Old White Un* had at long last met his match and as November was approaching, with the chance of rough weather, Ji and Ellis discussed the tactics to be used in a match with Bert's brilliant youngster. Ji argued that the inclement weather would give the older bird the edge in a slogging match where stamina would be needed. With this strategy in mind, they met Bert and proposed a match for an eight-mile place race, for a £20 stake. Bert willingly accepted and the match would take place on the last Sunday in November.

Ji's assumptions were not to be, the weather was reasonably warm, more like mid-summer than late autumn. The 'draw' did not help the older pigeon either, as the first miles to be flown were by general consensus to be the 'easy' mile places and would favour the young bird. The first race, from Shaw Lane, was won by Bert's young pigeon, with four seconds in hand. The second race, from Pogmoor Road, put the youngster a further three seconds in front, and another victory, this time from Redbrook put him further ahead. In the first three races Bert's pigeon, against all expectations, had gained himself a most handsome lead of nine seconds in winning the first three flights out of eight. On the fourth flight the *Old White Un* won by two seconds, bringing a little hope to Ellis and Ernest. Although the old pigeon was beginning to exert his superiority as the race progressed, he was never going to reduce the young pigeon's big lead in the contest, to have a chance of winning. The *Old White Un* won two of the last three races, but the young bird held on to win the match comfortably. The eight mile race was an epic, with experience against youth and speed. The young *Blue White Feather* won and there is no argument that he won on on merit, yet who knows what the outcome would have been if the barometer had read 'Stormy, Wind and Rain'.

The *Old White Un* lost nothing in defeat and fate was soon to place the old bird back on his pedestal. Fate also decreed that the young one would never be a champion. A few days after the famous match, Bert's cote was broken into and the *Blue White Feather* abducted, never to be seen again. Bert was heartbroken and gave up training because of this horrid crime against a harmless pigeon that could only have been done by the most despicable of men. Though his career was cruelly cut short, he was a big star in his first year of racing.

The magnificent speed and stamina of the *Old White Un* was on the wane, although his stud career was just beginning. He produced an exact replica of himself, a cock to be named *Persil,* who was to win many races. He also bred a neat *Blue White hen,* later to find fame as the mate of another outstanding pigeon owned by Ellis Wilde and partners, a pigeon who was also such a prolific winner, he was for all intents and purposes unbeatable. Records tell us that his winning margins were so great that his opponents withdrew from certain contests and fortified the prizes. This situation could not carry on and one by one the cotes closed down until the early 1960s when racing ceased at the Keel Field. Ji Dunnoo had noted a potential winner at Worsbrough and advised Ellis to buy him for the ridiculous price of £1. Ji said that the huge ungainly pigeon, if he responded to training would be a 'good un'. Ji also said he was big and daft and possessed a temperament that earned him the name of *Mad Pab.*

After a few weeks Ellis confided in Ji that the pigeon was no good as he could not stop *Pab* from 'wheeling'. The mystification increased when Ji told Ellis that the pigeon had done a complete wheel in a trial spin from the Bobbin Mill and yet broke the time record for that particular mile. Following that stunning performance the *Pab* went from strength to strength, he won the next leger, from the Thirty-two Steps and was never again defeated from that venue. His usual time from that particular mile place was around 1:05, against times of 1:15 by his rivals. Some of his accomplishments begger belief. In one race from Shaw Lane, with fifteen seconds in hand, he decided to alight among some foraging Rhode Island Reds, some 200 yards from home. Ellis was whistling and shouting for *Pab* who could be clearly seen paying courtship to a large rusty pullet. With five seconds to go, he took to the air again, touching down in time to win the leger by a good half second. Another race in which he astonished many spectators was from the short Bobbin Mill mile against a promising bird owned by Charlie Philips. Charlie's pigeon was the third home in a very good time of 52 seconds. *Mad Pab* was the last bird, and at the shout of 'ten' he could be seen hurtling through the gap between the terraced houses that bordered the Keel fields. It still looked impossible for the Pab at the shout of 'five', but somehow he threw himself down to his hen and won the race by half a second. I can still see Charlie in my imagination, as he came into view on his return to the paddock. From a distance he confidently shouted to enquire which pigeon had won. To the reply of '*Mad Pab*' he violently threw his pigeon box and his hat to the ground and proceeded to jump on both. He was heard to say that the *Pab* cannot have really won, because he had done a big

Figure 4. Pigeon cotes and 'sighting platform', *Royal Arms* paddock. *The Author*

'wheel' before setting off for home.

The *Pab's* achievements spread far and Ellis began to receive many challenges to his brilliant miler. One such challenge arose when two trainers proposed a race for £5 per bird, but only if they could have the choice of mile place. Ellis agreed and the challengers chose a one-and-a-half-mile race to give them the advantage of not only a new distance, but a completely strange race course. The chosen venue was from Bromley Bridge, just a half mile north of his favourite Thirty-Two Steps mile place. Ellis was more than suited by this choice and he knew that the Pab would beat his rivals, even over the longer distance. The race proved to be a complete triumph for the *Pab*, his winning time of 1:43 was eighteen seconds better than the second bird home and twenty-three seconds better than the third. Needless to say the *Pab* was never challenged again and remained the undisputed champion at Honeywell racing ceased there. The *Pab* did produce one really good offspring, a pigeon called *Cutneck* who was the image of his sire in appearance and not too far away in ability. His curious name was bestowed upon him following a bad accident in a collision with some telephone wires. Ellis saved his life by inserting sixteen stitches of cotton in a gaping wound in an effort to staunch the heavy bleeding. The pigeon recovered and went on to win races in all too short a career and was unfortunate in that racing ceased at Honeywell at the time he was making his mark.

There is no doubt that the *Pab*, by his superiority, initiated the end of racing at Honeywell. Measures to avoid similar situations were introduced by the racing clubs and a new type of race was designed. The simple system meant that trainers had to enter two pigeons in each race, prizes going to the lowest aggregate time. The system worked well and helped to spread the prize money more equally among the club members – no longer would one pigeon dominate the paddocks.

With the closure of Honeywell, Ellis sold off *Pab* and most of his stock, but kept two pair of the Pab's strain, along with the *Old White Un*. *Pab* went on to more success at Redbrook, then Ellis lost track of him. The *Old White Un* lived on for a couple of years, then vanished in mysterious circumstances. It was two years later that Ellis learned what had happened to his favourite white pigeon. A nearby allotment holder, digging out an old drain, found a pigeon's remains, just three white feathers and, more importantly, the identity ring of the *Old White Un*. It was a tragic end to a brilliant miler who apparently had fallen victim to a predator, possibly a cat. When the Honeywell Association finally ceased, a number of fanciers moved to a new site at the Royal Arms, Wakefield Road, where they still are, thirty years on (Figure 4). Ellis joined them a couple of years later, bringing with him his good stock and proceeded to win races, although he still has the descendants of the *Old White Un* and the *Mad Pab,* he has never had a pigeon who could compare with those brilliant milers. Old timers such as Joe Padgett (Figure 5) can recall the 1926 strike when they flew for joints of meat at Worsbrough Common. This sprightly

Figure 5. 'Shorty' and Joe Padgett 'boxing-up' before going to the mile place. *The Author*

seventy-six year old, along with the Short family, Ken Wood, Ken Sheard, Charlie Reid and a few other veteran flyers, keep the sport alive despite the fact that the younger generations do not wish to get involved. It seems likely that when these stalwarts are gone then so will miler bird racing disappear forever.

Acknowledgements

This article has been written from observations taken over the last fifty years, with special thanks to Ellis Wilde for answering many questions when my memory failed to recall names and incidents. Thanks are also due to Brian Elliott for editing and processing my original text.

15. BEFORE THE BAWDY COURTS: SCANDALOUS BEHAVIOUR AT ROYSTON c1660-c1800

by Brian Elliott

IMAGINE THE SCENE that took place on a May Sunday morning in 1705 during divine service in the parish church of Royston when a young women, 'bare-headed, bare-footed and bare-legged', wearing a white sheet 'wrapped about her from the shoulders to the feet' and carrying a white wand in her hand was, after the minister, Reverend St John Bingley had read from the Gospel, told to stand on a form or seat which had been placed by the churchwardens in front of the pulpit probably before a larger than usual congregation. If this shameful display – in front of family, neighbours and community was not enough, the offender then had to repeat the minister's words as follows:

> *Whereas, I* [Sarah Lister] *good People forgetting my Duty to Almighty God, have committed the detestable sin of Fornication with Robert Shillitoe and thereby have justly provoked the heavy wrath of God against me, to the great danger of my own Soul, and evil example of others, I do earnestly repent, and am heartily sorry for the same, desiring Almighty God for the Merits of Jesus Christ, to forgive me both this and all other of my offences, and also ever hereafter, so to assist me with His Holy Spirit, that I never fall into the like offence again, and for that end and purpose, I desire you all hear present to pray with me, and for me, saying,*

> *Our Father which art in heaven....*

The above must have been a dreadful experience for Sarah Lister and her family but penances such as this were regarded by the church courts as having a corrective as well as disciplinary purpose. The offender needed to publicly (though sometimes privately) acknowledge his or her sin and feel penitent. Sex before marriage as were other moral offences such as adultery and giving birth to an illegitimate child were deemed to be a sin against God and God's Church had a duty at the very least to admonish proven miscreants. The correction and punishment of the 'unquiet, disobedient and criminous' was embodied in the *Book of Common Prayer*.[1] How effective such punishments were is difficult to assess with any degree of certainty though this short study of church discipline, based on surviving records relating to Royston parish, may provide us with an insight into the nature and changing scope of moral and religious discipline and the role of the church courts, particularily during the Restoration period, from 1660 to about 1700.

From the medieval period a variety of church courts were established in order to deal with a growing number of what might be called 'spiritual and moral misdemeanours' or, more accurately 'ecclesiastical causes'. A 'cause' was when a person was seen by an archbishop or brought before an archbishop, bishop, archdeacon or other ecclesiastical judge. It has been estimated that between 1300 and 1800

Royston Parish Church, from an anon. oil painting, c. 1840.

around nine million cases were heard in ecclesiastical courts, representing about ten percent of the adult population of Britain.2 Although, as we shall see, there was some overlap with the temporal courts and their authority was on the wane during the eighteenth century, the church courts clearly could have a powerful impact on individuals, families, communities and society; and yet their records have been little used in local and family histories compared with other 'criminal' sources such as those found in quarter sessions.

Basically, the ecclesiastical courts' role was to take appropriate action in order to preserve the social and moral fabric of society. The types of 'offences' heard reflects this aim and can be summarised into seven main areas:

heresy, sorcery and witchcraft (abolished 1736 in Britain); *not attending church, not paying church dues etc violating moral code* (social and sexual matters); *defaming a neighbour* (was heard until 1855); *perjury* (extant until 1823); *violence to a clergyman whilst taking divine service and brawling in consecrated precincts* (the latter two dealt with by common law from 1860).

The behaviour of incumbents was also of course subject to ecclesiastical discipline. This could range from a relatively mild admonishment for not wearing the correct clothes to excommunication for serious sexual scandal. In the 1630s a named vicar was 'found guilty' of showing off parts of his anatomy and successfully enticing ladies to join him. He was excommunicated, fined the huge sum £500 and ordered to pay the court costs.[3] Punishment options for the clergy might involve 'suspension', a temporary withholding of 'privileges such as taking divine service, receiving the sacrament; 'sequestration' which meant loss of the profits of office; 'deprivation' or permanent withdrawal of office which could be extended to the taking away of holy orders and therefore reduction to laity status; and the dreaded excommunication, the most serious spiritual sentence for both clergy and laity. In its most extreme form excommunication barred the offender from the company of other Christians and also stripped the individual of civil liberties and rights.

For the laity, sexual offences were often punished by penance which could be public, usually performed in church but in some cases in the market place or private, in the presence of the incumbent and churchwardens. For the few that could afford it, a penance could be waived by means of a monetary payment to charity. The lightest censure took the form of a warning or admonishment whereby an individual was formally warned not to commit the offence again.

At local level most ordinary or non-controversial cases were of a straight forward 'corrective' nature, heard via presentments at the annual visitation of the archdeacon and via summary procedure in the archdeacon's court, usually held at a set place within the parish church. There was a wide range of cases but the sexual content of proceedings led to the popular appellation 'Bawdy Court'.[4] The accused was made to answer on oath as to the accuracy of the charges but he (or she) could call upon 'character' witnesses – five or six friends or neighbours willing to swear an oath to say that he (or she) was innocent and the case was then dismissed. If found guilty sentence, often in the form of a penance was passed, recorded and sent to the parish priest who had to countersigned it after the penance had been performed. The document was then filed.

This study is based on records from the archdeaconry of York (West Riding) housed at the Borthwick Institute of Historical Research at York, in particular the court books that contain records relating to presentments and visitations.[5] Boxes 3 to 17 were examined, covering

Figure 1. Court Presentments for Royston Parish, 1664-1730

Reason for presentment	1664 -1690	1691-1730	1731-1800	Totals
Absence from church/not receiving sacrament	6	-	-	6
Absence from church (Quakers)	11	-	-	11
Refusal to pay church tax	1	6	-	7
Adultery	1	1	-	2
Clandestine Marriage/Living scandalously together	3	1	-	4
Fornication	7	21	14	42
Incest	1	1	-	2
Bearing a bastard child	-	1	3	4
Bad language/Defamation	2	-	-	2
Refusal to appear at court	-	1	-	1
Absentee cleric	-	1	1	2
Totals	32	33	18	83

	1664 - 80	1681 - 90	1691 - 1700	1701 - 10	1711 - 20	1721 - 30	Totals
Courts held	5	10	7	7	3	5	37
Presentments	9	23	14	9	4	6	65
Persons named	42	123	19	17	6	11	218

Figure 2. Court Presentments for Royston Parish, 1731-1800

the period 1664 (the courts resumed at the Restoration after a lapse during the Civil War) to 1796. The information for Royston parish was extracted from records relating to the rural deanery of Doncaster though, for comparative purposes, some extracts were also made for three neighbouring chapelries: Woolley (a chapelry of Royston parish) and to a lesser extent for Worsbrough (Darfield) and Barnsley (Silkstone). Since Quakers appeared frequently in the post-Restoration records for Royston, note was also made of Quaker presentments right across the deanery. Box number 10 (for 1733) consisted of a 'correction book' for papists. A summary of the infor-mation relating to cases that would have been heard in Royston from its townships of Chevet, Notton, Carlton, Cudworth, Monk Bretton and Royston itself is shown at the end of this study.

The documents used relating to Royston parish actually date from 1667-1792, a period of 125 years. Some 53 court papers were exam-ined concerning 83 individuals and groups (usually Quakers) and a total of 245 named persons. However, most (218) as can be seen by reference to Figures 1 and 2 relate to the six decades before 1730. Excluding Woolley, the population of the parish consisted of only about 160-180 households by the end of the seventeenth century in the period when 'most business' was being recorded so the courts did involve – over two generations – a surprisingly high proportion of the adult population, especially before 1690 in villages such as Monk Bretton where there were significant numbers of resident Quaker families.6 In 1684 Quaker presentments were fairly widespread throughout the deanery, appearing at Adlingfleet (8), Aston (2), Darton (7), Fishlake (4), Hatfield (1), Kirk Smeaton (3), Sheffield (15), Attercliffe (4), Ecclesall (6), Thorne (15) and Whiston (6). Two years earlier sixteen people, probably Quakers, were presented to the archdeacon in St Mary's church, Barnsley 'for not receiving the sacre-ment'. After 1688 Quakers had won the legal right to worship without persecution by the church courts hence the marked decline in the number of presentments but in any event the numbers of Quakers declined markedly during the eighteenth century. At archbishop

	1731 - 40	1741 - 50	1751 - 60	1761 - 70	1771 - 80	1781 - 1800*	Totals
Courts held	5	1	1	4	1	4	16
Presentments	5	1	2	4	1	5	18
Persons named	6	2	4	8	2	5	27
* 20 year period							

Figure 3. Reasons for Presentment, Royston Parish, 1664-1800

Herring's visitation of 1743 the incumbent, Reverend George Wood, stated that there were 185 families in the parish only two of which were Quakers 'who assemble once ev'ry Sunday: But they are few in Number, & very rarely any Teacher.'

As we have already noticed, the frequency of courts held and the number of presentments markedly declined during the eighteenth century, a trend that was to continue into the next century when several areas hitherto subject to ecclesiastic judgement were either abandoned or came under the jurisdiction of the temporal courts.

A summary of the reasons for presentments can be seen by reference to Figure 3. Cases involving absence from church and not receiving the sacrament are confined to the pre-1690 period, almost all of them being Quakers. Any punishment issued for to such offenders had little effect. Well-known Quaker families such as the Milners, Silvesters and Broadheads of Monk Bretton were typical in ignoring frequent warnings issued by the court via Reverend Dutton. Indeed, they were also summoned to appear before the Barnsley Quarter Sessions such was the level of persecution at this time. Perhaps significantly it was during this period, in fact in the same year of 1688 that two cases of bad language and defamation were heard. William Popplewell and William Ibbotson (both probably from Cudworth) had to answer 'for common curses and sweares' whilst 'words of defamation spoken at Mr Dutton' by George Bramhall of Royston may have been treated more seriously.

The great majority of presentments after 1690 related to sexual matters especially fornication which appears to have been almost the sole reason for presentments during the later years of the eighteenth century when the power of the court was in decline. For such cases it appears to have been standard procedure for the woman to be named first and then the man, if he was known. In 1682, for example, Helen Fryer of Royston was cited 'for fornication with George Thompson'.

Three years later 'Ellen Fryer' was named with a group of Quakers who refused to attend church and as 'Ellen Frere' appeared 'for fornication' yet again (the man not named) in 1686. In close-knit communities involving thirty or so households a network of gossip is likely to have ensured information being made available to the parson but there must have also been successful secrecy for a variety of reasons with the more promiscuous and dissenting groups such as Quakers running the greater chance of being reported. In the case of Helen or Ellen Fryer, if she was a Quaker, her appearances for fornication may have been a consequence of an unrecognised marriage, though 'clandestine marriage' or 'living together' was not mentioned in her case. In 1691 George Colley of Royston 'who is fled' was named but obviously not available to face the court for fornication with Maria Ellis of Notton. In 1699 Mary Broadley of Carlton appeared for fornication with Robert Stafford who was described as 'dead' and in the same year Mary Addy of Cudworth appeared for fornication with an unnamed soldier. A similar case was cited in 1703 and another in 1736 between Anne Marshall of Royston 'and a Dragoon'. At this time most of the presentments involving fornication appear to have resulted in public penance or excommunication though a 'Certificate of Innocence' was produced for a Monk Bretton widow, Elizabeth Crookes and her neighbour, William Crabtree.

In 1726 the incumbent was cited 'for not residing upon his living', a situation that was also reported to the archdeacon in 1733, otherwise there are no instances of presentments against Royston vicars.

At St Mary's chapel in Worsbrough township Francis Wood was ordered to appear before the archdeacon in 1738 'for entertaining disorderly people in his house in the time of divine service he keeping a publick house and suffering persons to tipple therin.' Wood was 'admonished' – warned against his future behaviour for this offence against the church.

The prospect of public disgrace in the form of a penance may have been an effective form of church discipline for much of the seventeenth century but there was increasing overlap with common law which also had public and more brutal resources. In about 1778 John Bedford was charged at Barnsley Quarter Session with entering Royston Church and escaping with the communion plate which he hid in the lane leading to Carlton. His punishment was to be publicly whipped at three market towns on their respective market days. Bedford had previously done penance in Royston Church for bastardy.[7]

York Diocesan Archives at the Borthwick Institute of Historical Research (University of York), St Anthony's Hall, York.

Archdeacons Records of Visitation. Court Books, [Y.V/CB]
Rural Deanery of Doncaster: Parish of Royston.
1664-80 [Y.V/CB 3]

Year

1667   George Cooper of Burton[Monk Bretton] and Francis Oxley
for very seldom frequenting the church to hear divine Service.
Anna Oxene, Brian Sanderson for having a child begotten in
Adultery which she fathered upon George Cooper.
Robert Leedom, William Silvester, Jonathan Broadhead, Jane
Ainsley, George and Maria Ellis, Gamaliel Milner, Mary
Broadhead, Richard White, George and Alice Scamadine, and
Thomas Dodson [of Royston parish] for standing excommu
nicate and not coming to the church being Quakers.

1674   Francis Scamaden [and] Thomas Scamaden of Cudworth,
Richard Stafford of Monk Bretton Smithies, Jacob Hill alias
Willey [and] Gilbert Royston of Monk Bretton for not goeing
to church nor receiving the sacrement.

1675   Thomas Cusworth of Royston for being clandestinely
married.
Marian Fierd [?], William Aycroyd of Carlton, Gamaliel
Milner, Isabella Milner, Ellen Milner, William Silvester [and]
Elizabeth Silvester of Monk Bretton for not coming to
church.
Anne White of Cudworth and Thomas Roebuck of Darfield
for fornication.

1679   William Broadhead and Alice Hill of Burton [Monk Bretton]
for not coming to church.

1679   Francis Middleton and Anne Watson of Woolley for fornication together.

1680   William Silvester, Elizabeth Silvester, Alice Hall, Jonathan
Brodehead, Bartholemew Cooper, William Brodehead [and]
Gilbert Royston [all] of Monk Bretton[;] Francis Scamaden
of Cudworth reputed Quakers for standing Excomunicate.

1681-90 [Y.V/CB 4]

1681   William Colley, Anne Moore, Susanna Moore [all] of

Notton[;] Jonathan Broadhead and Jane Broadhead, William Broadhead, William Silvester and Elizabeth Silvester, Alice Hill, Gilbert Royston and Francis Scamaden [all of Monk Bretton] for not coming to church nor receiving the Sacrement.

1682   Jonathan Broadhead and Jane Broadhead; William Silvester and Elizabeth Silvester; William Broadhead and Alice Broadhead; Alice Hill, Gilbert Royston, Joseph Sanderson; Francis Scamaden and Maria Scamaden; Matthew Addy, Anna Moore [and] Susanna Moore [all of Royston parish] for standing Excommunicate being reputed Quakers.

1682   Ann Moore, Susanna Moore, Jonathan Broadhead and William Broadhead, Alice Hill widow, William Silvester and Elizabeth Silvester, Gilbert Royston, Francis Scamaden, Maria and Matthew Addy [of Royston parish being] Quakers for not coming to church.
        Helen Fryer of Royston for fornication with George Thompson.
        Joshua Bramhall and Sara Moore [both] of Royston for a clandestine marriage.

1683   Jonathan Broadhead, Alice Hill, William Broadhead, William Silvester, Francis Scamaden; Maria Addy and Matthew Addy; Susanna Moore and Anna Moore [all of Royston parish] for standing excommunicate.
        George Addy and Grace Holden of Cudworth for suspicion of incest the said Grace Holden having a bastard child in ye house of ye said George Addy not declaring the father.

1684   Anne Moore and Susanna Moore of Notton; Jonathan Broadhead and Jane Broadhead, Alice Hill, Guileehumus Broadhead and Hannah Broadhead, William Silvester and Elizabeth Silvester [all] of Monk Bretton for not repaireing to the Church and not receiving the sacrement being Quakers.
        Francis Scamaden, Maria and Matthew Addy of Cudworth for the same.
        Alice Foster of Burton [Monk Bretton] for the same.

1685   Ellen Fryer, Anne Moore, Susanna Moore, Francis Scamaden, Maria and Matthew Addy, Jonathan Broadhead and Jane Broadhead, Alice Hill, William Silvester and Elizabeth Silvester[all of Royston parish] for not coming to church.

1686   Thomas Holgate and Sara Cooper of Burton and Matthew

Addy of Cudworth for not receiving the sacrement.
Jonathan Broadhead, John Broadhead, Alice Hill, William
and Elizabeth Silvester, Nathan Broadhead, Elizabeth
Broadhead [all] of Burton for not coming to divine service.
Susanna Moore of Notton, Maria and Matthew Addy and
Francis Scamaden of Cudworth for the like.
Ellen Frere of Royston for fornication.
Ruth Willey for the like.
Matthew Addy [of Cudworth] and Maria Rogers for fornication.

1687   Susanna Moore of Notton; William and Elizabeth Silvester,
Jonathan and Jane Broadhead, Henry and Margaret Ellis,
Alice Hill, Nathan and Martha Broadhead, Sara Cooper [all
of] Burton; Francis Scamaden, Matthew and Maria Addy
[all] of Cudworth for standing excommunicate being reputed
Quakers.

1687   Maria Thompson of Carlton and Thomas Addy of Wintersett
for the like. [fornication]
Michael Addy and Susanna Pitt for a clandestine marriage.

1688   Matthew Addy [of Royston parish] for refusing to pay
any assessments on him towards the repairs of the church.
William Popplewell and William Ibbotson for common curses
and sweares.
George Bramhall for words of defamation spoken at Mr
Dutton [parish priest]..

1689   Dorothy Marshall of Carlton and Richard Turton for
fornication.

1691-1703 [Y.V/CB 5]

1691   Maria Ellis of Notton for fornication with George Colley of
Royston who is fled.
Daniel Pitt and Hannah Pitt of Carlton for incest and fornication.

1692   Jane Broadhead of Burton for refusing to pay her assessments
to the church being 3s.3d.
Mary Hayforth for the like being 3s.9d.
Sara Kirkby for fornication.

1693   Excommunications in Doncaster Deanery: Royston parish:
Matthew Addy and Edward Shirtcliffe of Cudworth for not
paying their church layes.
William Batley and Sara Smith of Notton for fornication.

1693   Margaret Ardsley [of Royston parish] for fornication with
Caleb Thompson.

1694   Francisca Walker [of Royston parish] for being cladestinely
        marryed.
1697   Edward Shirtcliffe of Cudworth for not paying his church
        assessts.
1699   Mary Broadley of Carlton for fornication with Robert
        Stafforth dead.
        Mary Addy of Cudworth for the like with a soldier.
1700   Maria Gee [of Royston parish] for fornication.
1701   Anne Kingstone of Burton for fornication with Joshua
        Flockton of Oulton [near Wakefield].
        Jane Wildman for the like with William Fish of Featherstone.
1702   Henry Ellis of Burton, Grizilla Ellis of Darfield for not paying
        their assessts.
        Jonathan Broadhead gent, William Crookes gent, John
        Wadsworth and John Cooper for refusing to sign the
        assessmts paid for the reimbursing of the church gardens [all
        of Burton].

1704-1710 [Y.V/CB 6]

1703   Maria Mellor[of Royston parish] for fornication with a
        soldier.
1705   Robert Shillitoe and Sara Lister [of Royston] for fornication.
1706   John Atkinson and Elizabeth Atkinson [of Royston] for
        fornication before marriage.
1707   Richard Middleton and Maria [of Royston] for fornication
        before marriage.
1708   John Ibbotson and Maria Shepherd [of Royston] for a clan
        destine marriage, or rather for living scandalously together.
        Excommunicated by St John Bingley [parish priest of Royston].

1711-20 [Y.V/CB 7]

1711   Caleb Charlesworth [of Royston] for not appearing at ye
        vistation.
1715   Joanne Colley [of Royston] and William Webster of Wragby
        for fornication.
        Maria Denton [of Royston] for bearing a bastard (father not
        known).
1718   Maria Holden and Thomas Green [of Royston] for
        fornication.

1721-29 (Y.V/CB 8]

1721   Maria Thompson [of Royston] and Robert Rushforth of
        Mirfield for Adultary fornication together he a married man.
        Anne Cusworth [of Royston] and Henry Bond fornication
        together.
1726   Keith Trcburn [?] for not residing upon his living.
1728   John Gelder and Maria [of Royston] for fornication before
        marriage.
1728   George Browneld [of Royston] and Martha Moody of High
        Hoyland for fornication.
1729   Anne Gelder [of Royston] and Jacob Askwith of Pontefract a
        Quaker for the crime of fornication together.

1730-36 [Y.V/CB 9]

1733   All well. The office against Wm Keith clerk the vicar
        [Royston] for not being resident upon his living.
1736   Anne Marshland [Royston] and a Dragoon for fornication.

1737-44 [Y.V/CB 11]

1737   Sarah Mokeson of Carlton for the crime of fornication with
        Charles Bingley who hath done penance (Excommunicated).
1738   Sara Musgrave of Chevet widow having a bastard child the
        father not known (Excommunicated).
1741   Sussana Wadsworth and William Armitage [Royston] for
        fornication (Excommunicated).

1744-47 (Y.V/CB 12) {no information}

1747-59 [Y.V/CB 13]

1752   Elizabeth Crookes of Burton widow and William Crabtree of
        Burton for the crime of fornication. Certificate of innocence
        produced.
        Thomas Wainwright of Burton for fornication with Mary
        Fawcett now dead the said Thomas and Mary being in the
        lifetime of the said Mary fully and duly published in order for
        speedy Matrimony in the parish church of Royston in case
        the said Mary had not died (Appeared and confessed).

1759-66 [Y.V/CB 14]

1763   Mary Horner for fornication and a bastard child (App. confessed against John Hutchinson father. Penance).

1765   Martha Hawcroft [Royston] for fornication (App. and confessed against John Hutchinson father. Penance).

1766   Thomas Smith and Anne Bramhall [Royston] for fornication [were married. Declaration required].

1767-75 [Y.V/CB 15]

1767   George Allen [Royston} and Elizabeth Tomlinson for fornication (Letter received. Penance. She excommunicated).

1772   William Peckett [Royston] and Jane Thompson for fornication (App. and confessed. Penance).

1775-85 [Y.V/CB 16]

1785   Betty or Elizabeth Rothwell of Monk Bretton for fornication (App. and confessed. Penance).

1786-96 [Y.V/CB 17]

1788   Sarah Steel of Monk Bretton for fornication (Penance). Margaret McGowan of Carlton for fornication (Penance).

1791   Mary McGowen of Carlton for fornication (App. Posp).

1792   Anne Rhodes of Carlton for fornication .

Notes and References

1. Chapman C R (hereafter 'Chapman')*Ecclesiastical Courts, Their Officials and Their Records* (Chapman Record Cameo Series), Lochin Publishing, 1992, p.2.
2. Chapman, p.7.
3. Chapman, p.19.
4. Chapman, p.61.
5. Borthwick Institute of Historical Research (University of York), Y.V/CB, Records of Visitation.
6. For information relating to the population of Royston parish see Elliott B, *Royston People of an Ancient Parish* (Issue One), Royston Comprehensive School, 1985; the Monk Bretton Quakers are discussed in 'The Early Quakers of Monk Bretton, 1657-1700: A Sudy of Dissent in a South Yorkshire Village', *Transactions of the Hunter Archaeological Society*, X, 1977; also see Elliott B *The Making of Barnsley*, Wharncliffe Publishing, Barnsley, 1988, pp 251-275.
7. Jackson R *The History of the Town and Township of Barnsley*, London, 1858, p.132.

Acknowledgement

I am grateful to the staff at the Borthwick Institute of Historical Research for help with access to records and for permission to quote from visitation papers

CONTRIBUTORS

1. WARTIME AT THE TOWN HALL

Eileen Umpleby was born in the Barnsley and educated at Barnsley

Girls' High School and Barnsley Technical College. Her early employment, from 1939-46, was at the Education Department in the Town Hall, mostly as secretary to the Director. She married Tom Umpleby and had three children. Later, Eileen qualified as a primary school teacher at Wentworth Castle Training College, thereafter teaching at schools in Barnsley, London and Sheffield. After retirement she studied for a B.A. (Hons) with the Open University. A contribution under the title 'Open All Hours' was also made to *Aspects of Barnsley 4* (1996).

2. THE INVASION SCARE OF AUGUST 1805

Harold Taylor was born in Staincross. After attending Barnsley

Grammar School, he studied Geography at Cambridge University before entering a career in schoolteaching. Since retiring he has followed his interest in local history. Tracing his own family history in Staincross-Mapplewell led him to make a study of the hand-made nail industry of the village and to research the influence of the nonconformist chapels on the musical, social and educational activities there in the nineteenth century. Membership of the South Yorkshire Industrial History Society, and especially of its Field Recording

Group, led to the study of the former linen industry of Barnsley and subsequently of the social history of the town. Harald has written articles for all five volumes of *Aspects of Barnsley*.

3. THE DEVELOPMENT AND DECLINE OF THE BARNSLEY CANAL

Roger Glister was born a stone's throw away from the Sheffield and South Yorkshire Navigation at Sprotbrough. The close association with the 'cut' has resulted in a life-long interest in inland waterways about which he writes extensively. He is a long-standing member of the Waterway Recovery Group, the national body for the organisation of voluntary labour for canal restoration. Lately his efforts have concentrated on the two Barnsley Canals. Educated at Mexborough Grammar School and the Doncaster College of Technology, he is an engineer by profession and a specialist in church heating. His other interests include fell-walking and vintage cars. Roger is a regular contributor to the *Aspects Series*.

4. UP WAKEFIELD ROAD: COLLIERY DEVELOPMENTS

John Goodchild is a native of Wakefield and was educated at the Grammar School there. He has been active in local historical research since about the age of thirteen, and is the author of over 140 books and published essays on aspects of the history of the West Riding. He was founder-curator of Cusworth Hall Museum and subsequently Archivist to Wakefield MDC; in his retirement he runs a Local History

Study Centre which houses his immense collection of manuscripts and research materials, and which is open to use, free of charge, by appointment. Mr Goodchild holds an honorary M Univ from the Open University from the Open University, awarded for academic and scholarly distinction and for public services. He is a regular contributor to the *Aspects Series*. Outside historical research, his interests lie in Freemasonry and in Unitarianism - and his dog.

5. A History of Barnsley Trams

Trevor Polding was born at Pindar Oaks nursing home, just yards from

Barnsley electric traction's tram shed. Spending his childhood at Gawber, he attended Wilthorpe School and won a scholarship to Barnsley Grammar. Afterwards he served an engineering apprenticeship with R W Crabtree of Leeds which allowed lunch-times to be spent studying Leeds' fascinating tramway system or helping with work on the locks of the Leeds-Liverpool Canal which ran just behind the factory. He then served three years in the RAF, mainly in the Middle East, starting work as a jig-tool draughtsman on demob with David Brown Gears of Huddersfield. Trevor moved to live in Huddersfield after marriage to Barbara but retains strong Barnsley connections. Recently retired, after 40 years at Browns, he is busy photographing all aspects of rail and industrial archaeology including the mill chimneys near his home in the Colne valley.

6. FROM PLOUGH BOY TO CHEESE FACTOR

Athron 'Dick' Bedford was born in the Barnsley area in 1907 and still

lives near to the town centre. From farming stock, he continues to keep interested in agricultural matters and since his retirement has travelled widely. Dick's memories of his early life on the land, his private education at Wakefield Boys' Grammar School and his entre-preneurial business activities make him a worthy 'subject' for the *Aspects Series*. His autobiographical contribution, at the age of 90 plus is a remarkable achievement and example of putting life-long learning to good use.

7. BUNS BUT NO BEER: BARNSLEY COFFEE TAVERNS

Coral 'Kate' Taylor was born in Wakefield in 1933 and educated at the

Girls' High School before going on to St Anne's College, Oxford, where she read English Language and Literature. After teaching in Leeds, at West Park C S School and the City of Leeds and Carnegie College of Education, she took up a post as Principal Lecturer in English at Wentworth Castle College of Education at Stainborough. Following the closure of the College she became Vice-Principal (Community) at Barnsley Sixth Form College when it opened in 1979. Since her retirement in 1990 she has spent her time researching local history, in particular in the field of entertainment. Her book *Right Royal: Wakefield Theatre 1776-1994* was published in 1995. She works part-time as a tutor for the Open University and is the Hon Managing Editor of Wakefield Historical Publications, President of Wakefield Historical Society and Chair of the Mercia Cinema Society.

Kate has written articles on theatre history for *Aspects of Barnsley 4* (1996) and *Aspects of Doncaster 1* (1997)and is currently editing the forthcoming first volume of *Aspects of Wakefield.*

8. MEMORIES OF BARNSLEY'S THEATRE ROYAL

Pamela Watford was born in the Smithies area of Barnsley. Educated at Athersley schools and at Longcar Central, her first job was as a clerk/typist at Wood Brothers Glass Company, working in the invoice export department for eleven years. After two years as a clerk/receptionist with a plant hire company, Pamela did varied temporary and part-time work for some years. Pamela admits to having had a strong interest in writing and in art from her childhood years and subsequently some of her articles have appeared in a variety of publications. Her other interests include music and the theatre. This is Pamela's first contribution to *Aspects of Barnsley.*

9. A SPONSORED MIGRATION FROM STAFFORDSHIRE TO HOYLAND IN THE MID-NINETEENTH CENTURY

Melvyn Jones, who is also the editor of *Aspects of Rotherham* and the *Aspects of Sheffield* series, was born in Barnsley and educated at the Holgate Grammar School and the universities of Nottingham and Leeds. He taught for seven years at Myers Grove, Sheffield's first comprehensive school, and then for nine years at Sheffield City College of Education before its amalgamation into Sheffield City Polytechnic in 1976. He has recently retired from the post of Head of

Academic Resources in the School of Leisure and Food Management at Sheffield Hallam University. He is now pursuing a long-delayed career as an independent author and consultant. He has written extensively on the economic, social and environmental history of South Yorkshire. Publications include *A Most Enterprising Thing* (an illustrated history of Newton Chambers at Thorncliffe) and the widely acclaimed *Sheffield's Woodland Heritage. Rotherham's Woodland Heritage,* published by Rotherwood Press in 1995, won fourth place in the prestigious Allan Ball Local History Awards in 1996. He is co-author of *Chapletown and High Green* (1996) and *Chapletown, High Green, Grenoside and Ecclesfield* (1998) both in Chalford Publishing's Archive Photograph series. He has contributed articles to all the volumes in the *Aspects of Barnsley* series. He is currently working on a book on the history of South Yorkshire's countryside.

10. GEORGE ORWELL AND THE ROAD TO POGMOOR SANDS

Rose Johnstone grew up in Monk Bretton. In the 1960s she helped

her mother to run a fish and chip shop there, before going to St Hilda's College, Oxford to read English. She qualified as a lawyer and in the 1980s went to Hong Kong where she represented clients on Legal Aid, mainly workers injured in accidents. On her return she moved back to South Yorkshire with her husband, a Scot. She has had articles on various topics including travel, books and humour published in magazines in the UK and overseas. Her article on Orwell is based on a lecture given at Barnsley Literary Society in National Libraries Week, 1997 and is her first contribution to the *Aspects of Barnsley* series.

11. ELSECAR: THE MAKING OF THE INDUSTRIAL REVOLUTION, 1750-1830

Ian Medlicott was born in Doncaster where he spent his early years before moving to Sheffield. Educated at High Green Secondary Modern School, Barnsley College of Technology, and Ecclesfield Grammar School, and after qualifying as a school teacher taught in primary and secondary schools in Sheffield and Barnsley. Ian gained a BA (Hons) and an M Phil with the Open University. For a long time he has been interested in local history, especially early coal mining in South Yorkshire, with articles published in archaeological journals. This is Ian's first contribution to the *Aspects of Barnsley* series.

12. PENISTONE MARKET AND CLOTH HALL

David Hey is Professor of Local and Family History at the University of Sheffield, where he teaches in the Division of Adult Continuing Education. Originally from Penistone, he now lives in Dronfield Woodhouse. He was educated at Penistone Grammar School and Keele University and obtained part-time MA and PhD degrees at the Department of English Local History at Leicester University. His books on South Yorkshire include *The Making of South Yorkshire* (1979), *Packmen, Carriers and Packhorse Roads* (1980), *Yorkshire From AD 1000* (1986) and *The Fiery Blades of Hallamshire: Sheffield and its Neighbourhood, 1660-1740* (1991). He has also written *Family History and Local History in England* (1987) and *The Oxford Companion to Local and Family History* (1996). He is, with Martin Olive and Martin Liddament author of *Forging the Valley* (1997), outlining the remarkable story of Sheffield's

Lower Don Valley and has recently completed a new *History of Sheffield.* (forthcoming).

---

13. JOHN WHITWORTH, ARCHITECT AND SURVEYOR OF BARNSLEY

Alan Whitworth trained at Bradford College of Art, from 1977, after a number of years in the world of printing and graphic design and then predominantly turned his attention to promoting the preservation of English parish churches, founding and running a charity to that end, writing and lecturing on the subject, mounting many exhibitions and organising the first national conference dealing with churches and tourism; and yet his interests are wider, and his regard for old buildings and history has led in one area to the founding of the Yorkshire Dovecote Society after a study of dovecotes and pigeon lofts, about which he has written and lectured often. He now writes and lectures about local history subjects and his books include *Yorkshire Windmills* (MTD Rigg Publications, 1991); *Village Tales: A History of Scalby* (Alan Sutton, 1993); and *Exploring Churches* (Lion Publishing, 1993). Alan is also editing the forthcoming *Aspects of the East Yorkshire Coast* for Wharncliffe Publishing.

---

14. MINERS AND MILER PIGEON RACING

Jack Wilde was born in Union Street, Barnsley in 1922, the son of a miner who was commended for bravery at Ypres in 1915. Jack attended Holy Rood Elementary School until the age of fourteen when he started underground work at Woolley Colliery studying mining at night school. Jack has devoted a great deal of time to community work, being branch secretary, for thirteen years, of a Health

Service Union and a local Councillor for eight years, retiring in the mid-1980s. He is involved in voluntary work, at present a member of the Roundhouse Community Partnership and member of the New Lodge Tenants and Residents Association. Married for more than fifty years, he has three daughters, eight grandchildren and three great-grandchildren. Jack is currently writing his autobiography.

15. BEFORE THE BAWDY COURTS: SCANDALOUS BEHAVIOUR AT ROYSTON

Brian Elliott was born in Royston and spent his childhood in the village of Carlton where he attended the primary School, and then Edward Sheerian School at Athersley. After an undistinguished spell as an apprentice professional footballer he obtained a proper job, working for Barnsley Corporation in a Dickensian office next to the Public Cleansing Department. Whilst Head of Geography at Royston Comprehensive School he also tutored adult education courses for the WEA and University of Sheffield and published short histories of Royston parish. He researched his own town for an M Phil, awarded by the University of Sheffield in 1990. His popular book *The Making of Barnsley* (1988) was the first published historical account of the town since 1858. Brian founded the acclaimed Aspects of Local History series, edits *Aspects of Barnsley and Aspects of Doncaster* and advises Wharncliffe on local books. Recent publications include *Barnsley's History From the Air, 1926-1939* (1994), *Barnsley's Sporting Heroes* (as editor, 1997) and *Discovering South Yorkshire's History* (forthcoming). Articles on Barnsley's photographic history have recently been published by the Royal Photographic Society. Brian works at Rother Valley College where he is Head of School (General and Community Education).

Index of Places

Index of People